Exploring Virtuality within and beyond Organizations

TECHNOLOGY, WORK AND GLOBALIZATION

The Technology, Work and Globalization series was developed to provide policy makers, workers, managers, academics and students with a deeper understanding of the complex interlinks and influences between technological developments, including information and communication technologies, work organizations and patterns of globalization. The mission of the series is to disseminate rich knowledge based on deep research about relevant issues surrounding the globalization of work that is spawned by technology.

Also in the series

ICT AND INNOVATION IN THE PUBLIC SECTOR
Edited by Francesco Contini and Giovan Francesco Lanzara

KNOWLEDGE PROCESSES IN GLOBALLY DISTRIBUTED
CONTEXTS
Edited by Julia Kotlarsky, Ilan Oshri and Paul C. van Fenema

OFFSHORE OUTSOURCING OF IT WORK
Edited by Mary C. Lacity and Joseph W. Rottman

GLOBAL SOURCING OF BUSINESS AND IT SERVICES
Edited by Leslie P. Willcocks and Mary C. Lacity

GLOBAL CHALLENGES FOR IDENTITY POLICIES
Edited by Edgar Whitley and Ian Hosein

E-GOVERNANCE FOR DEVELOPMENT
Edited by Shirin Madon

Exploring Virtuality within and beyond Organizations

Social, Global and Local Dimensions

Niki Panteli and Mike Chiasson

palgrave
macmillan

First published in 2008 by
PALGRAVE MACMILLAN
Houndmills, Basingstoke, Hampshire RG21 6XS and
175 Fifth Avenue, New York, N.Y. 10010
Companies and representatives throughout the world.

PALGRAVE MACMILLAN is the global academic imprint of the Palgrave
Macmillan division of St. Martin's Press, LLC and of Palgrave Macmillan Ltd.
Macmillan® is a registered trademark in the United States, United Kingdom
and other countries. Palgrave is a registered trademark in the European
Union and other countries.

ISBN-13: 978–0–230–20128–6
ISBN-10: 0–230–20128–8

This book is printed on paper suitable for recycling and made from fully
managed and sustained forest sources. Logging, pulping and manufacturing
processes are expected to conform to the environmental regulations of
the country of origin.

A catalogue record for this book is available from the British Library.

A catalog record for this book is available from the Library of Congress.

10 9 8 7 6 5 4 3 2 1
17 16 15 14 13 12 11 10 09 08

Printed and bound in China

To
Nikolas, Vasilis, Maria, and
Mark for inspiring our work

CONTENTS

LIST OF TABLES

LIST OF FIGURES

ACKNOWLEDGMENTS

The authors wish to acknowledge a number of people who have made this book possible: the senior editors of this Palgrave Macmillan series, Leslie Willcocks and Mary Lacity; Stephen Rutt, Alexandra Dawe, and their colleagues at Palgrave Macmillan; the workshop participants at the first IFIP 9.5 workshop in June 2006 on "Virtuality and Society: Emerging Themes" at the London School of Economics. Special thanks also go to all the contributors of this book for their efforts and enthusiasm in exploring with us the nature of virtuality.

Technology is all too often positioned as the welcome driver of globalization. The popular press neatly packages technology's influence on globalization with snappy sound bites, such as "any work that can be digitized, will be globally sourced." Cover stories report Indians doing US tax returns, Moroccans developing software for the French, Filipinos answering UK customer service calls, and the Chinese doing everything for everybody. Most glossy cover stories assume that all globalization is progressive, seamless, intractable, and leads to unmitigated good. But what we are experiencing in the twenty-first century in terms of the interrelationships among technology, work, and globalization is both profound and highly complex.

We launched this series to provide policy makers, workers, managers, academics, and students with a deeper understanding of the complex interlinks and influences between technological developments, including information and communication technologies, work organizations, and patterns of globalization. The mission of this series is to disseminate rich knowledge based on deep research about relevant issues surrounding the globalization of work that is spawned by technology. To us, substantial research on globalization considers multiple perspectives and levels of analyses. We seek to publish research based on in-depth study of developments in technology, work, and globalization and their impacts on and relationships with individuals, organizations, industries, and countries. We welcome perspectives from business, economics, sociology, public policy, cultural studies, law, and other disciplines that contemplate both larger trends and micro-developments from Asian, African, Australian, and Latin American, as well as North American and European viewpoints.

The first book in the series, *Global Sourcing of Business and IT Services* by Leslie Willcocks and Mary Lacity is based on over 1,000 interviews with clients, suppliers, and advisors and 15 years of study. The specific focus is on developments in outsourcing, offshoring, and mixed sourcing practices from client and supplier perspectives in a globalizing world. We found many organizations struggling. We also found other practitioners adeptly creating global sourcing networks that are agile, effective, and cost efficient. But they did so only after a tremendous amount of trial-and-error and close attention to details. All our participant organizations acted in a context of fast moving technology, rapid development of supply side offerings, and ever-changing economic conditions.

Knowledge Processes in Globally Distributed Contexts by Julia Kotlarsky, Ilan Oshri, and Paul van Fenema, examines the management of knowledge processes of global knowledge workers. Based on substantial case studies and interviews, the authors – along with their network of coauthors – provide frameworks, practices, and tools that consider how to develop, coordinate, and manage knowledge processes in order to create synergetic value in globally distributed contexts. Chapters address knowledge sharing, social ties, transactive memory, imperative learning, work division, and many other social and organizational practices to ensure successful collaboration in globally distributed teams.

Offshore Outsourcing of IT Work by Mary Lacity and Joseph Rottman examines the practices for successfully outsourcing IT work from Western clients to offshore suppliers. Based on over 200 interviews with 26 Western clients and their offshore suppliers in India, China, and Canada, the book details client-side roles of chief information officers, program management officers, and project managers and identifies project characteristics that differentiated successful from unsuccessful projects. The authors examine ten engagement models for moving IT work offshore and describe proven practices to ensure that offshore outsourcing is successful for both client and supplier organizations.

Exploring Virtuality within and beyond Organizations by Niki Panteli and Mike Chiasson argues that there has been a limited conceptualization of virtuality and its implications on the management of organizations. Based on illustrative cases, empirical studies, and theorizing on virtuality, this book goes beyond the simple comparison between the virtual and the traditional to explore the different types, dimensions, and perspectives of virtuality. Almost all organizations are virtual, but they differ theoretically and substantively in their virtuality. By exploring and understanding these differences, researchers and practitioners gain a deeper understanding of the past, present, and future possibilities of virtuality. The collection is designed to be indicative of current thinking and approaches, and provides a rich basis for further research and reflection in this important area of management and information systems research and practice.

ICT and Innovation in the Public Sector by Francesco Contini and Giovan Franceso Lanzara examines the theoretical and practical issues of implementing innovative ICT solutions in the public sector. The book is based on a major research project sponsored and funded by the Italian government (Ministry of University and Research) and coordinated by Italy's National Research Council and the University of Bologna during the years 2002–2006. The authors, along with a number of coauthors, explore the complex interplay between technology and institutions, drawing on multiple theoretical traditions such as institutional analysis, actor network theory, social systems theory, organization theory, and transaction costs economics. Detailed case studies offer realistic and rich lessons. These cases studies include e-justice in Italy and Finland, e-bureaucracy in Austria, and Money Claim On-Line in England and Wales.

In addition to these first five books, several other manuscripts are under development. These forthcoming books cover topics of ICT in developing countries, global ICT standards, and identity protection. Each book uniquely meets the mission of the series.

We encourage other researchers to submit proposals to the series, as we envision a protracted need for scholars to deeply and richly analyze and conceptualize the complex relationships among technology, work, and globalization.

Leslie P. Willcocks
Mary C. Lacity

Notes on the Contributors

Mike Chiasson (m.chiasson@lancaster.ac.uk) is an Advanced Institute of Management (AIM) Innovation Fellow, and a Senior Lecturer in the Department of Management Science at Lancaster University. Prior to this, he worked at the University of Calgary in Canada, and as a post-doctoral fellow at the University of British Columbia, after obtaining his PhD in Information Systems. Mike's research examines the relationships between institutional contexts and the implementation of information systems. His work has included various approaches and topics that address this question: action research methods for organizational change; user involvement and the participants' view on systems; the diffusion and influence of IT in professional organizations; social issues related to IS (privacy, criminal activity, intellectual property, and IT outsourcing conflict); and philosophical and social foundations of IS development and use. He has published his work in various book chapters and journals, including: *Management Information Systems Quarterly, Information & Organization, Information Systems Journal, European Journal of Information Systems, Information Technology and People*, and *Data Base for Advances in Information Systems*. His current research is focused on the use of web systems to support patient–clinician dialogue in the care of chronic disease.

Katherine M. Chudoba (kathy.chudoba@usu.edu) is an Associate Professor of MIS at Utah State University. Dr Chudoba's research interests focus on the nature of work in distributed environments, and how ICTs are used and integrated into work practices. Her research has been published in journals such as *MIS Quarterly, Organization Science, Information Systems Journal, Information Technology & People*, and *Journal of the Association of Information Systems (JAIS)*. She earned her PhD at the University of Arizona, and her bachelor's degree and MBA at the College of William and Mary. Prior to joining academe, she worked for eight years as an analyst and manager in the information technology industry.

Keith Dixon (K.R.Dixon@bath.ac.uk) has more than twenty years' experience in the IT and high-tech sectors. His roles have spanned technical, operational, strategy and senior management in organizations ranging from start-ups to major, global companies such as Cap Gemini, Motorola, and Sybase. He holds a PhD in Management and first-class Honours BSc in Control Engineering from the University of Bath and a Masters in

Business Administration from Brunel University. His research interests focus on virtuality, boundaries, and the development of intellectual capital in teams. He has presented aspects of this work at conferences in Boston, Toronto, and Hawaii, and is currently writing up his thesis at the School of Management at the University of Bath.

Paul Dunning-Lewis (p.lewis@lancaster.ac.uk) has taught and published on systems thinking and the design of new technologies for over twenty years, and was closely involved with the development of Soft Systems Methodology. His academic career followed experience as a programmer, systems analyst, and database designer in the oil industry and work as a consultant. A consistent theme of his research has been the need for collaboration with real-world practice through the use of Action Research.

Jeremy Hunsinger (jhuns@vt.edu) is completing his PhD in Science and Technology in Society at Virginia Tech and is a Visiting Assistant Professor in the Department of Communication at University of Illinois at Chicago. His research agenda unites theory with practice on the political economy, ethics, and knowledge cultures of the internet, learning environments, cyber-infrastructures, higher education, and research. At Virginia Tech, he was one of the founders of the Center for Digital Discourse and Culture and a 2006 Scholar Fellow. He attended the Oxford Internet Institutes 2004 Summer Doctoral Programme and was Graduate Fellow of the NSF Workshop on Values in Information Systems Design. He is a Ethics Fellow at the Center for Information Policy Research a the University of Wisconsin, Milwaukee in 2007–2008.

Maria Katsorchi-Hayes (m.hayes1@lancaster.ac.uk) is a Research Associate in Lancaster University Management School. She holds a PhD in Information Management from the Judge Institute of Management at the University of Cambridge, her postgraduate degree from Lancaster University and her undergraduate degree from Athens University of Economics and Business. Her current interests are in the social implications of implementing technological change at individual and organizational level in private and public sector companies.

Susanne Kinzler (susanne.kinzler@htw-aalen.de) is Professor of International Accounting at the Hochschule Aalen, Germany. Her research interests include telesupport, remote working, and eProcurement in the automotive sector.

Julia Kotlarsky (JKotlarsky@wbs.ac.uk) is Assistant Professor of Information Systems at Warwick Business School, UK. She holds a PhD in IS and Management from Rotterdam School of Management Erasmus (the Netherlands). Her main research interests revolve around the social and technical aspects of managing globally distributed IS teams and IT outsourcing. She has published her work in such journals as *Communications of the ACM*, *European Journal of Information Systems*, *Information Systems Journal*, *Journal of Information Technology*, *MISQ Executive*, *Journal of Strategic Information Systems* and others.

Dr David Kreps (d.g.kreps@salford.ac.uk)is an "early adopter", pioneering thinker, and commentator, with a fascination for technology and its impact upon society. A web developer since 1995, he did his PhD thesis on Cyborgism, and has become an expert on web accessibility, and explorer into the philosophy of virtuality. As an arts centre director for Tamworth Borough Council, and then Portsmouth City Council, during the 1990s, as chairman of Kaos Theatre since 1997, and as principal investigator on the recent Combating eDiscrimination European Social Fund project into the accessibility of employment websites, David has managed a wide range of projects in the public sector. His background in Cultural Studies and Sociology foster a critical approach to his research in IS. David Lectures in Web Development, eGovernment and Technoculture at the University of Salford.

Ilan Oshri (IOshri@rsm.nl) is Associate Professor of Technology and Strategic Management at Rotterdam School of Management Erasmus, the Netherlands. He holds a PhD in Technological Innovation from Warwick Business School, UK. His main research interest lies in the area of learning and innovation in global teams. He has widely published his work in journals and books, including *IEEE Transactions on Engineering Management*, *Communications of the ACM*, *European Journal of Information Systems*, *Journal of Strategic Information Systems*, *Journal of Information Technology*, *Information Systems Journal*, *MISQ Executive*, and others.

Niki Panteli (N.Panteli@bath.ac.uk) is a Senior Lecturer in Information Systems and Director for the Centre for Information Management at the University of Bath School of Management and the Chair of the IFIP W.G. 9.5 "Virtuality & Society." Her main research interests lie in the area of IT-enabled transformation, virtual teams, and computer-mediated communication. Within this field, she has studied issues of trust, conflict, and collaborations in virtual, geographically dispersed environments. She has published articles in numerous journals, including *Decision Support Systems*, *Information & Organization*, *Information and Management*, *IEEE Transactions on Professional Communication*, *Behaviour and Information Technology*, *European Journal of Information Systems*, *Futures*, *New Technology, Work and Employment* and the *Journal of*

Business Ethics. Further, her work has appeared in book chapters and conference proceedings.

Patchareeporn Pluempavarn (pp225@bath.ac.uk) is a PhD candidate in Information Systems at the School of Management, University of Bath. She received her MSc degree in Management from the University of Bath, Master in Public Administration (MPA) and her BA first-class honour in Government from Chulalongkorn University in Thailand. Her research interests are in the field of information and communication technologies. She is currently involved in research on virtuality and identity, and has a specific interest in blogging communities. Her research was presented at the UK Academy for Information Systems conference 2006.

Angeliki Poulymenakou (akp@aueb.gr) is an Assistant Professor (tenured) of Information Systems at the Department of Management Science and Technology of the Athens University of Economics and Business. Previously, she has served as lecturer in Information Systems at the London School of Economics and Political Science. Her research interests focus on the study of the processes and impacts of technological intervention in a variety of contexts. Over the years, she has conducted research in advanced systems analysis practices, IT-enabled organizational change, and e-commerce, while more recently she has been working in the areas of e-learning and knowledge-management adoption, IT-enabled collaboration and organizational networks, and virtual communities of practice. Her related work is interwoven with her participation in and coordination of European- and national-funded research projects She has served as scientific coordinator of various national- and European-funded projects in the wider context of socio-economic research on ICTs. She has been the member of the program committees of several international conferences, the co-chair of the IFIP WG8.2 international conference in Athens (2003), and a member of the editorial board in two international journals. She has published three books, and more than 50 scientific papers in peer-reviewed journals and conferences.

Ann McCready (a.mccready@gcal.ac.uk) has been a Senior Lecturer in the Business School at Glasgow Caledonian University (UK) since 1997. Her teaching and research interests focus on the organizational and social aspects of e-commerce and e-business, particularly the development of online business in the context of small businesses, and virtual teams.

Julian Newman (j.newman@gcal.ac.uk) is Professor of Computing at Glasgow Caledonian University, UK. His research interests include virtual organizations, computer-supported collaborative work, theories of information, security and the representation of argumentation structures.

Anthony Papargyris is a PhD candidate in the Department of Management Science and Technology at the Athens University of Economics and Business, Greece. He holds a first degree in Business Computing (Teesside, UK), and an MSc degree in Information Systems (AUEB). His current research is focusing on collective action and meaning construction, virtual communities, and learning. His general research interests are in online interactive learning games, philosophy of science and information systems, and knowledge management.

Christin Schmidt (christin.schmidt@htw-saarland.de) is a member of the staff as well as a lecturer in the Department of Business Administration at HTW – Hochschule für Technik und Wirtschaft des Saarlandes (Saarbruecken, Germany). In parallel, Christin is currently pursuing her doctorate at Glasgow Caledonian University, UK. She has an interdisciplinary working background in academia and business. Her research interests include organizational, social, and psychological aspects of information and communication technology.

Bryan Temple (b.k.temple@gcal.ac.uk) is a Senior Lecturer in the School of Engineering and Computing at Glasgow Caledonian University, UK. He is co-director of the university's CSCW laboratory (with Julian Newman, below). He has worked in both the business and academic sectors and has research interests that cover small businesses, new product design and development, project management, and related issues.

Mary Beth Watson-Manheim (mbwm@uic.edu) is an Associate Professor in the Information Decision Sciences Department and Director of the Center for Research in Information Management in the College of Business Administration at the University of Illinois, Chicago. She obtained her PhD in Information Technology Management from Georgia Institute of Technology. She is actively involved in research on issues related to the use of information and communication technologies (ICT) in virtual teams. Her work has been published in *MIS Quarterly*, *Journal of Management Information Systems*, *Information Systems Journal*, *Information Technology and People*, *MIS Quarterly Executive*, *IEEE Transactions on Professional Communications*, *Group Decision and Negotiation*, and others. Her research has been funded by Intel Corporation, IBM Corporation, Lotus Development Corporation, and various university centers. Prior to obtaining her PhD, she worked in the telecommunications industry.

Velvet Weems-Landingham (Vweemsl@kent.edu) PhD is currently an Assistant Professor at Kent State University, USA. Her dissertation work, entitled "The Role of Project Manager and Team Member Knowledge, Skills and Abilities (KSAs) in Virtual Team Effectiveness," was completed at Case Western Reserve University's Weatherhead School of Management in 2004. Dr Weems-Landingham has taught over a dozen courses at the undergraduate, graduate, and professional levels. In addition, she possesses more than a decade of experience designing, developing, and managing distance learning initiatives within a wide array of organizations, ranging from pharmaceuticals and hospitals to manufacturing and not-for-profit agencies.

Leslie Willcocks (L.P.Willcocks@lse.ac.uk) is Head of the Information Systems and Innovation Group and Professor of Technology, Work and Globalization at the London School of Economics and Political Science. He holds a PhD from the University of Cambridge and is a Visiting Professor at Erasmus and Melbourne Universities. He is also co-editor of the *Journal of Information Technology*. He has co-authored 26 books and over 180 refereed papers on information systems management, IT and business process outsourcing, IT-enabled change, IT evaluation, and social theory and philosophy for information systems.

Lin Yan (l.yan@lamp.ac.uk) is a lecturer at the Department of Management and Information Technology, University of Wales Lampeter, UK. She holds an MPhil and a PhD in Management Studies from University of Cambridge, UK, and has years of experience in international management. Lin researches in the area of virtuality, particularly on issues concerning identity and power in distributed settings. Currently, she is investigating the formation process of organizational identification in small, innovative, international organizations, and the interplay between this process and its contextual factors, such as use of technology, organizational structure, and power and politics. Lin is a member of the Academy of Management, European Group for Organizational Studies (EGOS), IFIP Working Group 9.5. (Virtuality & Society), and the British Association for Chinese Studies.

CHAPTER 1

Rethinking virtuality

Niki Panteli and Mike Chiasson

Why a study on the nature of virtuality?

Over the last few years, there has been considerable interest in the "virtual" – teams, organizations, groups, and communities – in management research and practice. The focus of attention has generally been on how to improve collaboration and knowledge sharing, how to develop trust and cohesiveness within virtual teams and communities, and how best to support virtual interactions. Underlying this research is the assumption that we possess sufficient understanding about the nature of virtuality and the ability to distinguish what is virtual, and what is not. Even though several researchers have attempted on various occasions to make a contribution in this field, we increasingly recognize that the nature of virtuality has neither been well conceptualized nor fully explored.

Part of the reason for this is that researchers often compare the virtual (i.e., global, geographically dispersed, and electronically linked) to the traditional (i.e., local, collocated, and face-to-face) environment. While a useful starting point, we question this primarily technological distinction, while recognizing that virtuality, through an IT-enabled system, is increasingly extending its reach, and becoming more global, more dispersed, and more pervasive across all spheres of society. Schultze and Orlikowski (2001) explain that "global, electronic workspaces or information devices ... together make up the unseen and sprawling empires of virtual organizations" (p. 57). The advancement of information and communication technologies (ICTs) has been related not only to the emergence of the virtual society, but also to the development of the virtual empire, which is purported to have an enormous impact on how people work, communicate and share their knowledge. Fulk and DeSanctis (1995) have identified several features of communication technologies, which "offer important advancements in organizations" (p. 338). These include the speed of communication, the dramatic reduction in the costs of communication, the increase in communication bandwidth, the vastly expanded connectivity with people and machines throughout the world, and the integration of communication with computing technologies. These effects include more reach, fluidity, and flexibility in everything we do as individuals, organizations, communities, and societies. The location of work and our coworkers is now considered irrelevant. It is not surprising therefore that virtuality has been linked to globalization, which "is quintessentially about the death of distance" (Woolgar, 2002 p. 19). However, as van Binsbergen (1998) puts it: "globalization is not about the absence or dissolution of boundaries, but about ... the opening up of new spaces and new times within new boundaries that were hitherto inconceivable" (p. 875).

> Globalization as a condition of the social world today revolves around the interplay between unbounded world-wide flow, and the selective framing of such flow within localizing contexts; such framing organizes not only flow (of people, ideas and objects) and individual experience, but also the people involved in them, creating more or less enduring social categories and groups whose collective identity as supported by their members' interaction creates an eddy of particularism, of social localization, within the unbounded global flow. (van Binsbergen, 1998, p. 875/6)

It follows that to view virtuality as being merely a global phenomenon provides us with only a partial understanding of its impact and pervasiveness. Virtuality is also a local phenomenon that needs to be examined from a micro-level analysis as well as a macro-level analysis. Therefore, despite the distance-*less* and boundary-*less new* world of virtuality, Woolgar (2002) suggests that virtual interactions are still realized in the particular local settings of individuals, which influences the way they manage and use virtual systems. For example, individuals live, think, and breathe in their local physical, psychological, and sociological circumstances, and this affects and shapes their virtual work, interactions, and interpretations. Woolgar has argued that "instantiations of global communication and identity depend critically on attention to the local setting ... . It is not just that local context affects uptake and use. Instead, the very effort to escape local context, to promote one's transcendent global (and/or virtual) identity, actually depend on specifically local ways of managing the technology" (p. 19).

As virtuality and our experiences with it changes and expands, the local and the global are intertwined (Panteli et al., 2007). Increasingly, there are clear instances, such as the Accoplir case, where the local and global meet both in the virtual and real – where an idea and a project emerge in a computer-mediated and virtual space, but the implications are realized and affect a local context. Accoplir is the Paris Resident Association that has used the virtual world of Second Life to get ideas for a new garden in the city centre. It did this in order to put pressure on the officials to speed up the redevelopment process, which had started in 2004 but had failed to produce new designs because of limited consultation with residents. The competition was announced in April 2007 and the decision was made at the end of June. People in China, Canada, and Germany took part and came up with ideas for a new garden. The winner was a French citizen who received 275,000 linden dollars (785 Euros, £530, ~US$ 1, 000). Apart from the main prize, smaller prizes were also awarded, including 40,000 linden dollars to a six-year-old in the children's play area category. The winning prize included ambitious water features and an ice-rink (BBC News, June 2007).

It follows from this example that increasingly we live and breathe virtual possibilities on a day-to-day basis. Some of us may be more reluctant, skeptical, and critical in spending much time in virtual spaces such as Second Life, but we have to acknowledge that many today are growing up with the virtual world and swimming in virtual waters as a natural part of their lives. This new generation is what Rymaszewski and his colleagues (2007) have called the "digital natives". Therefore what may be considered global to us, is for these digital natives, their local. This is one of the reasons why we should examine the different varieties and experiences of virtuality; because we feel that our interpretations and realizations of it in local contexts are changing and increasing. As technology and social practices change, we have more opportunities to "enter" and experience different forms of virtuality, and, in the process, our understanding and conception of virtuality changes. We believe therefore that other varieties of virtuality research and practice are important and necessary for both understanding and extending the future possibilities for the "virtual" in managerial and information systems research and practice. These changes and possibilities are what we explore in this book.

With this edited collection, we argue that there has been a limited conceptualization of virtuality and its implications on the management of organizations. Our aim is to go beyond the comparison between the virtual and the real-traditional-concrete, to explore the different types, dimensions and perspectives of virtuality. We posit that almost all organizations are virtual, but that they differ theoretically and substantively in their virtuality. It is by exploring and understanding these differences that researchers and practitioners will be able to develop a deeper understanding of the past, present, and future possibilities of virtuality. We need to rethink, therefore, what virtuality is and the roles it plays in managing and theorizing contemporary organizations. The aim of the book is to examine, to appreciate, and to debate the nature of virtuality in organizations, exploring a range of virtuality topics that challenge traditional social and technical imperatives in our research.

This book provides illustrative cases, empirical studies, and theories of virtuality, with individual, group, organizational, and interorganizational examples, drawn from a wide range of settings. Theories of virtuality are applied and developed, and the implications for the management of virtuality are discussed. The collection is designed to be indicative of current thinking and approaches, and to provide a rich basis for further research and reflection in this important area of management and information systems research and practice. The complex and dynamic nature of virtuality requires collective and collaborative efforts toward a better appreciation of the broader social, cultural, geographical and technological characteristics that surround it (Webster, 2005). In what follows, we will explore the different conceptualizations of virtuality provided in the general management, information systems (IS) and other literatures. Different varieties of virtuality will then be identified and discussed. Reference will be made to variations of virtuality that exist *within* organizations (e.g., virtual individual members and virtual teams) but also *beyond* organizations (e.g., interorganizational and online communities, markets). It is upon these different variations of virtuality that the book chapters are presented. Chapters 2–7 will present virtuality as it appears and is conceptualized within organizations and Chapters 8–12 will present and conceptualize virtuality as it appears in studies beyond organizations.

Developing our understanding of virtuality is of significant importance for managers and organizations wishing to seek and use both their human and technological resources to explore virtual work and working. The book achieves this objective by asking each author to discuss the practical implications of their study.

Finally, we would like to note that the idea for this edited book was born following a workshop that was organized in June 2006 at the London School of Economics. The theme of the workshop was to survey the globality of virtuality, the complex, emergent, and changing nature of this field, and to act as a location for transdisciplinary work on virtuality. The workshop was under the auspices of the International Federation of Information Processing (IFIP) Working Group 9.5 (Virtuality and Society), which explores virtuality, through information and communication technologies and other means, and its intertwining relationship with individuals, groups, organizations, and society. It brought together researchers and practitioners of virtuality to sketch out a joint agenda on virtuality research. The present edited collection captures some of these interests, while also making a general call for new approaches to the subject.

Virtuality or virtualities

Although there has been an overwhelming interest in virtual environments within the management, organizational and information systems literatures, the terms "virtual" and "virtuality" have received diverse attention (Woolgar, 2002). The *Oxford English Dictionary* lists three possible definitions for virtuality. The first defines virtuality as "the possession of force or power" or "something endowed with virtue or power." The second possible definition is "essential nature of being, apart from external form or embodiment." The third definition, which also corresponds to the common usage of the word, is "a virtual (as opposed to an actual) thing, capacity, etc; a potentiality." Based on this latter understanding, Turoff (1997) has defined virutality as "the potential for a virtual system to become part of the real world" (p. 42).

Overall, definitions of virtuality vary, with some adopting a philosophical view (e.g., Nelson, 1980) and others seeing virtuality as a computer representation. For example, the philosopher Michael Heim (1993) defines "virtual" as "A philosophical term meaning 'not actually but just as if'." Drawing upon Heim, Sotto (1998) posits that "the term 'virtual' can be said to mean: not actually existing but as if actually existing. In this sense, a virtual artefact is an event or entity that is real in effect but not in fact" (p. 79).

Within the general management and organizational literature, it is more difficult to find clearly stated definitions of virtuality. Instead, a prevailing assumption is that virtuality is harnessed by traditional organizations in order to take advantage of advances in information and communication technologies (see Rockart, 1995; Wiesenfeld et al., 1998). Virtual organizations are often seen as extensions of the traditional physical and structural bounded groups, enabled by technological advancements. This conceptualization, however, does not embrace the full articulation of virtuality that is possible (Panteli and Dibben, 2001). Virtuality is not simply an extension of the traditional physical and structural, such as something that already exists, but it could also be a new and emergent entity. Due to its emergence, it is difficult to put a singular definition around it because this may constrain what virtuality is, has been, and may become.

With particular reference to organizations, Zigurs and Qureshi (2001) posited that virtuality involves activities that can take place anytime, anywhere, with no physical, geographical, and structural constraints. They believe that virtuality is the "elsewhere," something that is not here because we can not see or experience its physical presence. It is a space and not a place because it is not fixed. A place is static and has walls and boundaries, whereas the virtual is fluid and flexible, though it connects and associates people, things, and objects. With virtuality, individual choices are believed to be expanded to numerous and new possibilities, unrestricted by local constraints. For example, it can involve an expansion of the way people shop, work, and play, loosening their local and physical ties which restrict what is available to them.

We found the following statement illustrative of the expansion we wish to pursue:

> We [humans] are able to step [into virtuality] through the looking glass. We are learning to live in virtual worlds. We may find ourselves alone as we navigate virtual oceans, unravel virtual mysteries, and engineer virtual skyscrapers. But increasingly, when we step through the looking glass, other people are there as well. (Turkle, 1995, p. 9)

There are several issues that arise from Turkle's statement. The virtual world is unbounded and nonlinear, with a free flow of movement. It expresses the flexibility, fluidity, and creativity that are embedded in virtual context. In fact, an inherent part of virtuality is said to be that of "playfulness" (Sotto, 1997). As Rheingold puts it (1991, p. 373) "[play] is the first thing most people do when they find themselves immersed in a virtual world." Being playful, according to Romanyshyn (1989) allows individuals to get away from the "real" world, to "lift off," "depart from earth," "escape death," and "turn on the dream" (in Sotto, 1997, p. 46). Such potential for freedom and flexibility is purported to enable a fluid exchange of ideas and information, improving opportunities for learning (thus, unraveling virtual mysteries) and creativity (thus, engineering virtual skyscrapers). There is also an perception that an electronic link, a computer system, acts as the "looking glass." Information technology has indeed been considered vital in building and maintaining virtual organizations (Fulk and DeSanctis, 1995; Rockart, 1995). An expanded view of virtuality is that an information system, enabled by new forms of IT, produces computer-generated representations of the world (Jackson, 1999). But moving beyond deterministic view of IT, we believe that virtuality is not only about information technology. It is also about interacting with people whom we may not know, but who share the same interest and conceptual space as us. Therefore, even though computer-mediated communication is an important contributor to virtuality, IT does not dictate virtuality. Rather it is engaging and being a part of a social and conceptual network which is important, and it is within these revised networked spaces where we wish to explore virtuality.

Panteli and Dibben (2001) following Sotto (1998), have described virtual teams as "topos"[1] for the exchange of discourses where their fixity is not determined by their location but rather by the social orders and flows that constitute them. To function, virtual teams require the presence, or more accurately the telepresence, of individuals as virtual workers. According to Steuer (1992), telepresence is the experience of presence in an environment by means of a computer-mediated communication. Rethinking virtual teams as a group of individuals who experience telepresence contributes to a better articulation of virtuality since this specifies the unit of analysis for a study as the individual. In doing so, it shifts the locus of attention from technology and the organization, to the individual and how she perceives her role in the virtual environment, and her relations with other virtual team members. Clearly, virtual teams are neither effective only because of technology nor as a result of organizations wanting to extend their boundaries, but also and most importantly because individuals are able to trust, and thus interact and work together in these electronic and nontraditional environments. An initial focus in the literature on technology has tended to overlook this point.

Variaties of virtuality

Virtuality as a matter of degree

The notion that virtuality is a matter of degree is becoming widely used among researchers in this field, and is acknowledged by the contributors in this book. Zigurs and Qureshi (2001) have explained the different degrees of virtuality with reference to the internal orientation and the external orientation to virtuality: "Internally, an organization might include isolated individuals who work primarily through IT and are rarely physically present … Externally, an organization may interact via IT with suppliers and/or customers" (p. 129).

With specific reference to the literature on virtual teams, there is an increasing acknowledgment that virtual teams fall along a continuum from traditional face-to-face to completely distributed (Crowston et al., 2005; Kirkman and Mathieum, 2005). As Schmidt, Temple, McCready, Newman, and Kinzler (Chapter 5) show, a wide range of teams are left in the middle of this continuum and these are often called "hybrid" teams; a concept also adopted by Oshri, Kotlarsky, and Willcocks in this collection. Acknowledgment of the hybrid nature of virtual teams is also made in the contribution by Dixon and Panteli (Chapter 8) in their attempt to explore the nature of virtuality in teams which combine face-to-face and technology-mediated interactions.

Virtuality as a matter of dimensions

There seems to be a general agreement that virtuality is multidimensional (Gibson and Gibbs, 2006). For example, according to Shin (2004), virtuality is the degree to which a group has temporal, cultural, spatial, and organizational dispersion, and communicates through electronic means. Similarly, Chudoba et al. (2005) posit that virtuality depends on disconti-nuities in geography, time zone, organization, national culture, work practices, and technologies. Gibson and Gibbs define virtuality "as a multi-faceted higher-order construct comprising four independent defining characteristics identified in previous literature: geographic dispersion, electronic dependence, dynamic structural arrangements, and national diversity" (2006, p. 455). Their study found that these features need to be seen in their own right as they are not always interrelated. For example, geographically dispersed teams are not always structurally dynamic, but instead consist of the same members that operate in a stable environment.

Virtuality within and beyond organizations

Even though it follows from the above discussion on variations of virtual-ity that the emphasis of our current understanding has remained with the organization and its surroundings, it is also important to go beyond this setting to explore the role and effects of virtuality beyond organizations. Our argument is that exploring virtuality both within and beyond organi-zations will provide a better understanding of the nature of virtuality. In what follows, therefore, reference will be made to variations of virtuality that exist within organizations (e.g., virtual dispersed individuals, distrib-uted teams, and organizations) and beyond organizations (e.g., online communities, markets).

Virtuality within organizations

During the last decade there has been an increasing literature on virtual organizations and virtual teams. This body of research generally agrees that virtual organizations (Quinn and Jackson, 1996) and virtual teams (Lipnack and Stamps, 1997; Jarvenpaa and Leidner, 1999) consist of a collection of geographically dispersed individuals who work on joint projects or common tasks, and who communicate electronically. Various types of virtual teams (Panteli, 2004), virtual organizations (Davenport and Pearlson, 1998), and virtual alliances (Burn, Marschall, and Barnett, 2002) have been identified.

Given the explosive growth of virtual teams, virtual intra-organizations and interorganizational alliances, virtual arrangements constitute an increasingly important aspect of contemporary organizations. Indeed, the growth of virtual work arrangements has highlighted the role of computer-mediated communication and the diverse tools which support virtual work interactions. The first part of the book presents a collection of studies that explore the nature of virtuality within organizations. The aim here is to gain insight as to how virtuality affects organizations and its members. Issues of shared expectations and understanding among virtual team members, as well as collaboration and cooperation, are discussed. These issues are crucial in understanding an promoting virtual work arrangements.

The recent organization and information systems literature has given overwhelming attention to virtual teams, their effectiveness, dynamics, and communication patterns. Virtual (i.e. distributed) teams require and are challenged to produce effective communication, especially in collaborative and knowledge-intensive projects. Oshri, Kotlarsky, and Willcocks (Chapter 2) argue that developing and coordinating expertise in globally distributed contexts is far more complex than in co-located teams because of knowledge asymmetries, coordination challenges, and communication issues. Therefore, companies that engage in globally distributed work need to be able to find a balance between distributing expertise, and coordinating and integrating expertise through a process of socialization where one "learns the company's ropes." In a globally distributed environment, this process should be ongoing and should be supported by a series of technology-mediated activities beyond face-to-face meetings.

Chudoba and Watson-Manheim (Chapter 3) highlight a common assumption within the virtual team literature, that work is harder in these teams because members must communicate across temporal and spatial boundaries. However, some research suggests that a lack of shared work practices is a more significant impediment to successful performance in the virtual work environment than these various boundaries. In their chapter, they attempt to shed light on the role of shared practices by first looking at the relationship between the use of the communication media repertoire – the collection of communication channels and shared routines of media use across members of a team – and the processes of building and maintaining mental models in a virtual team. They consider the consequences of virtuality as a perceptual rather than an objective phenomenon. In other words, members of a team may work across objective boundaries (e.g., multiple time zones, different organizations), but the boundaries are not always perceived as problematic. Their discontinuity construct, they argue, is a factor contributing to perceptions of problems at the boundaries, which means that increased effort by the team is required to accomplish work because of the differences in expectations introduced at the boundary. These differences must be negotiated and resolved in order for work to be accomplished.

The study by Weems-Landingham (Chapter 4) assesses virtual team cooperation from a contingency perspective, proposing that performance tactics are moderated by the degree of perceived virtuality. Through illustrative examples of virtual team experiences, this work provides an evaluation of virtual project manager behaviors associated with team effectiveness and virtual team cooperation. It is found that successful virtual project managers are relationship-oriented, and that they use both formal and informal networks in ensuring that critical resources are available, accountable, and responsive.

Schmidt, Temple, McCready, Newman and Kinzler, in Chapter 5, discuss the phenomenon of virtuality in team-based environments from an interdisciplinary perspective. They posit that virtuality occurs in different degrees and constitutes multiple configurations of organizational design in the hybrid workplace, somewhere between traditional and fully virtual environments. Using quantitative and qualitative methods, they found that virtuality is not significantly related to the economic effectiveness of a team's output, but rather to indicators of social and psychological efficiency. The study also found that although identity and identification is positively related to the degree of virtuality experienced within each team, the general level of virtuality in the sample shows that this effect is not exploited to its full potential.

Issues of identification are discussed by Yan (Chapter 6). Given geographic dispersion, virtual organizations find it difficult to rely on direct control and coordination. Instead, they bind the organization through shared values and norms. Organizational identification therefore moderates the often difficult social relations that exist in virtual organizations. This study highlights the social nature of virtuality by illustrating the role of ongoing and political interactions in developing shared understanding in a geographically distributed organization.

Lewis and Katsorchi-Hayes's chapter (Chapter 7) examines the consequences of diverging views of virtuality in practice, and specifically examines differences in relation to customer and supplier relationships in a competitive and commercial context. They argue that understanding virtuality in contemporary organizations requires understanding the business context and norms of those organizations. Their discussion is based upon a three-year study, contrasting various visions of what was technically feasible and organizationally desirable in the UK chemicals industry. Through interviews with managers and staff of companies, the research provides insights into the different meanings that organizations attribute to the virtuality of work and to the acceptability of potential implementations of a middleware technology. It was found that interpretations of virtuality among the potential users and participants were strongly influenced by established work practices, and by previous experiences of relationships-at-a-distance with suppliers and customers. There was also a sharp contrast between the enthusiastic visions of virtual work by technical developers, and the negative views of users who perceived internet-only interaction as rigid, alienating from well-established ways of working with suppliers and customers, and unworkable. They conclude that virtual work needs to pay attention to the norms and values in the local context, and how ICTs will affect and be affected by these influences.

Dixon and Panteli's chapter (Chapter 8) draws on recent research into the growing phenomena of virtuality in organizational teams, particularly collaboration. In particular, this chapter uses the concept of virtuality in teams, not in technological terms, but as discontinuities. Using data from an interorganizational case study, the chapter highlights the multiple levels of discontinuities that lie beyond those traditionally associated with technology-oriented views of virtuality. The discussion emphasizes that it is this complexity of discontinuities that increasingly matters in our understanding of virtuality.

Virtuality beyond organizations

The second part of the book presents a collection of chapters on the nature of virtuality beyond organizations. Here the emphasis shifts from virtuality within organizations and their subgroups (e.g., virtual teams) to inter-organizational and societal instances of virtuality. These include empirical studies on online communities and conceptual studies on the phenomenon of virtuality in general, from both a theoretical and research perspective.

There is no doubt, as DeSanctis and Monge (1999) argued that the changing nature of information and communication technologies in organizations will be different in the long run than in the short run. Indeed, only recently have we seen the emergence of new online communities offering different social realities and virtual experiences for its members. Blogs or Blogospheres, for example, have been shown to be substantially different to online chatrooms. Herring et al. (2005), in a content-analysis study of 203 blogs, describe them as hybrids, because they allow social interaction while giving authors control over the communication space – such as the what, how, and frequency of contributions. Further to enhancing social networks, blogs have been presented as an upcoming corporate communication medium (Lee, 2006) and an open-source source of information (Blumenthal, 2005) due to the vast amount of information that they carry.

Pluempavarn and Panteli (Chapter 9) argue that there is a need to examine how the social identity of individual bloggers influences and is being influenced by the blogging community. Bloggers are active in selecting to participate in those communities that match their interests, and they can be members of more than one group. Furthermore, specific blogging communities create social identities, which affect members' participation and interaction with others inside and outside the group.

Papargyris and Poulymenakou (Chapter 10) explore the case of massively multiplayer online games (MMOG) on the internet, as a virtual world where players participate in virtual communities, engage into collective actions, and construct intersubjective understandings of their relationships with others and the virtual world. Their ethnographic study suggests that players acting collectively in a MMOG share an enjoyment but also an agony in making sense of the virtual game setting and, as a result, employ various instruments and strategies in order to negotiate their understandings. Such instruments include various metaphors, game rules, and players' roles, while common strategies include petitions, propagandas, and peripheral discussions. In these communities, players learn the game's rules and mechanisms through continuous experimentation. The meaning of the virtual world is gradually constituted through repetition of trial-and-error practices. Indeed, the social distribution of knowledge of the virtual world is acquired directly by engaging in meaningful actions, or by sharing it with other players that, for example, were present at a past event.

Moving away from empirical studies, the remaining chapters aim to develop conceptually the nature of virtuality. A critique of the existing literature is that much of it has been simply extensions of nonvirtual research, with a few complications regarding space and time (Robey, Schwaig, and Jin, 2003). We question virtual work as simply an extension of traditional work – a social imperative – while acknowledging that both global (virtual) and local (real) is important in anchoring and directing virtual outcomes.

Chiasson (Chapter 11) discusses alternative conceptions of the local, global, and virtual, through Shields (2003) and others, in order to loosen a typical focus on electronic channels as virtual-global, and face-to-face communication as concrete-local. The result is a shift towards other *luminal* spaces "in between" all three, but also back to virtual possibilities before ICTs, mediated through language and meaning. He argues that ICTs are only an evolution and not a revolution in virtuality. Based on this, the virtual is no longer tied only or even primarily to an electronic medium, but to the ideal-present concepts that influence and are influenced by absorbed individuals. As a result, every moment of our life is filled with the virtual and concrete – behaviors in particular circumstances (the concrete), the talking and influence of others using electronic text (virtual), the exploration and realization of future actions (probable), with the intent of forming new social movements, friendships, and contacts (abstract).

Along a similar line of inquiry, Kreps (Chapter 12) deals explicitly with the question "Are the real and the virtual truly as opposed to one another as might at first appear?". His chapter – perhaps the most philosophical in the current collection – questions whether the real and the virtual are really so opposed, and, in the course of various arguments which examine this issue, he questions whether virtuality can indeed be regarded as any kind of threat to the mental health or psychological development of those engaged in it – or indeed to a society that embraces it. He concludes that virtuality may even be inherent in the nature of what it is to be human.

Acknowledging the diversity and variety that exists in virtuality research, Hunsinger (Chapter 13) presents the case that virtuality is best approached from a transdisciplinary perspective. The area of research that constitutes virtuality is already multidisciplinary and interdisciplinary, but he argues that transdisciplinarity will benefit the field by creating a new axiology – a new common set of understandings – that will make sense of the field to its broader audience. This audience for virtuality research is global and constantly changing, so fixing a set of common axioms and conventions into our research will enable the global research community to grow and encompass the field, while maintaining its legitimacy in the face of disciplinary fragmentation.

Conlcuding comments

Collectively, this book questions the technological emphasis in definitions and approaches to virtuality, and, through them, the destruction and loss of the local worlds in which users live. At the same time, the book recognizes that virtuality increasingly extends and transforms practices within and beyond organizations, through the far-reaching effects of ICTs.

This edited book demonstrates that virtuality not only increasingly extends and transforms organizational and societal practices; it also extends and transforms its own nature, its varieties and dimensions. Virtuality is not just what we experience when we go through the electronic looking glass. This is only the beginning, as the virtual experience can be considered to start both before and after one crosses the electronic threshold and finds the other people there.

A multitude of interpretations could be given to "virtuality." Virtuality is manifested symbolically, metaphorically, materially, mentally and physically. What a better example than the case of MMOGs presented by Papargyris and Poulymenakou, who show that the virtual world is a province of meaning where, through a scenario-driven MMOG (material), players enjoy and share a life, negotiated through their "life-worlds" in which they celebrate their agony (mental) and triumphs in this imaginary and virtual world. Diversity in the way we approach and explore virtuality is important in order to capture the current and future diversity of virtuality itself.

With this book we have aimed to bring together a collection of studies that show the complex nature of virtuality, as well as the varieties of virtuality. Though there has been overwhelming attention on the possibilities that virtual world has created, there has been little discussion on the current state of research in this field that is embracing the characteristics of the virtual society. To advance research and discussions on the topic, we sought papers that addressed the variety of perspectives and research issues in the field of virtuality within and beyond organizations. The contributors to this edited book have, in different ways, identified and discussed critical issues on virtuality. Collectively, they assist in unraveling the mystery of the virtual world and in showing that the virtual mystery is a project under constant construction! These chapters allow us to reflect on research practices and help us in developing an agenda for further research in this area. We will do this in our last chapter, "the epilogue."

Notes

1. In Greek, "topos" means "a place." Here, it is used as a social setting rather than as a physical environment.

References

BBC News 28 June 2007.

Blumenthal, M.M. (2005) Toward an Open-Source Methodology: What we can learn from the Blogosphere, *Public Opinion Quarterly*, 69(5), Special Issue, 655–669.

Burn, J., Marschall, P., and Barnett, M. (2002) *E-business Strategies for Virtual Organizations*, Butterworth-Heinemann: Oxford.

Chudoba, K.M., Wynn, E., Lu, M., and Watson-Manheim, M.B. (2005) How virtual are we? Measuring virtuality and understanding its impact in a global organization. *Information Systems Journal*, 15, 279–306.

Crowston, K., Howison, J., Masango, C., and Eseryel, U.Y. (2005) Face-to-face interactions in self-organizing distributed teams, Academy of Management Conference, August 5–10, Honolulu, Hawaii, USA.

Davenport, T.H., and Pearlson, K. (1998) Two Cheers for the Virtual Office, *Sloan Management Review*, Summer: 51–65.

DeSanctis, G., and Monge, P. (1999) Introduction to the Special Issue: Communication Processes for Virtual Organizations, *Organization Science*, 10(6), Special Issue: Communication Processes for Virtual Organizations (Nov.–Dec., 1999), 693–703.

Fulk, J., and DeSanctis, G. (1995) Electronic Communication and Changing Organizational Forms, *Organization Science*, 6(4), July–August: 337–349.

Gibson, C.B., and Gibbs, J.L. (2006) Unpacking the Concept of Virtuality: The Effects of Geographic Dispersion, Electronic Dependence, Dynamic Structure, and National Diversity on Team Innovation, *Administrative Science Quarterly*, 51, 451–495.

Heim, M. (1993) *The Metaphysics of Virtual Reality*, Oxford University Press: Oxford.

Herring, C.S., Schiedt, L.A., Bonus, S., and Wright, E. (2005) Weblogs as a Bridging Genre, *Information, Technology & People*, 18(2), 142–171.

Jackson, P. (Ed.) (1999) *Virtual Working: Social and Organizational Dynamics*, London: Routledge.

Jarvenpaa, S.L., and Leidner, D.E. (1999) Communication and Trust in Global Virtual Teams, *Organization Science*, 10, 791–815.

Kirkman, B.L., and Mathieum, J.E. (2005) The Dimensions and Antecedents of Team Virtuality. *Journal of Management*, 31(5), 700–718.

Lee, S. (2006) Corporate Blogging Strategies of the Fortune 500 Companies, *Management Decision*, 44(3), 316–334.

Lipnack, J., and Stamps, J. (1997) *Virtual Teams: Reaching Across Space, Time, and Organizations with Technology*, John Wiley: New York.

Nelson, T. (1980) Interactive Systems and the Design of Virtuality, *Creative Computing*, November, pp. 56–62.

Panteli, N. (2004) "Situating Trust within Virtual Teams," in S. Reddy (Ed.), *Virtual Teams: Contemporary Insights*, 20–40, ICFAI University Press: Hyderabad, India.

Panteli, N., Chiasson, M., Yan, L., Papargyris, A., and Poulymenakou, A. (2007) Exploring the Nature of Virtuality: An Interplay of Global and Local Interactions, in K. Crowston, S. Sieber, and E. Wynn (Eds), *Virtuality and Virtualization*, Springer: NY.

Panteli, N., and Dibben, M.R. (2001) Revisiting the Nature of Virtual Organizations: Reflections on Mobile Communication Systems, *Futures*, 33(5), March, 379–391.

Quinn, J.J., and Jackson, P. (1996) Control in the Virtual Organization, Paper Presented at the British Academy of Management, Aston University, Birmingham, 16–18, September, 1996.

Rheingold, H. *Virtual Reality*. London: Mandarin, 1991.

Robey, D., Schwaig, K.S., and Jin, L. (2003) Intertwining Material and Virtual Work, *Information and Organization*, 13, 111–129.

Rockart, J.F. (1995) Towards Survivability of Communication-Intensive New Organization Forms. *Journal of Management Studies*, 35(4), July: 417–420.

Romanyshyn, R. (1989) *Technology as Symptom & Dream*, London: Routledge.

Rymaszenski, M., Au, W.J., Winters, C., Onndrejka, C., and Cunningham, B.B. (2007) *Second Life: The Official Guide*, John Wiley: New Jersey.

Schultze, U. and Orlikowski, W.J. (2001) Metaphors of Virtuality: Shaping an Emergent Reality. *Information and Organization*, 11(1), 45–77.

Shields, 2003, *The Virtual*. Routledge: London.

Shin, Y.Y. (2004) A Person-Environment Fit Model for Virtual Organization, *Journal of Management*, 30, 725–743.

Sotto, R. (1997) The Virtual Organization, *Accounting, Management and Information Technology*, 7(1), 37–51.

Sotto, R. (1998) The Virtualization of the Organizational Subject, in R. Chia (Ed.), *Organized Worlds: Exploration in Technology and Organization* with Robert Cooper, Routledge: London.

Steuer, J. (1992) Defining Virtual Reality: Dimensions Determining Telepresence. *Journal of Communication*, 42(4), 10.

Turkle, S. (1995) *Life on the Screen: Identity in the Age of the Internet*, Phoenix: London.

Turoff, M. (1997) Virtuality, *Communications of the ACM*, September, 40(9), 38–43.

van Binsbergen, Wim (1998) Globalization and Virtuality: Analytical Problems Posed by the Contemporary Transformation of African Societies, *Development and Change*, 29, 873–903.

Watson-Manheim, M.B., Chudoba, K., and Crowston, K. (2002) Discontinuities and Continuities: A New Way to Understand Virtual Work, *Information Technology and People*, 15, 191–209.

Webster, F. (2005) Making Sense of the Information Age: Sociology and Cultural Studies, *Information, Communication & Society*, 8(4), December, 439–458.

Wiesenfeld, B.M., Raghuram, S., and Garud, R. (1998) Communication Patterns as Determinants of Organizational Identification in a Virtual Organization, *Journal of Computer-Mediated Communication*, 3(4), June: http//jcms.hugi.ac.il/vol3/issue4/wiesenfeld.html

Woolgar, S. (2002) *Virtual Society? Technology, Cyberbole, Reality*, Oxford University Press: New York.

Zigurs, I., and Qureshi, S. (2001) The Extended Enterprise: Creating Value from Virtual Space, in G.W. Dickson and G. DeSanctis (Eds), *Information Technology and the Future Enterprise – New Models for Managers*, Prentice Hall: New Jersey.

PART I

Virtuality within organizations

CHAPTER 2

Socialization in a global context: Lessons from dispersed teams

Ilan Oshri, Julia Kotlarsky, and Leslie Willcocks

Introduction

Recent years have witnessed the globalization of many industries. Consequently, globally distributed collaborations and virtual teams have become increasingly common in many areas, but in particular in software development (e.g., Kotlarsky and Oshri, 2005; Krishna, Sahay, and Walsham, 2004; Herbsleb and Mockus, 2003; Battin, Crocker, and Kreidler , 2001; Carmel, 1999). Ongoing innovations in Information and Communication Technologies (ICTs) have made it possible to cooperate in a distributed mode. From originally quite small projects, enabled by ICTs, companies now embark on major complex software development projects across multiple locations.

For example, more and more companies in developed nations are outsourcing parts of their IT services and business processes to developing nations (Carmel and Agarwal, 2002), which results in strategic projects on a large scale and with a longer lifespan. Specific examples include DuPont, the US-based global corporation, that in 2006 signed a sourcing contract with CSC and Accenture to develop and implement SAP Enterprise Resource Planning software and systems globally across more than 20 locations at a cost exceeding $1 billion. Another example is a Tata Consulting Services (TCS) outsourcing project, in which globally distributed teams would provide support and application enhancement services to ABN AMRO Bank over five years. These teams provide support and application enhancement from centers in Mumbai, Bangalore, Sao Paolo, Luxemburg, and Amsterdam.

Overall, a high degree of global collaboration has been evident since the 1990s. Friedman (2005, p. 176), in his book *The World is Flat*, describes how a global, web-enabled playing field has been created as a result of the convergence of ten flattening factors (e.g., the introduction of search engines, such as Netscape and Google, and of workflow applications, and the growing tendency to outsource and offshore work), which offer a real-time platform for collaboration and knowledge sharing to almost anyone on the globe.

Collaboration and team performance depends, to some extent, on the socialization of the dispersed team members (Andres, 2002; Govindarajan and Gupta, 2001; Maznevski and Chudoba, 2000). *Socialization* refers to the process by which individuals acquire the behaviors, attitudes and knowledge necessary for participation in an organization (Ahuja and Galvin, 2003; Goodman and Wilson, 2000). Through socialization, the norms, identity, and cohesion between team members develop, enabling team members to effectively communicate and perform (Ahuja and Galvin, 2003; Hinds and Weisband, 2003).

By and large, the existing research on socialization is based on co-located teams. In the context of non-co-located teams, research has emphasized the unique conditions under which socialization can be supported. For example, electronic communications can enhance the socialization of a newcomer in a virtual team (Ahuja and Galvin, 2003). Nonetheless, non-co-located teams may vary in their degree of virtuality (Crowston et al., 2005), in the length of the project and in the number of remote counterparts involved. In this regard, in addition to creating and maintaining socialization, distributed teams, especially those with a long lifespan, may need to reacquire norms and resocialize as the project progresses. Therefore, the key objective of this chapter is to understand how globally distributed teams (GDTs) support the reacquisition of norms and attitudes over time.

To do so, data were drawn from several globally distributed software development projects at SAP, LeCroy and Baan. The results of the case analyses suggest that indeed various activities were carried out before, during and after face-to-face meetings to support socialization between remote counterparts. Furthermore, these activities were at the individual, team, and organizational levels. As a conclusion, the lifecycle of socialization in GDTs is described and suggestions to practitioners and for further research are made.

Following this introduction, the next two sections provide reviews of the literature relating to socialization in teams in general and in globally distributed teams in particular. The next sections describe and analyze two cases of strategic GDTs from LeCroy and SAP, emphasizing on the mechanisms employed before, during and after face-to-face meetings.

These cases are then compared with the Baan case, where a different approach to socialization was carried out. The following section discusses the findings of this study and offers a framework to consider the lifecycle of socialization in distributed teams. Lastly, practical implications and possible future research are discussed.

Socialization and teams

Socialization is the process through which one "learns the ropes" of a particular organizational role (Wooldbridge and Minsky, 2002). Most studies refer to organizational socialization as a process that is based on interactions between a newcomer and members of the organization (e.g., colleagues, superiors or subordinates). Through such interactions, an employee is taught and learns what behaviors and views are customary and desirable at their workplace, and becomes aware of those that are not, as well as acquiring the knowledge and skills needed to perform his or her job (Taormina and Bauer, 2000). Research has consistently shown that organizational socialization has been positively associated with the organization's strategic effectiveness, intercross-functional coordination capabilities (Wooldbridge and Minsky, 2002), team performance (Hinds and Weisband, 2003), and employee retention (Bigliardi et al., 2005). Activities that support socialization between members of a team have been widely described in the literature and include bonding exercises, training programs, and mentoring schemes. By and large, the literature on socialization is in the context of co-located teams. Only recently have some studies considered socialization in non-co-located teams (e.g., Crowston et al., 2005; Ahuja and Galvin, 2003; Goodman and Wilson, 2000). These studies have emphasized the unique contextual settings involved in non-co-located teams that result in a socialization process that is different from the process observed in co-located teams. For example, Ahuja and Galvin's (2003) study suggests that electronic communications can enhance the socialization of a newcomer in a virtual team, because of the comfort "provided by a lean and faceless electronic communication medium" (ibid., p. 161). For exocentric groups such as incident response and flight crew teams, which are temporary and of short lifespan, Goodman and Wilson (2000) suggest replacing socialization within team boundaries with "substitutes for socialization" that take place beyond actual team boundaries. Such substitutes for socialization include structural substitutes, for example, the development of standard procedures and common sets of knowledge and skills, and learning substitutes based on shared databases and professional meetings through which members of a community can learn in advance how to work in a team.

Nonetheless, when examining non-co-located teams, it is evident that such teams may vary in terms of their degree of "virtuality" and lifespan. Indeed, as Crowston et al. (2005, p. 3) have observed, "teams fall along a continuum from traditional face-to-face to fully distributed, with many exhibiting a mixed mode of interaction." Furthermore, Ahuja and Galvin (2003, p. 170) have explained that some teams do not share a single, physical space since their members are spread throughout the world; however, these teams are not completely virtual because some of the sub-team members are co-located. Such teams are also referred to as "hybrid" teams (Lu et al., 2006). Members of a "hybrid" team are dispersed, but they maintain face-to-face meetings from time to time. Therefore, members of a "hybrid" team may create socialization with their remote counterparts through face-to-face meetings as well as by relying on ICTs. Nonetheless, establishing socialization in "hybrid" teams is not problem-free. In particular, challenges to socializing within "hybrid" teams may arise when such projects continue over a long time and when interpersonal ties may thus weaken. The following section discusses in more detail such challenges.

Socialization in globally distributed contexts: The challenge

One specific case of a "hybrid" team is a globally distributed software development team. Globally distributed projects involve two or more teams working together from different geographical locations to accomplish common project goals. In addition to geographical dispersion, globally distributed teams face time-zone and cultural differences that may include different languages, national traditions, values, and norms of behavior (Carmel, 1999) that may greatly reduce the extent of socialization between remote counterparts.

Socialization in globally distributed teams may take place through two key mechanisms. One is the application of ICT and the second is through face-to-face interactions. In terms of the application of ICT, research on globally distributed teams has widely reported the various electronic media needed to support connectivity between remote sites and to facilitate socialization. For example, Carmel (1999) has argued that a powerful ICT infrastructure is required to ensure connectivity and data transfer at high speed between remote sites. Additionally, generic collaborative technologies (e.g., groupware) are needed to enable remote counterparts to connect and communicate. The most commonly suggested collaborative technologies are e-mail, chat (e.g., instant messaging), phone/teleconferencing, videoconferencing, intranet, group calendar, discussion lists, and electronic meeting systems (Herbsleb and Mockus, 2003; Smith and Blanck, 2002). More recent studies have focused on integrating collaborative technologies into an integrated development environment in order to offer solutions that deal with breakdowns in communication among developers in dispersed software development teams (Cheng et al., 2004).

The literature relating to face-to-face meetings in globally distributed teams is also wide. For example, past research has confirmed that face-to-face meetings are important for the development of distributed teams through the establishment of interpersonal relationships (Crowston et al., 2005). Furthermore, such meetings were found to positively affect team collaboration (Ahuja and Galvin, 2003; Kanawattanachai and Yoo, 2002; Kraut, Butler, and Cummings, 2002; Child, 2001) and team performance (Andres, 2002; Govindarajan and Gupta, 2001; Maznevski and Chudoba, 2000), mainly through the enhancement of interactions between team members (Crowston et al., 2005). While past research has demonstrated that face-to-face meetings are imperative for developing interpersonal ties and socialization between remote counterparts, the literature has, so far, not considered certain challenges associated with face-to-face meetings in GDTs. For example, for budget reasons, it is likely that only a minority of the GDT will participate in a face-to-face meeting. Furthermore, such face-to-face meetings tend to be short and often revolve around technical and project management matters, leaving little time for socialization. These shortcomings relating to face-to-face meetings are summarized in Table 2.1.

Table 2.1 Socialization in GDTs: The challenges

Face-to face meetings are *short* and tend to offer only limited social space that accommodates cultural differences.
Most time spent in face-to-face meetings is dedicated to project procedures and technical issues (i.e., they are *formal* to a great extent).
Face-to-face meetings are *selective* in the sense that not all counterparts are invited to face-to-face meetings.
Short and infrequent face-to-face meetings offer *sporadic* interpersonal interactions between remote counterparts, which restrict the buildup of interpersonal relationships.
ICT offers limited opportunities for personal contact and social space, as compared to face-to-face meetings.
(Based on Robey, Koo, and Powers, 2000; Andres 2002; Nardi and Whittaker, 2002; Olson et al., 2002)

While face-to-face meetings assist in acquainting remote counterparts and in addressing project and technical issues, such meetings being sporadic, short, selective, and formal to a great extent (Andres, 2002; Nardi and Whittaker, 2002; Olson et al., 2002; Robey, Koo, and Powers, 2000) the nature of such meetings barely provides support for long-term socialization (Kraut, Butler, and Cummings, 2002). Furthermore, unlike exocentric teams with a short lifespan, some globally distributed teams cooperate on a lengthier basis, often over several years, while maintaining a "hybrid" mode of work. Such project teams (e.g., research and development teams in multinational organizations and outsourcing projects teams) tend to be large in scale, involving hundreds of remote counterparts who collaborate almost on a daily basis. In this regard, socialization, as a multistaged process that unfolds over time (Goodman and Wilson, 2000), starts when a team is formed or a newcomer joins, and continues throughout a team's lifetime. Indeed, in such teams, face-to-face meetings may assist in familiarizing remote counterparts in the early stages of a project; however, the interpersonal ties created during the initial socialization through face-to-face meetings may eventually degrade over time (Nardi and Whittaker, 2002). Consequently, the development of a long-lasting globally distributed team could be inhibited, as members of the team might experience challenges in progressing from the "forming to performing" through the "storming and norming" stages in the team development process (Furst et al., 2004). In this regard, a lack of processes and organizational mechanisms that support the reacquisition and re-norming of behaviors, attitudes, and knowledge could result in breakdowns in communication, and might negatively affect the productive participation of team members in organizational activities.

While the literature is clear about the positive impact that socialization has on team performance (Hinds and Weisband, 2003), it provides little evidence as to the processes through which socialization can be recreated and renewed. In line with such observations, this study investigates how globally distributed teams support the acquisition of norms and attitudes over time.

Research design and methods

Design and case selection

An in-depth study of globally distributed software development projects is provided in this paper. A qualitative, interpretive approach is adopted. According to Yin (1994), case study research is appropriate to investigate a phenomenon in its real-life context, to answer *how* and *why* questions, when the investigator has little control over the events. Therefore, a case study method was chosen as the most appropriate approach for this research. The case study method is widely used in Information Systems (IS) research. For example, Palvia et al. (2003) examined the usage of various research methodologies, based on an overview of leading management and IS journals, and observed a greater use of the case study method and other qualitative techniques over the years.

To correspond with the main interests of the research, only project teams that were globally distributed across at least two locations, and large in scale and long term time together, were considered for this study. A search for companies with such GDTs resulted in three companies, LeCroy, SAP, and Baan, who agreed to participate in this study. Initial inquiries about the way these GDTs collaborated revealed that SAP and LeCroy pursued an approach that encouraged interpersonal ties between members of their global teams, while Baan downplayed this aspect but emphasized the utilization of electronic media in its collaborative work. An in-depth study of these aspects then followed, to reveal the various aspects involved.

It is also important to mention that, while these GDTs were similar in terms of their size and geographical dispersion, there was one distinct difference between them. The SAP remote teams did not have a history of working together, while the LeCroy dispersed teams had been working together as a global team for a long time (since the mid-1980s). The Baan dispersed teams, on the other hand, had been working as a global team for about three years (since 1999). This variation in team age was seen by the researchers as an opportunity to examine the process through which socialization was created and renewed over time.

Data collection

Evidence was collected from interviews and documentation. Interviews were conducted at two remote sites per company: in India and Germany for SAP, Switzerland and USA for LeCroy, and India and the Netherlands (NL) for Baan. Interviewees were chosen to include (1) counterparts working closely from remote locations, and (2) diverse roles such as managers and developers. In total, 23 interviews (five at SAP, five at LeCroy, and 13 at Baan) were conducted (see interviewees' details in Appendix A). Interviews lasted one hour and 30 minutes on average; they were recorded and fully transcribed. A semi-structured interview protocol was applied, to allow the researchers to clarify specific issues and for follow-up questions.

Data analysis

Data analysis followed several steps. It relied on iterative reading of the data using the open-coding technique (Strauss and Corbin, 1998), sorting and refining themes emerging from the data with some degree of diversity (Strauss and Corbin, 1998; Miles and Huberman, 1994), and linking these to categories and concepts (see Appendix B). In the first round of analysis, three categories emerged from an initial screening of the data, namely: *face-to-face meetings activities*, *additional activities* (i.e., *beyond face-to-face meetings*), and *collaborative technologies*. Statements referring to these socialization activities *during face-to-face meetings*, *beyond face-to-face meetings*, and *collaborative technologies* were selected, coded and analyzed using Atlas.ti – qualitative data analysis software (Miles and Huberman, 1994).

As data analysis progressed, statements (i.e., codes) referring to socialization were grouped around the three above-mentioned categories. A careful examination of the statements revealed that the category of "beyond F2F meetings" actually contained activities that took place *before* and *after face-to-face meetings*. Following this, a second phase of data analysis was launched in which statements referring to socialization activities that took place *before* and *after* face-to-face meetings were selected, coded, and analyzed. Finally, we analyzed statements coded into *before*, *during*, and *after face-to-face meeting* categories, to distinguish between socialization activities that took place on individual, team, and organizational levels. Analysis of data collected at Baan followed a similar procedure. Nonetheless, as little evidence relating to socialization was evident, the researchers sought statements that also referred to the drawbacks associated with the socialization approach taken by Baan.

Case studies of socialization: SAP, LeCroy, and Baan

This section details the results of the three case studies carried out at SAP, LeCroy, and Baan. Based on the empirical evidence presented below, we argue that, despite the challenges faced by the teams, of LeCroy and SAP developed and sustained socialization through various activities that took place before, during, and after face-to-face meetings, which ensured the renewal of socialization over time. Baan, on the other hand, took a different approach: socialization activities were encouraged mainly when development problems became critical, and mostly between certain individuals. We first present the findings from SAP and LeCroy, followed by the Baan case.

The SAP case

This dispersed team was involved in the SAP Collaboration tools project developed by the Knowledge Management (KM) Collaboration group, which is part of the Enterprise Portal Division. The goal of the SAP Collaboration tools project was to develop a comprehensive collaborative platform that would enable both individuals and teams in different locations to communicate in real-time and asynchronously, and in order to support the teamwork of any distributed project teams. The SAP Collaboration tools were developed to be part of the next generation application and integration platform (that is, SAP NetWeaver), and to allow integration with various tools of different providers.

The development of SAP Collaboration tools started in September 2001. By June 2002, the first version of SAP Collaboration tools was released and the group was working on the second release.

The GDT in which the case study was conducted was made up of software engineers, architects, a project manager and team leaders. From a geographical perspective, the software team was distributed between three locations and consisted of four teams: two teams in Walldorf, Germany (ten people in each team), one team in Bangalore, India (six people), and one team in Palo Alto, USA (five people). Each team worked on a different part of the Collaboration tools (see organizational structure in Appendix C).

Before face-to-face: The challenges and socialization activities

When the project was launched in September 2001, key players (managers and architects) and team members from remote locations did not know each other. This team did not have a history of working together and only some of the team members had been previously engaged in global development projects.

Therefore, during the initial stages of the project the key challenge was to create awareness of the composition of the remote teams and their members. For this reason, an introduction of new team members was organized using videoconferencing (VC) sessions, which involved managers and developers in all three locations. One member of the team, Akhilesh, described this process:

> Whenever a new colleague joins our team or any of the teams in the other locations, we make sure that in the next VC, we will introduce this person. We actually do a round like "these are new colleagues that have joined." So, though you have not met them personally, you start learning about this person from that point in time.

Furthermore, interviewees indicated that teleconferences between managers and key members from the three locations were organized on a weekly basis in order to share the different perspectives about how the project should be run, and to create the dynamics for collaborative work between remote counterparts through exploring issues such as the project vision and its main objectives.

Another challenge that this team faced was to make sure that each remote counterpart knew who their contact person was. Indeed, once members of the team were introduced through the first VC session, information about the mini-teams and their contact persons was released. The reason for the formation of mini-teams was that team members did not know each other personally in the beginning and the process of getting acquainted took, in some cases, several weeks; therefore, the management established cross-continental mini-teams and a contact person was appointed for each remote team. For example, Christoph and Martin (development architects located in Walldorf) served as technical contact persons for the remote teams: Christoph was the contact person for the Bangalore team, and Martin was the contact person for the Palo Alto team. These contact people were the main contact points within the team and they ensured the smooth flow of information between dispersed teams and, as a result, facilitated knowledge-sharing processes between the Head Office in Walldorf and remote sites. Christoph described how the communication between teams was managed: "What I did in the past was – this was in the very early phase of the project – I sent requests only to Sudhir [team leader of Bangalore team] and he would distribute the issues between people."

This procedure, it was reported, reduced confusion and miscommunications with regard to who was supposed to deal with what. The contact persons made sure that communications between counterparts who did not know each other and were relatively unfamiliar with the roles within the teams would still occur despite these challenges.

During face-to-face: The challenges and socialization activities

There were numerous face-to-face meetings that took place during this project. For example, managers from Bangalore and Palo Alto flew to

Walldorf to meet for a "kickoff" meeting in late 2001. While blocking time to discuss project- and product-related issues was not a problem, freeing time for one-on-one sessions between counterparts had always been a challenge. For this reason, remote team members were encouraged to make time for one-on-one interactions with their counterparts so that they could get to know each other and become familiar with personal communication styles. For example, Stefan (Director of the GDT from Walldorf) described his experience with Sudhir in adjusting communication styles between them:

> What I did with Sudhir in the very beginning, I told him: "I am explicit; I am forgiving – but you have to tell me that something is going wrong in the very beginning. [...] it is not just me having to deal with an Indian team and it is not just me who needs to adapt my style totally. I will try to adapt, but because of time constraints I am not going to adapt exactly to what you are expecting." This is what we discussed during the F2F meeting when he [Sudhir] was here in Germany. Sudhir said that this is clear, and now we need to see that it works.

Additionally, to gain a better understanding of the local context of the Indian team, which is a common challenge in globally distributed contexts, in early spring 2002 key players from Germany and Palo Alto visited Bangalore to participate in a team-building exercise together with the local team. Some key outcomes from the team-building exercise were described by Sudhir: "It [the team-building exercise] is also about getting to know the infrastructure and the environment in which we work, because in a situation when there is a problem, then it's easy to visualise what is happening."

Also, during the team-building exercise, team members from the three sites met and spent time together, something that gave the entire team and each site a feeling of belonging, of being equally important, and of being part of the Collaborative Tools project team. Stefan, who participated in the team-building exercise, summarized the experience: "The team-building exercise was a way to show that we [headquarters] care about remote locations. The end result of that exercise was that the entire [globally distributed] team feels more comfortable to work together. Now we know each other and trust each other better."

One interesting outcome of this team-building exercise was that teams set up rules for communications and communication styles. Having discussed the direct personal style of communication exercised by the German team, the Indian team acknowledged this style and agreed to not take it personally. In return, German team members learned about Indian working and communication habits.

After face-to-face: The challenges and socialization activities

It was noted by interviewees that following the initial face-to-face meeting, communications became more informal, and also that in some cases it was unnecessary to communicate through the contact person any more. However, as this was a lengthy project, several activities and mechanisms were offered to members of the team to avoid losing touch with their remote counterparts. In term of activities, regular and frequent communications, such as teleconferences and VCs between remote counterparts, were carried out, more frequently (e.g., on a daily basis) between managers, architects and team leaders, as well as between individual developers working on a closely related issue, and less frequently between all teams.

Acknowledging that such communication means can be limited in terms by the richness of the media, short visits to remote locations were organized to ensure that remote counterparts shared information and in order to maintain a "one-team" spirit. Sudhir explained that managers of remote teams (Bangalore and Palo Alto) typically travelled at least once every three months to remote sites, because:

> Staying in Bangalore does not help. By staying here [in Bangalore] we may lose some information, mainly because people don't write every single piece of information in the e-mail. The best is to go out, work with your colleagues for one week to 10 days, keep asking a lot of questions and make sure you get good answers and knowledge.

The idea of individual trips was supported by other interviewees, who claimed that indeed it was challenging to maintain a "one-team spirit" in the long term after a face-to-face meeting. For example, developers located in Bangalore were also encouraged to visit the Head Office: "The idea was that every developer travels across [to Walldorf] and meets everybody at least once for the sake of getting to know each other in person rather than just by name (Sudhir)."

Through these activities, this GDT attempted to renew contacts between remote counterparts through individual trips, VCs and teleconferences. Attention, in particular, was paid to interpersonal contacts between developers and managers who carried out globally distributed collaborative work.

The LeCroy case

The project studied at LeCroy, called Maui, was distributed between two sites: Geneva (Switzerland) and New York (USA) (see organizational structure in Appendix C). There were about 10–15 people in Geneva and the same number in New York (NY). The project code "Maui" stands for massively advanced user interface. The goal of the Maui project was to develop and implement a software platform for new generations of oscilloscopes and oscilloscope-like instruments based on the Windows operating system. This case study covers the development of the Maui platform, and the development of the first products based on the platform. The project started in July 1997; in December 2001, when the data collection took place, LeCroy was launching a first product based on the Maui platform.

Before face-to-face: The challenges and
socialization activities

The software team had a long history of working together developing software for oscilloscopes (since the mid-1980s). At the time this study was carried out, the team had already gone through the initial stages of developing cohesion, learning the attitudes and behaviors of remote counterparts and developing strategies for working together across distance. However, the Maui project introduced new challenges to the GDT at LeCroy. The project involved switching to Microsoft COM technology, which was very different from the approaches LeCroy software engineers had used to develop embedded software for earlier products. Therefore, as with the introduction of the new technology, the norms, behaviors and attitudes common to the GDT were about to change, and one of the dilemmas LeCroy faced while developing the Windows-based Maui platform was how collectively to train embedded programmers located in different sites and yet ensure that this transition would not trigger disruptive communication problems or breakdowns.

Concurrently, another key challenge that this team faced was to integrate newcomers into the team. To overcome this challenge, newcomers joining the project were "introduced" to remote counterparts through transatlantic VCs. Such VCs became frequent during the time that the New York team joined the Geneva team in developing the Maui platform.

Another challenge that this team faced concerned language barriers between the Swiss and the rest of the team. To reduce language barriers, software engineers in Geneva, whose native language is French, were offered English language lessons. The language lessons appeared to improve significantly the communication between remote counterparts. It also positively affected the feeling of belonging to the entire project of the French-speaking team. Furthermore, interviewees indicated that overcoming language barriers, in addition to the introduction of remote counterparts through VCs, had been a key factor in creating direct and effective communication channels between dispersed teams.

During face-to-face: The challenges and
socialization activities

Numerous face-to-face meetings took place during this project. One key challenge that this team faced was to introduce a new technology in a way that further strengthened the interpersonal ties that already existed within the team. The options were to train each team separately in different geographical locations, which may have been cheaper, as opposed to training the team in one geographical location and using this event for additional activities. Eventually, project managers from the Geneva and NY teams decided to organize an event in the Alps that took place in August 1997 and combined training sessions in Microsoft COM technology and some social activities. Larry (director of GDT and manager of NY team) described this: "We all got together in the mountains of France and it was a real fun week. It had two purposes: one was to teach us all this new technology [Microsoft COM]. The other, which was equally important, if not more important, was to try to build relationships between people."

The social events organized during this face-to-face meeting had provided a space for participants to get to know each better. Anthony (manager of Geneva team) explained:

> In fact, I would say that the most valuable time spent is probably in the local bar rather than in the meeting room. Because getting to know someone happens over a few beers. And that develops into the professional [area]. I think that's an important thing, very important thing. That was the idea behind the meeting in the Alps, to get people in an environment where there was plenty time for that. It was pretty important.

This view was supported by other interviewees, who indeed argued that the meeting in the Alps was important from both a professional viewpoint and a social viewpoint. During this gathering, remote counterparts reestablished existing work attitudes and negotiated the way work would be conducted using the new development tools. Interviewees claimed that without meeting their remote counterparts face-to-face it would have been challenging for the entire global team to develop jointly a new platform, to meet the project deadlines and to achieve product success.

After face-to-face: The challenges and socialization activities

Similar to SAP, the LeCroy team was concerned with losing the momentum of socialization created during face-to-face meetings. For this reason, the team at LeCroy maintained frequent communications between the remote sites, utilizing various means of communication. While teleconferences between engineers were a matter of daily communications, VCs were held every several weeks to ensure that a team atmosphere was maintained. This means of communication was critical for the remote team in Geneva, as Anthony explained:

> What happened in Geneva is that among the guys there was a natural feeling that they are kind of unplugged from the rest of the company. Because it is an outpost! In order to handle that we organised regular meetings to let people know what is going on in the company, what everyone else is working on. It was a big help. Every several weeks we would have a transatlantic VC between the software teams in NY and Geneva. It helps everyone, I think, to feel we are working as a team and that they are part of the LeCroy team.

In addition, managers from Geneva and NY visited each other up to five times a year. Short visits and the temporary co-location of software engineers were offered by management so that counterparts could work and solve design problems together as well improve interpersonal contacts. The relocation of experts between remote sites served also as a mechanism that accelerated the sharing of knowledge and technical expertise of the Maui platform. Gilles (software engineer) was involved in the Maui project from the very beginning and was initially based in Geneva and during the transition to the Maui platform, was relocated to NY for one year. He explained:

> Initially only a few engineers from NY worked on the platform so they had always a lot of questions regarding the new platform. The NY engineers were constantly in touch with Geneva. When more and

more people in NY started to work on the new platform, it was decided for me to come over here [to NY] for one year to be the contact person for those who started working on the new platform. [...] this is because I know all the basics, the background of the platform. So, that's why I am here [NY] for one year to kind of teach all the other coworkers how to develop using the same tools.

Indeed, the relocation of experts has assisted in the sharing of knowledge as well as in tightening the links between the Geneva and the NY teams. Additional activities applied at LeCroy were the use of a wide range of collaboration technologies that allowed them to combine audio and visual cues, for example, doing design reviews using application sharing and the telephone at the same time. These, it was reported, reduced miscommunications and breakdowns in the design process.

The Baan case

The Baan globally dispersed team was involved in the development of an E-Enterprise Suite that was designed to let users extend their Baan manufacturing, financial, and distribution software on the Web, to allow them to collaborate better with customers, suppliers, and partners. At the time of data collection the E-Enterprise Suite consisted of seven products that were all based on one platform called E-Enterprise Server. Products included in the E-Enterprise Suite were developed to be stand-alone as well as to be integrated with the ERP package developed by Baan.

The development of the E-Enterprise Suite was organized by feature/ product function (see organizational structure in Appendix C). From a geographical perspective, the E-Enterprise group was distributed between two locations: Hyderabad, India (about 60 people working on five products of the E-Enterprise Suite), and Barneveld, NL (about 35 people working on two products and the common platform of the E-Enterprise Suite).

Socialization challenges and activities at Baan

The E-Enterprise group was established in 1999. Some people in Hyderabad had been working in a globally distributed environment before joining the E-Enterprise group, developing the Baan ERP solution. However, because of a general Baan policy to reduce travel expenses, and because the E-Enterprise organizational structure had changed several times since the group was established, team members had gradually come to know each other less well in person. These changes gave rise to particular challenges. First, the majority of the global team did not know their remote counterparts, and their workplace norms and attitudes. Second, differences relating to cultural backgrounds in terms of national culture (Dutch and Indian) and organizational culture (newcomers and people who had joined from Baan ERP group) were more difficult to bridge. The general manager of E-Enterprise based in Hyderabad explained:

> In E-Enterprise most of the people have not met face-to-face, except some key people. It is my perspective, I might be wrong, that E-Enterprise overall is not part of the Baan ERP culture. Especially in E-Enterprise Hyderabad, you find two sets of people [...]; People who worked for 3–4 years on ERP and moved into E-Enterprise [...], they understand the issues because they have also gone through them in the past; they also understand how the Dutch culture is. Newcomers, who have come directly from outside and started working on E-Enterprise products, have not undergone the process of maturity; they have not understood the Baan culture very well. They are not exposed to the Dutch culture.

Despite recognizing a lack of cohesion in terms of attitudes, norms and behaviors in the E-Enterprise group, Baan did not take actions to facilitate socialization between remote teams and within local teams. Furthermore, face-to-face interactions between remote counterparts in Baan were limited to high-level managers only, even though the value of interacting face-to-face was clear. The general manager reflected on the socialization process achieved in these limited meetings:

> After going through face-to-face discussions and starting to understand each other I could see a lot of change in the way we deal with things. Issues are still issues, but now the issues are tackled differently. [...] There is a change. During face-to-face we shared with each other what are the issues and discussed each other's wishes. So some kind of empathizing is coming in, understanding each other.

Nonetheless, Baan preferred to limit these face-to-face interactions for cost-saving reasons, as well as limiting the visits of certain individuals to remote locations only to those urgent occasions when it was not possible to deal with problems from a distance.

Last but not least, remote locations (e.g., Hyderabad office) found it difficult to access information generated in other locations (e.g. Barneveld office), such as updates about changes in requirements and dependencies between the products, and product and technology roadmaps.

To cope with such changes in the way dispersed teams collaborated and related to each other, the E-Enterprise group equipped its teams well with the technologies required to enable collaboration in a globally distributed environment. Technologies were considered very important to support collaborations despite the cost-cutting approach that significantly reduced face-to-face meetings between remote counterparts. As one manager from Hyderabad explained, "technology comes to our rescue in working in a distributed environment."

Indeed, various technologies were used to save on travel costs between the Netherlands and India. For example, e-mail would typically be used for brief queries and for describing a problem prior to a phone-call. The phone would be used in situations when an urgent response was required and to resolve potential conflicts. The product architect from Hyderabad described the use of these electronic means: "Telephone was usually involved when a lot of e-mails have exchanged and when certainly we feel that everyone is talking differently and it is taking too much time and no one is coming to any conclusions, then we start organizing a telephone call."

While the use of the phone was imperative for solving such problems, there was a general tendency, guided by management, to minimize the use of the phone because of the costs involved. This rule was applied to other communication means. For example, VC sessions took place between managers from dispersed locations, but in an infrequent manner, and application sharing tools (AST), in particular NetMeeting and Webex, were only occasionally in use, mainly for knowledge-sharing activities during meetings between sites and customers.

Socialization activities at Baan: The impact

The lack of face-to-face interactions and the limited use of electronic means generated discontent among members of the dispersed teams and exacerbated the lack of socialization across the remote sites. Interviewees claimed that there was a lack of team atmosphere between the teams in Hyderabad and Barneveld, which was evident in the way norms and atti-tudes were not shared. For example, the general manager of E-Enterprise in Hyderabad explained: "The major issue is that people don't perceive that on the other side, *they*'re not reciprocating *our* needs: what *we* want, during which time, what priority *we* have. *They* don't see the same priority as *our* people see, and vice versa. So there is always a gap."

Another example of tensions, as well as lack of cohesion (the problem of ownership), was given by a manager of two products in the E-Enterprise suite:

> When *we* [in Hyderabad] gained a lot of knowledge (for example myself: being consultant, I knew the product in and out), *we* realised that we in India could take the ownership of the entire product, one module at least, and create everything from scratch. So then *we* really had a huge problem with Holland to take ownership. *We* wanted to build a product in India without any influence from Holland, but *they* were not willing to give (Vijaya).

There was also a gap in the common understanding of processes, and resistance in following them. As the general manager of the E-Enterprise explained: "The processes are not really defined well, so still you find some gaps in having a common understanding on the processes. Slowly, slowly that is getting reduced, but still I can see an issue over that."

Furthermore, there was internal resistance to following processes, in particular with newcomers: "Whenever we start on a project we will say that these are the processes that we need to follow. But still we find some people are not very keen, they think that 'What advantage do we get if we follow this process?'" (Jeevan).

The impact of the approach taken by Baan to create socialization between remote counterparts, which was mainly based on occasional face-to-face meetings between certain individuals and a restricted use of rich media tools, resulted in discontent among members of the global team concerning their belonging to "one team," as well as their ability to cooperate and jointly develop products.

Collaborative Tools for socialization

Focusing on SAP and LeCroy, the evidence suggests that the tools and technologies employed by these GDTs were similar and included various means of media and collaborative technologies, such as phone, VC, and groupware technologies. Nonetheless, within these dispersed teams different tools and technologies were employed before and after face-to-face meetings. Asynchronous media (e.g., e-mail) were widely employed before the "kickoff" meeting. It has been claimed by interviewees that in the early stages of the project, remote counterparts did not always feel confident in contacting their remote colleagues by phone. The e-mail was the main collaborative tool employed at this stage. One flaw in this practice is that, during the early stages of a project, remote counterparts tended to engage in several rounds of sending e-mails, trying to clarify all the issues involved and to resolve misunderstandings. Once remote counterparts had met, the use of synchronous media (e.g., phone, VC, online chat, application sharing) increased. It was also reported by interviewees from both companies that VC was employed before and after face-to-face meetings to address the limited opportunities to meet in person.

In between face-to-face meetings, both companies utilized the telephone. LeCroy also relied on voice-chat as the main means of communication. SAP, for example, set up internal phone lines across the globe in which five-digit numbers between Bangalore and Walldorf were offered to the remote teams. Interviewees reported that the telephone was mainly used for urgent matters, for regular updates between managers, and the resolution of misunderstandings.

The e-mail, on the other hand, was employed to communicate low-priority tasks and issues, and tasks that could not or did not have to be completed in real-time because of time-zone differences.

Moreover, some remote counterparts, mainly those who enjoyed long-term interpersonal ties, tended to communicate more informally, using, for example, online chat applications. The global team at LeCroy, for example, communicated through MSN Messenger. Using this application enabled the team to have a real-time remote contact without having to use the telephone. Furthermore, at LeCroy MSN Messenger was used to inform team members about the availability of their remote counterparts in real-time. Table 2.2 summarizes the collaborative tools employed by remote teams at LeCroy and SAP.

Discussion of key findings

The main objective of this study was to understand how globally distributed teams resocialize through the reacquisition of norms, attitudes and behaviors. We have suggested earlier that such teams may need to "reacquire" norms, , and knowledge because of the unique characteristics of these teams. Indeed, evidence from LeCroy and SAP suggests that their GDTs needed to resocialize over time. For example, the introduction of a new technology at LeCroy created a need for the global team to reacquire norms and work attitudes relating to new practices, tools, and procedures. The first major face-to-face meeting at the SAP team only sharpened participants' awareness of the need for additional exposure to remote counterparts' attitudes and behaviors, and the need for innovative ways to

Table 2.2 Collaborative tools before, during, and after face-to-face meetings

	Before face-to-face	During face-to-face	After face-to-face
LeCroy	*E-mail* for clarifications/resolving misunderstandings *Phone* mainly between managers for updates *VC* for virtual meetings between managers and team members *Intranet* to post internal documents	Social spaces that enable face-to-face meetings and team-building exercises	*Online chat* to address short questions *E-mail* for clarifications *Phone* for resolving misunderstandings and conflicts and for helping in bug fixes (working around-the-clock) *VC* for virtual meetings between managers and team members *Application sharing* for helping in bug fixes *Intranet* to post internal documents
SAP	*E-mail* for clarifications/resolving misunderstandings *Phone* for urgent situations (mainly between managers) *VC* for virtual meetings between managers and team members	Social spaces that enable face-to-face meetings and team-building exercises	*E-mail* for clarifications *Phone* for resolving misunderstandings and conflicts and for helping in bug fixes (working around-the-clock) *VC* for virtual meetings between managers and team members *Application sharing* for knowledge sharing (e.g., slide shows) *Intranet* to post internal documents

update the team about evolving work attitudes and knowledge within the globally distributed team. On the other hand, the Baan team faced difficulties in developing socialization throughout the project lifecycle, not just in relation to mechanisms that could resocialize its remote counterparts. This team mainly relied on occasional socialization activities that were supported by electronic means, which resulted in disagreements and tensions between remote counterparts and had a negative impact on the ability of the GDT to collaborate. In this regard, the Baan global team failed to normalize and socialize newcomers in the first place, but, more importantly, failed to "resocialize" the entire global team. Thus, as the entire GDT faced difficulties in developing shared norms, attitudes, and behaviors, which created barriers to "reacquiring" norms and "resocializing" as the project progressed and as certain work practices changed.

Furthermore, our analysis suggests that the GDTs at SAP and LeCroy employed various mechanisms and implemented numerous processes to ensure that socialization would be created and maintained throughout the project lifecycle. For example, holding videoconferences to introduce team members to the global team was one element that interviewees indicated as important for collaboration prior to a face-to-face meeting. Making time during a face-to-face meeting for social activities as well as for one-on-one discussions were two additional components that assisted remote counterparts to acquire norms, attitudes, and behaviors. Reacquiring (changing) norms and attitudes required additional mechanisms in the form of short visits, relocations, and the use of rich media communication technologies. In this regard, SAP and LeCroy treated socialization as an organizational process that requires constant improvement and renewal, and which is part of the collaborative mode of work developed within these GDTs. Both LeCroy and SAP practiced temporary relocation of experts and offered short visits to remote sites, not necessarily in proportion to the degree of difficulty in collaborating that the team was facing. Opposed to the approach taken by LeCroy and SAP, Baan regarded socialization as a stand-alone process, separated from the daily mode of collaboration, which can be activated mainly when other mechanisms to support collaboration have failed. As described above, face-to-face meetings and videoconferencing at Baan were often organized in situations in which other communication means had failed to deliver a solution. Indeed, evidence from Baan suggests that this globally distributed team suffered from tensions, a lack of cohesion, and gaps in understanding attitudes, norms, and behaviors between remote counterparts.

In line with the existing literature (e.g., Crowston et al., 2005), the findings of this study suggest that face-to-face meetings are indeed important in creating interpersonal ties and facilitating a socialization process. However, evidence from the SAP and LeCroy cases also suggests that socialization in these GDTs was not supported by face-to-face meetings only. Rather, an array of activities that were offered and implemented by these companies before and after face-to-face meetings allowed these teams to socialize and, when necessary, to reacquire norms and attitudes. Furthermore, we observed that the team development process in GDTs indeed faces distinctive challenges induced not least by geographical and cultural differences, thus requiring management's intervention in supporting the timely development of a team from "forming, through storming and norming to performing" (Furst et al., 2004). But in anything other than a relatively small globally distributed project, and probably not even then, this cannot be a straightforward linear process. As global projects become more strategic in importance and larger in size, from a socialization perspective, the GDTs involved in such projects have to regularly reacquire norms and attitudes, mainly because, as we observed, newcomers join and affect the norms and attitudes within the teams, and disagreement and miscommunication may regularly arise even in late phases of projects. These soft factors can seriously delay projects, restrict productivity, and have quality and cost consequences, as other studies of complex IT projects regularly note. Therefore, based on the observations made in this study, we argue that socialization in GDTs should be an ever-evolving organizational process enacted on individual, team, and organizational levels and supported by an array of activities that go beyond face-to-face meetings.

Socialization in globally distributed teams: A proposed framework

It is important to note that our findings are based on three case studies and therefore, by definition, meet to only a limited extent the criteria of transferability (the extent to which the findings can be replicated across cases). Additional research across multiple case studies is needed in order to verify the insights reported in this paper. With this in mind we can explore the approach to creating, maintaining, and renewing socialization in globally distributed teams.

In line with the data analyzed above, we propose that the process of socialization in GDTs should be framed in three phases: *Introduction*, *Build-Up*, and *Renewal* (as shown in Figure 2.1). Each phase is associated with an array of activities that a firm may apply in order to move from the

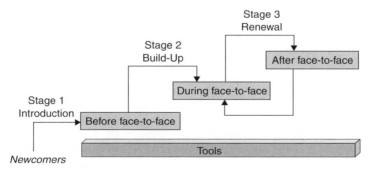

Figure 2.1 The lifecycle of social ties development in GDTs

introduction phase to the building up of socialization, and, finally, to the renewal phase. The first phase, *Introduction*, relates to the initial stage of a project or when a newcomer joins the GDT. During this phase, remote counterparts are being introduced to the norms, attitudes, and behaviors that should govern the collaboration mode within the global team. While such procedures are a standardized approach to collaboration, these rules can still be understood differently by remote counterparts or newcomers. Negotiating the meaning of work and communication procedures can be done during the introduction phase, and yet requires remote counterparts to overcome distance, cultural differences, and language barriers. Realizing the team composition and key rules, for example, can play a key role in the negotiation process, as team members refer to their remote counterparts with whom they will be corresponding when discussing aspects related to work and communication procedures. Reducing communication barriers is also critical in facilitating an initial negotiation of the meaning of work and communication attitudes. This can be achieved, for example, by overcoming language barriers and providing language lessons to local and remote sites. Yet, reducing possibilities for communication breakdowns and miscommunication is no less equally important, as remote counterparts and particular newcomers, may not have diffused the norms and attitudes of collaboration. Therefore, the role of a contact person and mini-teams in ensuring the flow of information between remote counterparts is critical.

The second phase, *Build-Up*, offers a stage to advance the socialization process through face-to-face meetings. Such a stage offers remote counterparts the opportunity to negotiate the meaning of work and communication procedures, and to resolve pending collaboration issues in a person-to-person manner. Typically, a major face-to-face meeting would take place early in the project and would involve a significant number of participants from remote locations. Additional face-to-face meetings would take place throughout the project lifecycle and would involve fewer remote counterparts in different roles. The negotiation of the meaning of work and communication procedures should be facilitated at various levels and through different channels, such as between corresponding remote counterparts and through a one-on-one meeting. Through such negotiations, the global team is going through a "storming" and "norming" process (Furst et al., 2004), during which remote counterparts examine existing work and communication procedures and assess their meaning in the team's local and global context. "Norming" the team would mean that members of the team can relate to the context within which their remote counterparts operate and agree on a shared understanding of norms, attitudes, and behaviors that support their collaborative work. Through such processes the global team facilitates (as in the SAP case) or refreshes (as in the LeCroy case) the acquisition of norms and attitudes at the individual and team levels through intensive interpersonal interactions and social activities.

The third phase, *Renewal*, refers to a later stage of the project, in which "resocialization" is needed. As the interpretation of work and communication procedures by remote counterparts may change over time, a "renorming" process of the team may need to take place. Having collaborated with each other for some time, the "renegotiation" of the meaning of work and communication procedures can be done through media-rich communication tools, but also through short visits and relocations. "Resocializing" the team requires the participation of remote counterparts in reflective sessions and other discussions. Through such participation, remote counterparts share their understanding of the team's work and communication procedures, consequently embarking on a "renegotiation" of these meanings until an agreement is achieved. This process "resocializes" the global team.

We observed that LeCroy's dispersed teams which had been working as a global team for a long time, invested mainly in activities associated with the *Renewal* step, that is, in "resocializing" this particular team. SAP, on the other hand, where remote teams had simply merged into one global team, advanced socialization by introducing activities associated with the Build-Up phase. Most companies will engage in activities associated with the Introduction phase either for the sake of introducing newcomers or when a new project is assembled and the counterparts do not know each other from the past.

In terms of hybrid teams, supporting and developing socialization is important within a co-located team and across virtual teams. In this regard, hybrid teams should invest in the three phases discussed above to ensure that socialization is supported both within co-located teams and across virtual teams. Yet, intra-team dynamics may affect interteam socialization processes. For example, a high employee turnover in one co-located team may have an impact on the set of values and norms commonly accepted by the entire virtual team. Therefore, re-norming hybrid teams would mean that project managers should "re-norm" co-located teams while "re-norming" the entire virtual team. Such a challenge requires project leads and managers to frequently communicate with their remote counterparts to ensure that they are exposed to local values and traits, while negotiating the norms, values and behaviors expected from the entire virtual team.

Practical implications

From a practical viewpoint, we argue that in order to achieve successful collaboration, firms should consider investing in the development of socialization despite the constraints imposed by global distribution. Socialization can be supported over time and at various levels within an organization, as shown in Table 2.3. We argue that such activities can be associated with the individual, team, and organizational level. Yet, in practice, each level contributes to the development of socialization across the entire organization and through the different phases (i.e., Introduction, Build-Up and Renewal). For example, language lessons offered before face-to-face meetings are likely to contribute to one-on-one interactions during face-to-face meetings, and these in return will support direct communications after face-to-face meetings. Therefore, we argue that the array of activities in Table 2.3 is imperative for understanding the multiple channels through which socialization is facilitated between remote teams.

Furthermore, we propose that firms should first assess the phase that the dispersed team is in, prior to embarking on introducing activities,

Table 2.3 Individual, team, and organizational activities supporting social ties before, during, and after face-to-face meetings

	Before face-to-face	During face-to-face	After face-to-face
Individual	• Offer language courses • Increase awareness of communication styles • Offer short visits of individuals to remote locations	• Create space for one-on-one interactions • Provide sense of importance of each member • Adjust communication styles	• Offer short visits to remote locations • Offer temporary co-location • Ensure real-time communication channels • Ensure mixed audio and visual cues
Team	• Introduction of new team members • Increase awareness of team composition • Offer virtual face-to-face meetings • Increase awareness of communication protocol • Set up mini-teams • Appoint contact person per remote team	• Conduct kick-off meeting • Offer space for multiple interactions between counterparts • Offer team-building exercises • Organize social events • Discuss differences in national cultures	• Facilitate reflection sessions • Facilitate around-the-table discussions • Facilitate progress meetings
Organizational	• Distribute newsletters • Create and offer shared cyberspaces	• Discuss organizational structure • Discuss differences in organizational culture	• Ensure direct communication channels

communication tools and procedures that aim at the creation and renewal of socialization. Dispersed teams that are in the *Introduction* phase (such as SAP and Baan in our research) require a different set of activities and tools to support the creation of socialization from teams that are in the *Renewal* phase (such as LeCroy). In assessing the phase that their team is in, managers should ask the following question: is there a reason to believe that the set of norms, work attitudes, and knowledge has changed since the team was formed?

In answering this question, managers should mainly consider two aspects. The first aspect is the shared histories of team members. A newly formed team whose members have little or no shared history of working together is more likely to be at the *Introduction* phase. This means that such a team would need to employ a set of activities and processes that ensure the acquaintance of remote counterparts with each other (e.g., through videoconferencing) and that support the flow of information, especially in the early stages of the project, with as few communication breakdowns as possible (e.g., through contact persons and communication protocols). A team whose members have previously worked together is likely to be in the *Renewal* phase. This team would require the employment of processes that ensure the reacquisition of norms (e.g., short visits and relocations) and offer a stage to negotiate the meaning of norms and work attitudes over time (e.g., through reflection sessions). The second aspect is technological change or innovation that a team may have experienced during the project, or in the beginning of a new project. In such a case, work attitudes and norms may have changed and their meaning might not be similarly perceived by remote counterparts. To overcome this, managers should provide a stage during which remote counterparts could discuss the meaning of the change in the context of their work and the implications for global collaboration. This can be achieved through reflective sessions via teleconferencing, videoconferencing or discussion boards on the intranet. On occasions when the change is significant, such as the switch to Microsoft COM technology at LeCroy, a face-to-face meeting between the remote counterparts involved should be considered.

Last but not least, we propose that managers consider staffing dispersed teams based not only on their set of skills but also on their shared past experiences. By doing this, GDTs will mainly focus on reacquiring norms and attitudes over time and on renegotiating the meaning of these norms and attitudes when change takes place.

While the focus of this study has been face-to-face meetings, we acknowledge that not all GDTs have the opportunity to develop socialization throughout the project lifecycle. Financial and project planning constraints may impede face-to-face meetings, thus resulting in fewer opportunities to develop interpersonal ties that support the reacquisition of norms and attitudes within the dispersed team. Despite these constraints, a GDT could still consider the activities described in Table 2.3 that will foster socialization without the support of face-to-face meetings.

References

Ahuja, M.K., and Galvin, J.E. (2003) Socialization in Virtual Groups, *Journal of Management*, 29(2), 161–185.

Andres, H.P. (2002) A Comparison of Face-to-face and Virtual Software Development Teams, *Team Performance Management*, 8(1/2), 39–48.

Battin, R.D., Crocker, R., and Kreidler, J. (2001) Leveraging Resources in Global Software Development, *IEEE Software*, 18(2), 70–77.

Bigliardi, B., Petroni, A., and Dormio, A.I. (2005) Organizational Socialization, Career Aspirations and Turnover Intentions Among Design Engineers, *Leadership & Organizational Development Journal*, 26(5/6), 424–441.

Carmel, E. (1999) *Global Software Teams: Collaborating Across Borders and Time Zones*, Prentice Hall: New Jersey.

Carmel, E., and Agarwal, R. (2002) The Maturation of Offshore Sourcing of Information Technology Work, *MIS Quarterly Executive*, 1(2), 65–77.

Cheng, L., De Souza, C.R.B., Hupfer, S., Patterson, J., and Ross, S. (2004) Building Collaboration into IDEs, *Queue*, 1(9), 40–50.

Child, J. (2001) Trust – The Fundamental Bond in Global Collaboration, *Organizational Dynamics*, 29(4), 274–288.

Crowston, K., Howison, J., Masango, C., and Eseryel, U.Y. (2005) Face-to-face Interactions in Self-organizing Distributed Teams, Academy of Management Conference, Honolulu, Hawaii.

Friedman, T.L. (2005) *The World is Flat*, Farrar, Straus, and Giroux: New York.

Furst, S.A., Reeves, M., Rosen, B., and Blackburn, R.S. (2004) Managing the Life Cycle of Virtual Teams, *The Academy of Management Executive*, 18(2), 6–20.

Goodman, P.S., and Wilson, J.M. (2000) "Substitutes for Socialization in Exocentric Teams," in M. Neale, B. Mannix, and T. Griffith (Eds), *Research in Groups and Teams*, Vol. 3, JAI Press, 53–77.

Govindarajan, V., and Gupta, A.K. (2001) Building an Effective Global Business Team, *MIT Sloan Management Review*, 42(4), 63–71.

Herbsleb, J.D., and Mockus, A. (2003) An Empirical Study of Speed and Communication in Globally Distributed Software Development, *IEEE Transactions on Software Engineering*, 29(6), 1–14.

Hinds, P., and Weisband, S. (2003) "Knowledge Sharing and Shared Understanding in Virtual Teams," in C. Gibson and S. Cohen (Eds), *Virtual Teams that Work: Creating Conditions for Virtual Team Effectiveness*, Jossey-Bass: San Francisco, pp. 21–36.

Kanawattanachai, P., and Yoo, Y. (2002) Dynamic Nature of Trust in Virtual Teams, *Journal of Strategic Information Systems*, 11(3–4), 187–213.

Kotlarsky, J., and Oshri, I. (2005) Social Ties, Knowledge Sharing and Successful Collaboration in Globally Distributed System Development Projects, *European Journal of Information Systems*, 14(1), 37–48.

Kraut, R. E., Butler, B.S., and Cummings, J. (2002) The Quality of Social Ties Online, *Communications of the ACM*, 45(7), 103–108.

Krishna, S., Sahay, S., and Walsham, G. (2004) Managing Cross-Cultural Issues in Global Software Outsourcing, *Communications of the ACM*, 47(4), 62–66.

Lu, M., Watson-Manheim, M.B., Chudoba, K.M., and Wynn, E. (2006) Virtuality and Team Performance: Understanding the Impact of Variety of Practice, *Journal of Global Information Technology Management*, 9(1), 4–23.

Maznevski, M.L., and Chudoba, K.M. (2000) Bridging Space Over Time: Global Virtual Team Dynamics and Effectiveness, *Organization Science*, 11(5), 473–492.

Miles, M.B., and Huberman, M.A. (1994) *Qualitative Data Analysis: An Expanded Sourcebook*, Sage: Thousand Oaks, CA.

Nardi, B., and Whittaker, S. (2002) "The Place of Face-to-Face Communication in Distributed Work," in P. Hinds and S. Kiesler (Eds), *Distributed Work* , MIT Press: Cambridge, MA, 83–110.

Olson, J.S., Teasley, S.D., Covi, L., and Olson, G.M.S. (2002) "The Currently Unique Advantages of Collocated Work," in P. Hinds and S. Kiesler (Eds), *Distributed Work*, MIT Press: Cambridge, MA, 113–135.

Palvia, P., Mao, E., Salam, A.F., and Soliman, K.S. (2003) Management Information System Research: What's There in a Methodology?, *Communications of the Association for Information Systems*, 11, 289–309.

Robey, D., Khoo, H., and Powers, C. (2000) Situated Learning in Cross-Functional Virtual Teams, *IEEE Transactions on Professional Communications*, 43(1), 51–66.

Smith, P.G., and Blanck, E.L. (2002) From Experience: Leading Dispersed Teams. *The Journal of Product Innovation Management*, 19, 294–304.

Strauss, A.L., and Corbin, J.M. (1998) *Basics of Qualitative Research*, Sage: Thousand Oaks, CA.

Taormina, R.J., and Bauer, T.N. (2000) Organizational Socialization in Two Cultures: Results from the United States and Hong Kong, *International Journal of Organizational Analysis*, 8(3), 262–289.

Wooldbridge, B.R., and Minsky, B.D. (2002) The Role of Climate and Socialization in Developing Interfunctional Coordination, *The Learning Organization*, 9(12), 29–38.

Yin, R.K. (1994) *Case Study Research: Design and Methods*, Sage: Thousand Oaks, CA.

Appendix A: Interviewees' details

1. SAP: Interviewees' details

Interviews were carried out between February and June 2002. Roles are correct for 2002.

Name	Role	Location
Stefan	Director of KM Collaboration Group	Walldorf
Sudhir	Development Manager	Bangalore
Christoph	Development Architect, contact person for Bangalore team	Walldorf
Akhilesh	Developer	Bangalore
Jyothi	Senior Developer	Bangalore

2. LeCroy: Interviewees' details

Interviews were carried out between November 2001 and January 2003. Roles are correct for 2002.

Name	Role	Location
Larry	Director of Software Engineering	NY
Anthony	Chief Software Architect	Geneva
Gilles	Software Engineer	Geneva
Adrian	Web-master	NY
Corey	Vice President Information Systems	NY

3. Baan: Interviewees' details

Interviews were carried out in March 2002. Roles are correct for 2002.

Name	Role	Location
Sjaak	Senior Process Engineer	Barneveld
Jeevan	General Manager of E-Enterprise	Hyderabad
Sridhar	Development Manager of Group 2 (Group 2)	Hyderabad
Phani	Product Architect of E-Service (Group 2)	Hyderabad
Sujai	Development Manager of Group 1 (Group 1)	Hyderabad
Srinivas	Product Architect of E-Service Remote (Group 2)	Hyderabad
Venkat	Product Manager of E-Service and E-Service Remote (Group 2)	Hyderabad
Ganesh	Process Manager for Hyderabad Group	Hyderabad
Vijaya	Product Manager of E-Time and Expense (Group 2)	Hyderabad
Maruthi	Product Architect of E-Procurement (Group 1)	Hyderabad
Johnson	Product Architect of E-Time and Expense (Group 2)	Hyderabad

Appendix B: Data analysis approach

The figure below illustrates the process through which codes describing specific socialization activities were associated with categories, and includes examples of the codes used for each category. A bottom-up, interpretive approach was used to associate codes with particular categories. Interview transcripts were analyzed using Atlas.ti software. During this process chunks of text that are partial or complete sentences or expressions describing socialization activities were assigned codes summarising the activity.

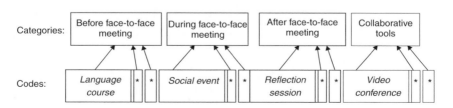

* more codes exist (not shown in the statement used as an example)

Appendix C: Organizational structure of GDTs

1. SAP: Organizational structure of KM Collaboration group (as of June 2002)

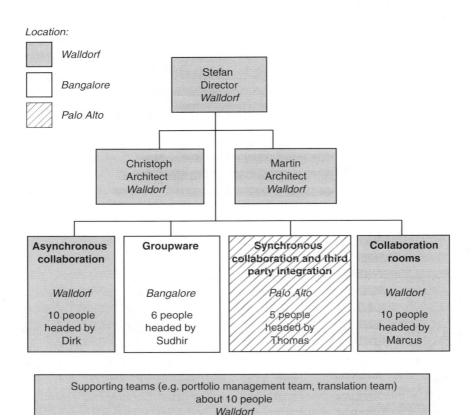

2. LeCroy: Organizational structure of global software team (as of January 2002)

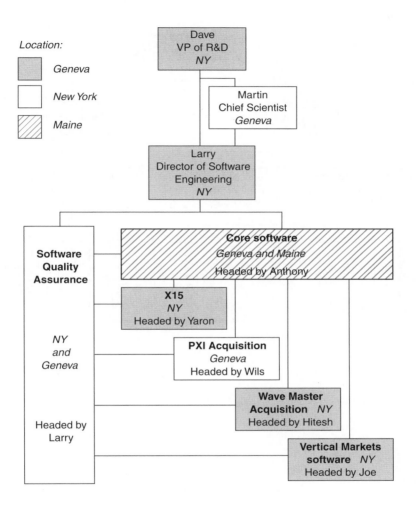

3. Baan: Organizational structure of E-Enterprise development group (as of March 2002)

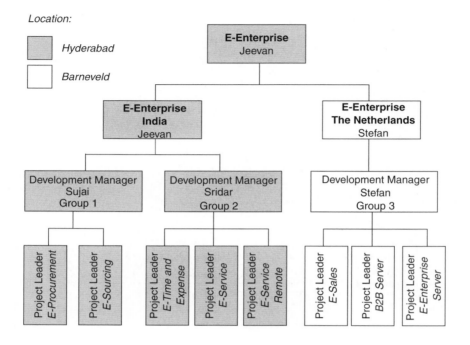

CHAPTER 3

Shared communication practices and mental models in the virtual work environment

Katherine M. Chudoba* and Mary Beth Watson-Manheim*

Introduction

Prior research underscores the importance of building and maintaining shared expectations in order for individual members of a team to coalesce and achieve successful team outcomes (Cohen and Bailey, 1997; Mignerey, Rubin, and Gorden, 1995). Expectations are part of an individual's mental model of a situation and are developed over time through attaching meaning to behaviors. Shared expectations lower communication costs and determine rules of behavior in organizations (Forsyth, 1998). The impact of virtuality on this process has produced equivocal findings in the literature. The common assumption is that work is harder because members must communicate across boundaries of time and space (Espinosa et al., 2003; Jarvenpaa and Leidner, 1999; Kiesler and Cummings, 2002); however, some research suggests that a lack of shared work practices is a more significant impediment to successful performance outcomes in the virtual work environment (VWE) than the simple presence of various boundaries (Chudoba et al., 2005).

In this chapter, we propose that shared expectations of ICT use, as represented in a team's communication media repertoire, are especially critical in the virtual environment where use of media is integral to accomplishing work activities. Maznevski and Chudoba (2000) found that shared understanding of temporal patterns of communication and rhythms of

* Both authors contributed equally.

meetings differentiated a successful global virtual team from less successful teams. However, little research has addressed the practices of media
use and development of shared expectations in the VWE.

We begin by first setting the context of the VWE and consider the
consequences of looking at virtuality as a perceptual rather than an objective phenomenon. In other words, members of a team may work across
objective boundaries (e.g., multiple time zones, different organizations),
but the boundaries may not always be perceived as problematic. Drawing
on the work of Watson-Manheim and her colleagues (2007), we view the
construct of discontinuity as a factor that reflects perceptions of problems
at boundaries. A discontinuity results in increased effort by the team members to accomplish work activities because of differences in expectations
introduced at the boundary. These differences must be negotiated and
resolved by the team members in order for work to be accomplished. Next,
we look at the relationship between the use of the communication media
repertoire (Watson-Manheim and Belanger, 2007) – the collection of communication channels and shared routines of media use across members of
a team – and the processes of maintaining and building mental models in a
virtual team. We propose that only when discontinuities are perceived at a
boundary will there be a moderating effect on the relationship between
communication mode repertoire and the processes of mental model maintenance and mental model building. Implications of our research model for
practice and research are also discussed.

Context: The virtual work environment[1]

The VWE has often been analyzed in terms of boundaries, which generally
have been understood as static demarcations that separate individuals and
create barriers to communication that can be bridged, in part, through the
use of ICT (Espinosa et al., 2003). Geography is the most obvious
boundary that is encountered in virtual work but people in these environments encounter numerous boundaries, such as time, organization, and
nationality, which are not usually present in more conventional work settings to the same extent. Orlikowski (2002) found boundaries to be particularly important in understanding how work was conducted in a
geographically dispersed high-tech organization. She identified seven
boundaries – temporal, geographic, social, cultural, historical, technical,
and political – navigated in Kappa. Members of the Kappa organization
adapted behavior regularly in order to deal with the multiple boundaries
they encountered in their daily work activities, as the boundaries were
being "reconstructed and redefined" (Orlikowski, 2002, p. 255).

Orlikowski's insight that boundaries were continually changing and redefined by Kappa members suggests that a boundary encompasses more than an objective concept that is either present or absent in the VWE – it also has a perceptual component. Further, because a shared work environment is dependent on interaction and coordination among its members (Stohl, 1995), boundaries are only problematic to the extent that team members in a VWE perceive that increased or unexpected communication is necessary in order to get work done. Watson-Manheim and her colleagues (2007) characterized the increased effort of crossing boundaries in order to get work done as a discontinuity. Nijkamp, Rietveld, and Salomon (1990) conceptualized this condition by looking at the effects of borders on physical flows of products and information across space. We tell a story to illustrate.

> Marie lives in the northeastern United States, near the border with Canada. She has the choice of traveling to a US city or a Canadian city for dinner and a movie. The geographic distance between US city or a Canadian city is the same, so distance alone does not play a role in her decision about where to enjoy a night on the town (see Figure 3.1). However, traveling to C means that Marie must cross a national border, and this requires a significant amount of effort. There are likely to be long lines as she waits to go through a border inspection and further delays if she is questioned by border or customs agents, perhaps even including a search of her car. Thus, while the geographic distance from A to C is no greater than the distance from A to B, the challenges of the border inspection mean that Marie perceives the national border to be a discontinuity – extra effort is required to cross the border. The sharp increase in effort required to traverse the discontinuity is represented by the steep vertical segment of the line, as seen in Figure 3.1. As a result of the perceived challenges of dealing with the discontinuity, Marie may decide to cross the border only when absolutely necessary. Most of the time, therefore, she'll decide to go to B for dinner and a movie.

Thus, a discontinuity is *the increased effort to accomplish a task through a communication interaction across a boundary*. By effort, we mean the additional difficulty an individual faces in trying to accomplish a given purpose. As a result, boundaries are objective (i.e., recognizable by all parties, even those not actually involved in the communication process), and discontinuities are subjective (i.e., relevant only as perceived by those involved in the communication process), although they may sometimes be measured (Nijkamp, Rietveld, and Salomon, 1990).

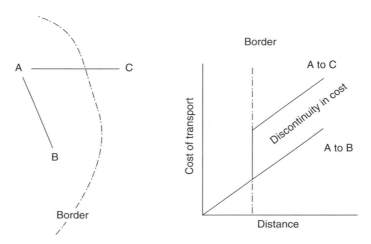

Figure 3.1 A border may create a discontinuity in the cost of transport (Watson-Manheim et al., 2007)

Individuals may experience a discontinuity at a boundary when action responses and flows of information are not as expected and hence are perceived as an impediment to communication. But this is not the only possible outcome in a shared work setting. When flows of communication and action are as expected and not perceived as cumbersome, the situation is considered to be ordinary and manageable. These routines or norms develop over time and form continuities that sustain interaction (Watson-Manheim et al., 2007). We continue with Marie's story.

> Marie and others living in the border towns of A and C are frustrated that it is so difficult to cross the border between the two countries. In response, the two national governments develop a process to make crossing the border easier for local residents. Initially, the new process requires some extra effort on Marie's part. First, she completes an application and submits it to her government. Once she is notified that she has passed this initial screening, Marie travels to the border in order to be fingerprinted, photographed, and interviewed by border and customs agents of both countries to ensure that she understands the regulations for traveling from one country to the other. In return for providing personal information and assurances that she will adhere to policies of both countries, Marie receives a commuter pass that allows her to travel across the border in the commuter lane. Usually, this entails minimal interaction with border and customs agents and

significantly less effort than those without commuter passes must expend in order to cross the border. The new routine enabled by the commuter pass, and shared expectations between Marie and the border agents about the guidelines for traveling between the two countries, serves as a continuity for Marie. The cost and effort of crossing the border increases linearly and is dependent on the distance traveled with little additional impact from having to cross a national border

The ease with which Marie can now traverse the border allows her to do things she would not have done before such as enjoy an impromptu dinner in C. Marie may even consider options that she would not have considered previously such as accepting a job in C. The boundary of the national border remains, but Marie now perceives crossing the border as a continuity because of the new routine enabled by her commuter pass.

Returning to the context of the VWE, various continuities such as previous virtual work experience, a strong institutional framework, or commonalities in background can provide common ground for work practices to develop and override differences (Watson-Manheim et al., 2007). Even if some differences are present, team members are able to resolve them with what is perceived as routine effort because of other factors that are common across the team. For example, Orlikowski (2002) described how the shared identity of Kappa employees permitted the teams to develop innovative products on time, within budget. The common understanding of Kappa goals enabled workers at different physical locations with different cultural backgrounds to successfully complete projects even though they may have had different specific understanding of precisely how to achieve their goals.

The way we work in Kappa is the same across locations because we're always shooting for the one goal, and this is to have a successful project. That's the bottom line. And people strive for that. We may differ sometimes on how to get to that goal. But the common goal of a successful product and a good product so our customer doesn't holler at us, is pretty much, I think, viewed by everybody as really important. And so whether the Americans want to go, you know, A, B, C, D to get there, or the Germans want to go A, F, E, D – as long as they come to that common goal, that's fine. And they do. It's the Kappa way. (Orlikowski, 2002, p. 258)

Thus, continuities are common expectations of work practices and patterns of interaction. When one or more continuities is present, the scripts for communication activities are clear within a team and shared by the members, based on common understandings and expectations of organizational norms, roles, and routine behaviors. While communication partners may not share the same precise meaning of events, there must be enough shared understanding to allow persons to make sense of the situation and to choose agreed-upon actions. This does not mean that all differences must be resolved but that all parties must at least have comparable understandings in order to undertake joint action (Weick, Sutcliffe, and Obstfeld, 2005).

As noted earlier, discontinuities and continuities are not static phenomena. What is perceived as a discontinuity or continuity at one point in time, may not always be perceived by team members in the same way. Returning to Marie's story, the discontinuity associated with the hassles of crossing the border dissipated as continuities associated with new border crossing procedures for local residents were implemented. The shift from discontinuity to continuity provides an opportunity for new routines or innovation. An example can be drawn from Maznevski and Chudoba's (2000) study of three global virtual teams. One of them, SellTech, an alliance between a US-based company and one of its major customers, crossed boundaries of time, space, and culture with members in the United States, United Kingdom, and northern Europe. Discontinuities formed around these boundaries early in the team's life because the sales manager, located in the United Kingdom, could not get the attention of the US-based engineers to address issues raised by the northern European-based customer. The presence of discontinuities was reflected in communication problems (e.g., US-based engineers would not return calls, e-mails, or even respond to face-to-face personal appeals) that threatened the viability of the corporate alliance.

When senior management realized that the SellTech strategic alliance was on the verge of failing, they instituted changes in the team's structure and communication practices to resolve the problems associated with the discontinuities. Specifically, a new team with senior representatives of both organizations was formed. The team initiated regular monthly telephone conference calls and, because of the presence of senior management, participation in the meetings by lower-level employees was expected. The new routine became a continuity that made it easier to resolve subsequent problems because key personnel were involved and gave the alliance appropriate attention. The objective boundaries of time, place, and culture were still present, but the discontinuities associated with those boundaries dissolved as continuities emerged. The shared expectations and expected action outcomes of the continuities mitigated any negative effects of communicating across multiple boundaries and supported effective ongoing operation of the SellTech strategic alliance.

An examination of discontinuities and continuities within the context of an ongoing team in the VWE requires attention to multiple levels of analysis. Discontinuities are an individual-level construct. When a team member perceives that increased effort is necessary to accomplish a given purpose, she must decide how to respond to the discontinuity. She may adapt her interaction in some way, such as by preparing minutes following audio-conference meetings with nonnative speakers to document discussion and agreed upon deliverables. She then observes the consequences of this change. If she perceives that the adaptation is successful, or reduces the problems associated with the discontinuity, she may continue its use. Through repeated use within the team, an individual's adaptations are recognized by the team as a new team-level routine of media use (Watson-Manheim and Belanger, 2007). The team now has a norm of preparing minutes following each of its meetings, which serves as a continuity that facilitates future interactions. Continuities are therefore a group-level phenomenon that are present or emerge as team members adapt to what individuals perceive as discontinuities.

Shared communication practices and mental models in the VWE

> Communication is the glue that holds the team structure together; it is the enzyme that allows the group process to function. (Applbaum et al., 1974, p. 9)

This observation is especially relevant for teams that operate in the VWE. Such teams are enabled by pervasive use of ICTs, but at the same time, ICTs do not provide for the same level of shared social settings as face-to-face interactions, thereby reducing the similarity of expectations and experiences (Forsyth, 1998). While virtual team members can combine the use of ICT to approach the richness of face-to-face communication (Zack and McKenney, 1995), team members usually still prefer face-to-face communication (McKinney and Whiteside, 2006; Orlikowski, 2002). We now consider one aspect of communication – a team's use of a communication mode repertoire – and its relationship to two specific team learning behaviors, mental model maintenance and

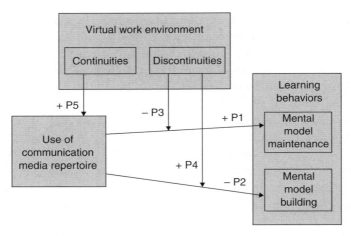

Figure 3.2 Research model

mental model building. We then look at these relationships within the context of the VWE and team members' perceptions of discontinuities and continuities. Our research model is shown in Figure 3.2.

Little research has examined the process through which individuals adapt media use behaviors in the VWE. We take a first step in examining this process from a cognitive learning perspective. A cognitive perspective implies a dynamic process where "learning emerges from the interaction of a stimulus and the mind of the learner, and results in a change to the learner's mental model" (Vandenbosch and Higgins, 1996, p. 201). We suggest that media usage adaptation can be investigated by examining the relationship between communication media repertoire usage with learning behaviors, mental model maintenance and mental model building. As depicted in the model, virtuality has a moderating influence on this relationship.

Communication media repertoires

Research has shown that norms of media use develop within work teams (Kraut et al., 1998). These norms influence understanding of the medium and shape appropriate usage patterns (Kraut et al., 1998; Watson-Manheim and Belanger, 2007). Thus, media use in the ongoing process of work activities is regulated through group or organizational norms. As individuals use media in the ongoing process of performing work activities, they learn when and how media use leads to more effective outcomes. Through this process of reflective usage, routines of usage are also adapted to accommodate situational variances (Orlikowski, 2000; Watson-Manheim and Belanger, 2007).

Organizational routines are integral to the process of performing work activities. Routines can be defined as: "repetitive, recognizable patterns of actions, carried by multiple actors" (Feldman and Pentland, 2003, p. 95). Rules and norms of behaviors enable teams to organize and coordinate activities efficiently (McGrath, 1984). Likewise, at the individual level, if processes are clear and well understood, individuals can pay more attention to the content of their work activities. Well-understood routines of behavior allow both individuals and teams to simplify the work environment and to perform work activities more productively.

Routines promote stability in the work environment but they have also been criticized as sources of inertia and stagnation (Feldman and Pentland, 2003). More recently, however, organizational routines have been conceptualized as a source of change in organizations (Feldman and Pentland, 2003). This conceptualization is based on the distinction between ostensive and performative aspects of routines. The ostensive aspect is the understanding of the routine, which may be codified in explicit procedures or may be an implicit norm of behavior. The performative aspect encompasses the actions taken when actually performing the routine. It is through the performative aspect that change initially occurs. While the ostensive framework for the routine remains appropriate, specific circumstances at the time of action may lead to an individual varying expected behavior.

To capture this duality as applied to the development and adaptation of media use routines, Watson-Manheim and Belanger (2007) proposed the concept of a communication media repertoire – the collection of communication channels and the routines of use of the media within a defined community of users. The repertoire concept provides a framework to investigate media usage in the ongoing performance of work activities. In their study of ICT usage in two different sales organizations with similar media choices, they found significantly different repertoires of media usage. While they identified similar patterns of use within the organizations, the two organizations differed significantly in their understanding of how and when the media should be used. They proposed that perceived differences in institutional conditions across the two firms reflexively influenced the development of the repertoire. In addition the use of media was posited to be influenced by previous usage decisions and by current situational conditions as perceived by the user. In other words, an individual's interpretation of the situation at the time of usage will influence the preference for a particular medium or combination of media.

Individual usage variations can ultimately lead to changes in the communication media repertoire of the community. Watson-Manheim and Belanger (2007) cite an example of the use of pagers at one firm in their research. The expectation within the user group was that the pager was used for urgent communication; however, it was sometimes used simply to get a timely response causing users to find alternate methods to convey urgency (e.g., cell phones). They propose that over time, if this behavior was repeated by multiple members of the group and became a common pattern of behavior understood by the group, a change in the communication routine for urgency would occur.

Learning behaviors

From a cognitive perspective, learning can be thought of in terms of mental models (Vandenbosch and Higgins, 1996). Mental models are used by people to frame events and develop expectations of behavior of others and to frame action choices in situations (Matlin, 1998). A similar cognitive construct of memory is a schema; schemas enable an individual to meaningfully organize information from a series of events that have happened across a period of time (Matlin, 1998). Mental models and schemas are emergent and evolving, developed in response to the experiences of the individual. When faced with uncertainty, people will try to associate the current situation with prior experience or information they have from other events. Learning occurs as the uncertainty is explored, new behaviors attempted, and responses are interpreted. Mental models are adapted to reflect the new information discovered from the trials.

Mental models are constantly evolving, however, as the level of uncertainty that individuals face in any situation varies. In some cases, problems faced are similar to previous experiences and routine responses produce successful outcomes. Alternatively, the situation faced may represent a radical departure from the past; routine responses are not adequate and if enacted produce unexpected results, or "surprise" (Schön, 1987, p. 28). Similarly, Vandenbosch and Higgins (1996) summarize research in cognitive theory and learning and propose two forms of learning, that is, mental model maintenance and mental model building. We adopt these two learning states in our research model.

Mental model maintenance is more likely a learning state than mental model building (Vandenbosch and Higgins, 1996). Individuals develop a model of expectations to apply to similar, but not necessarily identical, future events. In this state, known action routines within the community are considered appropriate for the situation. The individual's expectations about action responses are confirmed. Thus, it is possible for individuals to deal with some amount of ambiguity in well-practiced ways. Once expectations and mental models of a situation are developed, they are resistant to change. In this way, cognitive structures enable stability (House, Rousseau, and Thomas-Hunt, 1995).

While mental models reflect learning at an individual level, routines of behavior develop through mutual understanding, or shared mental models, within a social context. Thus, shared mental models within a work team refer to the overlapping of knowledge structures among team members that provides a means for them to choose actions consistent with team-mates' expectations (Mathieu et al., 2000), and are a group-level construct. The most critical components of shared mental models are the common expectations of the task and team behaviors (Cannon-Bowers, Salas, and Converse, 1993).

Communication media repertoire use and mental model maintenance

Communication media repertoires of team members provide a framework for media usage decisions. Individuals have preferences for media use to accomplish a communication purpose under different contextual conditions. Routines of media use in the group are shared by members if there is little unexpected variation among team members in their media preferences. While individuals may make minor adjustments, these adjustments and the consequences are similar to past experience. The rules understood by the group are then largely confirmed. In a study of three global virtual teams, Maznevski and Chudoba (2000) noted that the predictable rhythm of frequent communication supported "reinforcement of ongoing relationships and current routines and views [and] prevented inadvertent transitions from happening" (p. 488). Thus frequent and expected communication became instrumental in resolving uncertainty associated with working with others on a team. Thus, we posit the following:

> P1 – Greater congruence across team members' communication mode repertoire is associated with mental model maintenance.

Communication media repertoire use and mental model building

Alternatively, if there is variation among team members in their communication media repertoire, then individual usage decisions will vary and the group members will experience unexpected outcomes. This may happen for a number of reasons, for example, when a new team is formed whose members have not worked together previously. Each member will have their own preferences for media use. However, if these preferences for use do not lead to expected outcomes, the individual will vary actions in order to accomplish their communication purpose (Watson-Manheim and Belanger, 2007). Over time, expectations are reshaped and preferences are changed; that is, the individual's mental model is changed, to accommodate the new situation. Thus, we propose:

> *P2 – Less congruence across team members' communication mode repertoire (media preference by communication purpose and situational factors) is associated with mental model building.*

The influence of virtuality

The ongoing routine of a team characterized by a shared communication mode repertoire and stability of mental model maintenance can be disrupted with the introduction of discontinuities in the VWE. ICT makes it easy for people to join new work groups regardless of geographic constraints or other boundaries. People are expected to be a member of many teams concurrently (Chudoba et al., 2005), oftentimes resulting in fluid team membership as members move in and out, depending on current priorities. Members may perceive increased discontinuities from this fluid membership because schedules must be coordinated across changing sets of time zones, or because of new accommodations to include members who speak different first languages. Lack of understanding of the team's processes and culture and incomplete information requires a new member to incorporate beliefs that are beyond the control and knowledge of others (Louis, 1980; Oliver and Winer, 1987). New members may bring a set of preconceived perceptions and interpretations of the issues involved (Mohammed and Dumville, 2001), which result in other members' perception of increased discontinuity as existing routines are challenged. We posit:

> *P3 – The relationship between team members' communication mode repertoire and mental model maintenance will be weakened when members perceive the presence of discontinuities.*

On the other hand, discontinuities may enhance the relationship between communication mode repertoire and mental model building. "Mental models change only when new information is discrepant and not readily interpretable using the old model" (Rousseau, 1995, p. 28). As discontinuities are introduced, such as when membership changes, it creates uncertainty about the task, group hierarchy and governance structures, and the norms and values of other team members (Ostroff and Kozlowski, 1992). Less prior knowledge requires more communication for team members to gain insight about how other team members respond to given situations. In a study of 54 distributed teams across 26 companies, Majchrzak and her colleagues (2004) identified the importance of "induc[ing] a collection of strangers with little in common to function as a mutually supportive group" (p. 132). Teams accomplished this principle with frequent communication, by adopting a common language, and by blending individuals' work processes into team processes, which is reflective of the mental model building process.

In an examination of how expectations affect communication processes, Jablin (2001) notes that discrepancies between expectations and reality may increase surprises, as one's expectations can be realistic and accurate to varying degrees. Such surprises may be encountered by both new members of a team and ongoing team members (Pearson, 1995). Communication activities are driven then by an underlying negotiation process as team members strive to understand and resolve discrepant expectations. Uncertainty may create questions about the communication activities themselves, including what is communicated and how it is communicated (e.g., media choice, frequency of communication). These norms are included within both formal and informal rules of communicating that team members must discern (Gilsdorf, 1998). So team members engage in additional communication activities with people inside and outside the team, leading to the building or revision of a mental model of what membership in the team entails. For these reasons, we posit:

P4 – The relationship between team members' communication mode repertoire and mental model building will be strengthened when members perceive the presence of discontinuities.

Ongoing actions of team members influence the relationships the individual has with the team since experience helps the individual understand and predict the expected behavior of others (Lewicki and Bunker, 1996). As individuals experience more extensive team member knowledge, likely when continuities are present, it becomes easier to anticipate the reactions of team members, including how they make use of a communication media repertoire. The prior experience provides a basis for understanding what is expected from the team member as well as what can be reasonably expected from other members of the team. By having common perceptions, individuals can evaluate situations and make decisions that are more effective for the team because they will interpret the environment in ways that are compatible with the views of their team members (Cannon and

Edmondson, 2001). We propose:

> *P5 – Teams that perceive more continuities will also have greater congruence in their use of a communication media repertoire.*

Discussion and implications

The expected benefits of virtual work have been elusive for many organizations. In this chapter, we take a step toward understanding the effects of virtuality on work practices of teams, in particular as related to ICT use. While the addition of physically distant colleagues to a team is relatively easy to initiate with the use of ICT, interaction via ICT concurrently makes collaborative activities more complex and often leads to unexpected responses. ICT-mediated communication may increase the likelihood of misattribution and make it more difficult to maintain trust between team members (Cramton, 2001). For example, Hinds and Mortensen (2005) found that when distributed teams had coordination difficulties they experienced more conflict than collocated teams. So, in spite of the ease with which virtual teams can be formed, coordinating and performing joint activities is more complicated and often requires changes in work practices to realize the benefits that organizations want to achieve in VWEs.

We distinguish between boundaries in a VWE, for example, time, space, organization, and the perceived effects of the boundaries, which we term discontinuities. By linking the discontinuities with learning behavior in teams, we hope to shed light on how the benefits from virtual work can be obtained. This research has implications for both research and practice.

For researchers, distinguishing boundaries from their perceived effects may help to resolve some of the inconsistent findings on performance VWEs documented in previous research (Chudoba et al., 2005). The concept of discontinuities also needs to be further elaborated. We have proposed a general definition of discontinuity but have not distinguished the effects of different types of discontinuities. In addition, we have not addressed the number of discontinuities a team may face and how that may affect behavior and, ultimately, performance. In practice, it is common for teams to face multiple boundaries concurrently. For example, Griffith and colleagues (2003) proposed three dimensions of virtualness: technological, physical, and temporal. Using different combinations of these dimensions, they identify three categories of virtuality to differentiate teams being studied, that is, traditional, hybrid, and pure virtual. Hybrid teams and virtual teams may perceive discontinuities differently, for example, the intensity of effort may be different. Espinosa et al. (2003) cautioned researchers to take into account the presence of multiple boundaries and the effects of possible interactions between these boundaries in studies of virtuality.

Our research model proposes that virtuality has a moderating effect on the relationship between communication media use and learning behaviors. There is also indication from research that media practices have an indirect effect on perception of virtuality through learning behaviors. As ICT is routinely used in the performance of work activities, and understanding of how and when the technology can be used is developed, changes in the frame of understanding of the work environment occurs (Orlikowski, 2000; Watson-Manheim and Belanger, 2007). For example, the authors of this chapter have worked collaboratively for five years in different cities and times zones. We have conducted telephone interviews with employees of a global company who were located in many different countries. Our perception of the feasibility of conducting research virtually is likely to be much different than some of our colleagues, who have primarily worked with local colleagues. Thus, as usage practices and norms of media behavior change, perceptions of virtuality may also change.

For practitioners, this model is useful as it indicates that effective managerial strategies can help achieve the forecasted benefits of virtual teams. Strategies, including training and incentives, that support process experimentation can provide team members with an environment conducive to identifying the need for and making necessary changes in work practices. While mental model maintenance is preferred by individuals and teams because it is less risky and more certain, only through mental model building can significant innovation take place (Vandenbosch and Higgins, 1996). Strategies that explicitly focus on learning and innovation of processes may in fact exploit the potential for flexibility and responsiveness, which has been difficult for organizations to achieve.

Notes

1. Our description of the virtual work environment draws on ideas introduced by Watson-Manheim and her colleagues scheduled for presentation at the 2007 Academy of Management conference.

References

Applbaum, R.L., Bodaken, E.M., Sereno, K.K., and Anatol, K.W.E. (1974) *The Process of Group Communication*, Chicago, IL: Science Research Associates.

Cannon, M.D., and Edmondson, A.C. (2001) Confronting Failure: Antecedents and Consequences of Shared Beliefs about Failure in Organizational Work Groups, *Journal of Organizational Behavior*, 22, 161–177.

Cannon-Bowers, J.A., Salas, E., and Converse, S.A. (1993) "Shared Mental Models in Expert Team Decision Making", in N.J. Castellan (Ed.), *Individual and Group Decision Making*, Hillsdale, NJ: Lawrence Erlbaum, 221–246.

Chudoba, K.M., Wynn, E., Lu, M., and Watson-Manheim, M.B. (2005) How Virtual are We? Measuring Virtuality and Understanding its Impact in a Global Organization, *Information Systems Journal*, 15(4), 279–306.

Cohen, S.G., and Bailey, D.E. (1997) What Makes Teams Work: Group Effectiveness Research from the Shop Floor to the Executive Suite, *Journal of Management*, 23, 239–290.

Cramton, C. (2001) The Mutual Knowledge Problem and Its Consequences for Dispersed Collaboration, *Organization Science*, 12(3), 346–371.

Espinosa, J.A., Cummings, J.N., Wilson, J.M., and Pearce, B.M. (2003) Team Boundary Issues Across Multiple Global Firms, *Journal of Management Information Systems*, 19, 157–190.

Feldman, M.S., and Pentland, B.T. (2003) Reconceptualizing Organizational Routines as a Source of Flexibility and Change, *Administrative Science Quarterly*, 48, 94–118.

Forsyth, D.R. (1998) *Group Dynamics*, 3rd edn, Pacific Grove, CA: Wadsworth.

Gilsdorf, J.W. (1998) Organizational Rules on Communicating: How Employees Are – and are not – Learning the Ropes, *The Journal of Business Communication*, 35, 173–201.

Griffith, T.L., Sawyer, J.E., and Neale, M.A. (2003) Virtualness and Knowledge in Teams: Managing the Love Triangle of Organizations, Individuals, and Teams, *MIS Quarterly*, 27, 265–287.

Hinds, P.J., and Mortensen, M. (2005) Understanding Conflict in Geographically Distributed Teams, *Organization Science*, 16(3), 290–307.

House, R., Rousseau, D.M., and Thomas-Hunt, M. (1995) "The Meso Paradigm: A Framework for the Integration of Micro and Macro Organizational Behavior", in L.L. Cummings and B.M. Staw (Eds), *Research in Organizational Behavior*, Vol. 17, Greenwich, CT: Jai Press, 71–114.

Jablin, F.M. (2001) "Organizational Entry, Assimilation, and Disengagement/exit", in F.M. Jablin and L.L. Putnam (Eds), *The New Handbook of Organizational Communication*, Sage: Thousand Oaks, CA, 732–818.

Jarvenpaa, S.L., and Leidner, D.E. (1999) Communication and Trust in Global Virtual Teams, *Organization Science*, 10(6), 791–815.

Kiesler, S., and Cummings, J.N. (2002) "What Do We Know about Proximity and Distance in Work Groups? A Legacy of Research", in P.J. Hinds and S. Kiesler (Eds), *Distributed Work*, MIT Press: Cambridge, MA, pp. 57–80.

Kraut, R.E., Rice, R.E., Cool, C., and Fish, R.S. (1998) Varieties of Social Influence: The Role of Utility and Norms in the Success of a New Communication Medium, *Organization Science*, 9, 437–453.

Lewicki, R.J., and Bunker, B.B. (1996) "Developing and Maintaining Trust in Work Relationships", in R.M. Kramer and T.R. Tyler (Eds), *Trust in Organizations: Frontiers of Theory and Research*, Sage: Thousand Oaks, CA, 114–139.

Louis, M.R. (1980) Surprise and Sense Making: What Newcomers Experience in Entering Unfamiliar Organizational Settings, *Administrative Science Quarterly*, 25, 226–251.

Majchrzak, A.A., Malhotra, J., Stamps, J., and Lipnack, J. (2004) Can Absence Make a Team Grow Stronger?, *Harvard Business Review*, 82, 131.

Mathieu, J.E., Heffner, T.S., Goodwin, G.F., Salas, E., and Cannon-Bowers, J.A. (2000) The Influence of Shared Mental Models on Team Process and Performance, *Journal of Applied Psychology*, 85, 273–283.

Matlin, M.W. (1998) *Cognition*, Harcourt, Brace, & Company: Orlando, FL.

Maznevski, M.L., and Chudoba, K.M. (2000) Bridging Space Over Time: Global Virtual Team Dynamics and Effectiveness, *Organization Science*, 11(5), 473–492.

McGrath, J.E. (1984) *Groups: Interaction and Performance*, Prentice Hall: Englewood Cliffs, NJ.

McKinney, V.R., and Whiteside, M.M. (2006) Maintaining Distributed Relationships, *Communications of the ACM*, 49, 82.

Mignerey, J.T., Rubin, R.B., and Gorden, W.I. (1995) Organizational Entry: An Investigation of Newcomer Communication Behavior and Uncertainty, *Communication Research*, 22, 54–85.

Mohammed, S., and Dumville, B.C. (2001) Team Mental Models in a Team Knowledge Framework: Expanding Theory and Measurement across Disciplinary Boundaries, *Journal of Organizational Behavior*, 22, 89–106.

Nijkamp, P., Rietveld, P., and Salomon, I. (1990) Barriers in Spatial Interactions and Communications: A Conceptual Exploration, *Annals of Regional Science*, 24, 237–252.

Orlikowski, W.J. (2000) Using Technology and Constituting Structures: A Practice Lens for Studying Technology in Organizations, *Organization Science*, 11, 404–428.

Orlikowski, W.J. (2002) Knowing in Practice: Enacting a Collective Capability in Distributed Organizing, *Organization Science*, 13(3), 249–273.

Oliver, R.L., and Winer, R.S. (1987) A Framework for the Formation and Structure of Consumer Expectations: Review and Propositions, *Journal of Economic Psychology*, 8, 469–499.

Ostroff, C., and Kozlowski, S.W.J. (1992) Organizational Socialization as a Learning Process: The Role of Information Acquisition, *Personnel Psychology*, 45, 849–874.

Pearson, C.A.L. (1995) The Turnover Process in Organizations: An Exploration of the Role of Met-Unmet Expectations, *Human Relations*, 48, 405–420.

Rousseau, D.M. (1995) *Psychological Contracts in Organizations: Understanding Written and Unwritten Agreements*, Sage: Thousand Oaks, CA, London, New Delhi.

Schön, D. (1987) *Educating the Reflective Practitioner*, Jossey Bass: San Francisco .

Stohl, C. (1995) *Organizational Communication: Connectedness in Action*, Sage: Thousand Oaks, CA.

Vandenbosch, B., and Higgins, C. (1996) Information Acquisition and Mental Models: An Investigation into the Relationship between Behaviour and Learning, *Information Systems Research*, 7, 198–214.

Watson-Manheim, M.B., and Belanger, F. (2007) Communication Media Repertoires: Dealing with the Multiplicity of Media Choices, *MIS Quarterly*, 31, 267–293.

Watson-Manheim, M.B., Chudoba, K.M., and Crowston, K. (2007) Distance Matters: Except When It Doesn't, Presented at the Academy of Management Conference, Philadelphia, PA, 3–8 August 2007.

Weick, K.E., Sutcliffe, K.M., and Obstfeld, D. (2005) Organizing and the Process of Sensemaking, *Organization Science*, 16(4), 409–442.

Zack, M.H., and McKenney, J.L. (1995) Social Context and Interaction in Ongoing Computer-supported Management Groups, *Organization Science*, 6, 409–422.

CHAPTER 4

Building virtual cooperation: Guidelines for effective performance

Velvet Weems-Landingham

Introduction

Much of the research on virtual teamwork emphasizes the importance of developing trust (Handy, 1995; Jarvenpaa and Leidner, 1999; Jones and Bowie, 1998; Meyerson, Weick, and Kramer, 1996). Trust, however, is merely a reason to believe critical resources will be available and committed to interdependent performance (Das and Teng, 1998; Gallivan, 2001; O'Leary, Orlikowski, and Yates, 2002), but this may be simply a perception (Biocca and Delaney, 1995: Lombard and Ditton, 1997; Steuer, 1992). When trust is substantiated, the probability of virtual team success increases. When it is not, other tactics must be enlisted in its place.

Tactics are defined as attempts to influence others (e.g., expert human resources) to feel, think, or behave in a desired fashion. Success in influencing others has been deemed a primary determinant of group effectiveness (Elron and Vigoda, 2003). Thus, understanding tactics that influence member behavior, thinking, and feeling is imperative. Elron and Vigoda (2003) suggest,

> there are many possible tactics of social influence, and the choice of specific tactics can depend on the social and physical context, the qualities and status of the individual or group we are trying to influence, the goal of our influence, our own dispositions, and the organizational atmosphere and culture in which the influence attempts to take place. (p. 319)

Tactics consequently must be contingent upon the situation or degree of virtuality, and thus the degree of social presence within virtual contexts.

The nature of virtuality has been historically conceptualized in accordance with the use of ICT. When using ICT, virtuality is generally said to exist. When it is not, virtuality is said to be nonexistent. In comparison, this study conceptualizes virtuality not in accordance with the use of technology, but the degree of perceived availability and commitment demonstrated by individuals whose expertise is deemed necessary for interdependent virtual performances. This perspective emphasizes the importance of human resources and their virtual connections. Technology simply represents the tool for enabling interdependent performance.

The degree of virtuality is not solely determined by media richness (Daft and Lengel, 1986) but by the virtual manager's ability to foster availability and commitment among members. This conceptualization of virtuality is grounded within the social presence literature (Daft and Lengel, 1986; Short, Williams, and Christie, 1976, etc.). Social presence is articulated as a sense of connectedness, being attentive, aware, and willing to engage with others regardless of physical proximity (Jarvenpaa and Leidner, 1999; Kahn, 1992; Panteli, 2004). The present study uses social presence to describe the desired relationship between virtual project managers and the support resource upon which they rely.

Virtuality is an evaluative measure, which describes the situation managers face when attempting to assemble and coordinate effective virtual teams. Weems-Landingham's (2004) research corroborates the importance of social presence within virtual contexts, conjecturing that perceived availability, accountability, and responsiveness of critical resources precede interdependence. These findings and others (e.g., Panteli, 2004) highlight the need to understand and promote virtual cooperation.

Lurey and Raisinghani (2001) put forth best practices for virtual teamwork. They determine that team processes and team relationships present the strongest link to virtual team performance and member satisfaction. This suggests that managers evoke tactics that facilitate the development and utilization of positive, instrumental relationships. Relationships that are grounded not in physical but psychological proximity promote the strongest bonds (Goleman, 1998). And members cooperate because they get along, like, and connect with each other. The ensuing relational networks are not random but carefully synchronized to command the necessary expertise for each distinct situation.

Virtual teams will and do struggle with interdependent performance. The question remains, what management tactics can be enlisted to enhance virtual cooperation. O'Leary, Orlikowski, and Yates' (2002) research on distributed work implies that tactics for enhancing virtual cooperation should be rooted in the interpersonal processes related to socialization, communication, and participation. Hence, by assessing member interactions we can properly identify those tactics that enhance availability and commitment from the critical resources deemed necessary to complete interdependent performance objectives.

This study uses critical incidents within organization-based virtual teams to determine the tactics that enhance cooperation and interdependent performance. Particular emphasis is given to those processes associated with locating and commandeering expert or critical team member resources. This research assesses virtual team cooperation from a contingency perspective, proposing that tactics for performance are moderated in accordance with the degree of perceived virtuality. Major contributions of this work include an evaluation of virtual project manager behaviors associated with effectiveness, a review of data excerpts which support the findings, and the presentation of a contingency approach to virtual cooperation.

The remainder of this chapter is structured as follows. I begin by offering a theoretical framework for conceptualizing virtual cooperation and its impact on team effectiveness. This is followed by a case description. Next, an analysis of data and findings are presented along with a discussion of proposed guidelines for building virtual cooperation. Following this, an assessment of guidelines is presented, including excerpts for critical incidents that support the findings. I then present a contingency approach to building virtual cooperation designed to increase the efficiency and effectiveness in attaining availability and commitment from critical resources. Finally, I conclude by offering implications for practice and research.

Framework for conceptualizing virtual cooperation

Hackman's (1983) model of group effectiveness serves as a theoretical framework for studying virtual cooperation. It is a proven, valid, and a widely accepted model, which demonstrates the contribution of organizational context, group design, group synergy, process criteria of effectiveness, and material resources to team performance. Furst, Blackburn, and Rosen (1999) acknowledge the significance of this framework as a basis for exploring virtual team cooperation and heterogeneity. They assert the need for a direct study of the tactics associated with virtual cooperation, stating: "as virtual team membership becomes more heterogeneous in response to more complex and varied virtual team tasks, successful management of team co-ordination and co-operation will become increasingly important" (Furst, Blackburn, and Rosen, 1999, p. 261).

Members of a team are said to be cooperative when their efforts are systematically integrated to achieve a desired collective outcome. With greater integration come higher degrees of cooperation and performance. Therefore, managers attempting to enhance virtual cooperation must attend to member connections. Research on synergy reveals the importance of member cooperation in maximizing the outcomes associated with member involvement (Lawler, 1986) and team effectiveness (Hammer and Champy, 1993). It therefore represents the greatest opportunities for advancing research in this area.

Team synergy captures the many ways in which members coalesce to maximize integrated performances. Daft (2005) defines synergy as the combined action that occurs when members work interdependently to create new alternatives and solutions. It increases in accordance with the perceived strength of members' psychological proximity (Furst, Blackburn, and Rosen, 1999). Therefore, the use of management tactics which increase positive feelings of connectivity among virtual members is critical. Antecedents and potential tactics to enhance synergy include: building trust (Meyerson, Weick, and Kramer, 1996), establishing team identity (Gaertner et al., 1989), and generating cooperation (Nemeth, 1993; Tsui et al., 1992; Watson et al., 1993).

Research clearly acknowledges the importance of gaining virtual effectiveness through the utilization of trust (Corpola, Hiltz, and Rotter, 2004; Jarvenpaa and Leidner, 1999; Panteli and Duncan, 2004). Although control mechanisms are viewed as an alternative to trust, these controls (e.g., organization-based norms, cultures, rules, etc.) have proven fairly ineffective within virtual contexts. O'Leary and colleagues (2002) conclude that neither trust nor control is sufficient for distributed work, and they should not be perceived as diametric opposites but complements existing along the same continuum. For this reason, both should be considered when formulating tactics for enhancing virtual cooperation and performance.

Reliance on trust, although consequential, limits interdependent performance in situations where it is largely absent. Instead, establishing team identity as a means to increase affiliation is one alternative (Lipnack and Stamps, 1997; Yamagishi and Cook, 1993). Team identity is defined by Gaertner et al. (1989) as the acceptance of interdependent goals and collective commitment. Tactics thought to promote team identity include face-to-face orientation sessions, online team building exercises, and other intricate socialization efforts. Unfortunately, however, systematic research has not been conducted to substantiate the value of these efforts.

Barring trust and the establishment of group identity, virtual project managers are left to devise tactics that facilitate the integration of individual member performances. Regrettably, little in the way of systematic research devoted to understanding those tactics has been offered to date (Bordia, 1997). The heterogeneous nature of virtual teamwork has been noted to both increase conflict, due to varying spheres of expertise (Dougherty, 1992), and enhance effectiveness (Bettenhausen, 1991; Guzzo and Dickson, 1996). Given these and other competing findings, additional research must be conducted to determine management tactics that enhance virtual team members' abilities to cooperate effectively. The first step toward this end is developing a clear understanding of the expertise needed to fulfill performance objectives.

To be effective, virtual project managers must locate experts with the appropriate knowledge, skill, and ability (KSA) to complete interdependent performance objectives. Only after can they begin to devise strategies for garnering availability and commitment. Hackman's (1983) fifth variable, material resources, depicts the importance of attaining resources. This model of group effectiveness emphasizes the significance of tangible resources (i.e., tools, technologies, time, physical space, and money) exclusively. This approach, however, predates virtuality and discounts the impact of human and social capital as key resources within knowledge-based industries. The successful identification and attainment of expertise rests in managers' abilities to develop human and social capital. Human capital refers to each member's productive potential, knowledge, and action. Social capital (e.g., friends, peer groups, champions, advisors, etc.) expands individual capabilities by utilizing strong relationships, goodwill, trust, and other cooperative efforts to achieve performance objectives. Building human and social capital is paramount to virtual team success and must occur before team synergy can be established.

Co-located team research notes the difficulties associated with gaining collective commitment and performance from expert resources. Although integral to interdependent performance (McGrath, 1984), opportunities for cooperation must first be recognized (Littlepage, Robison, and Reddington, 1997) and then expert resources attained (Hollenbeck et al., 1995; Stewart and Stasser, 1995). Managers involved in the development of team meaning must firmly establish mutually desirable outcomes before experts will be willing to participate. This step between recognition and attainment, however, often proves problematic (Bunderson, 2003). Furthermore, problems are exacerbated within virtual contexts where

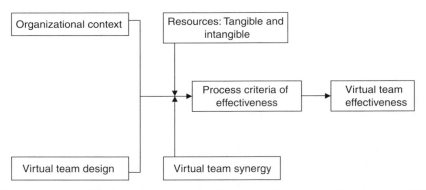

Figure 4.1 Modified version of model of group effectiveness (Hackman, 1983)

heterogeneity results in conflicting realms of expertise (Dougherty, 1992) and inequalities attenuated by limited socialization (Bordia, 1997).

The location and amassing of human and social capital must occur before gaining collective commitment or performance. Consequently, it becomes imperative to first understand tactics associated with determining and/or enhancing availability and commitment from critical resources, such as those individuals with the potential to act. The timely completion of this process allows virtual project managers to move beyond assessing situations to developing networks necessary to perform effectively. Figure 4.1 offers a revision of Hackman's (1983) model to illustrate the impact that acquiring human and social capital has on virtual team effectiveness. The resulting enhanced cooperation creates opportunities for synergies, which in turn moderate processes required for effective performance.

Tactics for building virtual cooperation: A case study

[We must] win friends and influence people. But the trick is figuring out where people are coming from, trying to get the point across in the least alienating way possible. ... Being a virtual person often means you are not someone's top priority. So, you have to wait due time before you start escalating [problems]. If you escalate every-thing ... nobody listens to you. You have to be tactful. ... Give people enough time to respond. You also have to be persistent enough to be in people's "faces" and not feel like a pest. (E-learn Virtual Project Manager 2)

This study is the result of 23 semi-structured interviews with virtual project managers, representing over 100 distinct virtual teams. Membership within teams varied from three to twelve people, depending upon the expertise needed to complete interdependent tasks. The tasks varied. Some teams were formed to exchange information and advice. Others engaged in complex decision-making and problem-resolution activities. Each team had one virtual project manager whose responsibility was to assess situations and to amass the necessary expertise to resolve client concerns. All managers were located in the United States or Canada and possessed two-plus years experience overseeing virtual projects at E-learn.

E-learn was a multinational software development company headquartered in San Francisco, with development centers in Dublin, Ireland. Other locations included: Germany, France, South Africa, Japan, and Australia, to name a few. Virtual teamwork had been a way of life since the company's inception in 1985. At one time the world's largest supplier of computer-based training software, E-learn specialized in the creation of content for many Global 500 companies. During its early years, the company placed emphasis on content development, enlisting rudimentary deployment tools (e.g., CD and diskette) to facilitate product distribution. The company employed a significant number of developers but relied heavily on joint ventures with industry leaders to provide the subject-matter expertise required for content development.

In an effort to expand its offerings, E-learn began developing internet- and intranet-based deployment tools necessary to service clients within distributed contexts. This vertical diversification strategy absorbed critical resources and resulted in escalating client concerns and internal resource scarcity. As quality concerns escalated, the company responded by diverting critical expertise away from client-related concerns to address ancillary issues. Managers responded with attempts to enlist human and social capital needed to address mounting concerns. Efforts to obtain support, however, were often thwarted by swelling resource demands. Ultimately, strategies of E-learn to expand its business ensnared the company E-learn in a vicious cycle of providing inadequate products and support necessary to satisfy client needs.

Interviews were conducted with virtual project managers to determine the support behaviors considered significant to interdependent performance outcomes. Managers were asked to identify times when they felt effective and ineffective when working virtually. They were prompted to provide as much detail as possible regarding each incident. This included personal thoughts, feelings, and actions; team member involvement and contribution; and perceived outcome. A total of 143 critical incidents were assessed to determine team member behaviors deemed necessary for success. Guidelines for enhancing virtual cooperation were generated based upon managers' demonstrated attempts to garner availability and commitment from critical resources.

Guidelines for enhancing virtual cooperation

Since research on tactics for enhancing virtual team cooperation is limited (Furst, Blackburn, and Rosen, 1999), the approach taken in this study was exploratory. A Critical Incident Interview (CII) methodology (McClelland and Daily, 1972) allowed for the assessment of team member support behaviors perceived as significant to overall team performance. Research has shown this technique to be a reliable and valid method for obtaining accurate descriptions of work behavior (Motowidlo, 1992; Ronan and Latham, 1974). In addition, it provides the means for collecting behavioral data in virtual work environments where investigators have limited access and control (Creswell, 1998; Ragin, 1987; Yin, 1994).

Thematic analysis was enlisted to develop a coding scheme of team member behaviors thought to impact virtual effectiveness (Boyatzis, 1998; Eisenhardt, 1989; Strauss and Corbin, 1990). Seventy-seven effective and 66 ineffective incidents were coded for both positive and negative occurrences of behavior. Mann-Whitney U statistical analysis determined those critical resource behaviors significantly contributing to interdependent performance outcomes. Results from this analysis showed that only negative perceptions of team member availability, competence, empathy, and facilitation proved consequential.

Virtual teams were deemed ineffective when managers perceived support resources as unavailable, apathetic, incompetent, and non-facilitative. Further review of the data revealed the importance of management behaviors associated with cultivating relationships necessary to garner availability and commitment from critical resources. Combined, these findings advocate management tactics that enhance cooperative behavior among virtual team members. Table 4.1 presents management guidelines for enhancing virtual cooperation.

Developing a comprehensive understanding of existing situations is critical to determining alternative courses of action deemed necessary to achieve interdependent performance objectives. The development of alternatives, hinges upon the manager's abilities to maneuver organizational and political hurdles and control harmful disruptive emotions. Meyerson and colleagues (1996) determined that swift trust, although fleeting, has

Table 4.1 Management guidelines for enhancing virtual cooperation

Develop a comprehensive understanding of situations
- Use trust where possible
- Understand alternatives
- Possess organizational awareness
- Possess political awareness
- Manage personal emotions

Use social competence to build bonds
- Ingratiate yourself to others
- Use preexisting and new relationships
- Seek out champions
- Use empathy

the ability to enhance virtual team cooperation and performance. Therefore, virtual project managers should be directed to use trust when possible. Although the existence of trusting relations facilitates cooperation, managers must be mindful that trust is not without cost or consequence. The following excerpts depict the fleeting nature of trust and the angst accompanying dependence upon it.

I'm emotional about it [the problem], ... because of my need to have others trust me. This person trusted me! And, because of that, her job and her career are on the line. (E-learn Virtual Project Manager 4)

I took the blame on that. I said, "It's my fault. I thought that we could do it. I should have researched it more ... I apologize." [My thinking was that] I had put enough credibility and time into this account that they trusted me. ... I thought they were okay with it. (E-learn Virtual Project Manager 5)

Trust can dissipate as quickly as it is bestowed. The effective manager does not wait in vain, but wisely develops alternatives necessary to ensure cooperation. Devising strategies reflects the virtual manager's ability to adjust to unforeseen challenges and difficulties. With increased adaptability comes a greater range of alternatives. The generation of alternatives increases the probability that virtual cooperation will occur. The following excerpts depict the value of developing alternative strategies to virtual cooperation. The first represents positive sentiments accompanying the development of viable choices. The latter, describes one manager's failure and the resulting process that ensued to gain availability and commitment from critical resources.

> What is wonderful is that I'm working with them on very complex strategies. To do that, I've got all my ducks in a row. It's really just a matter of getting all the choices out of the way. Then we can go have fun and implement the strategy. (E-learn Virtual Project Manager 14)

> I had to talk to each one of the players: my boss, the account manager, the technology manager, and a couple other people from development. … We all sat down on the conference call. I sent out the information and said we need to talk. We just had a strategy meeting. All of us gave our synopsis of what happened. It was a brainstorming session of "Where do we go from here?" Personally I felt almost awkward or ashamed that it had escalated to this level. I should have been able to manage more of what the customer was expecting. But, then [I] came to the realization that a lot of this stuff was out of my control. And, I just need the support. So it didn't matter how I felt at that point. It was just getting somebody to help me get through these things. (E-learn Virtual Project Manager 11)

The course of action and ultimately degree of success depends upon the manager's organizational and political awareness. Organizational awareness represents the manager's abilities to build relational networks and use political prowess to formulate effective virtual teams. These managers rely upon their knowledge of the organization to harness the critical resources necessary for team membership and its facilitation. In order to accomplish interdependent objectives, the virtual project manager must have a clear understanding of their organization's structure and culture. This would include using formal and informal controls to their advantage. The following excerpts illustrate the currents of organizational life and tactics enlisted to enhance performance therein:

> She [my sales manager] is a more aggressive than I am. I wanted to throw some ideas out to her because I didn't know who to go to. Also, this one guy I'm working with, he's got some clout. But, I knew that there were two, three or more people that he reported to that had more power. They were the decision-makers. (E-learn Virtual Project Manager 10)

> I contacted my manager to find out how to escalate within her management structure. I was trying to find resources that could be allocated to the project. I made sure to stress the criticalness of the

problem. ... And that the account was at risk. This enabled me to escalate it quickly. ... Brenda immediately got the [Toms], the [Dicks],
and the [Harry's] ... you know, all "the untouchables" engaged
quickly so that we could [provide] ... what was needed. People who
were involved were senior enough in our organization that action
would happen. (E-learn Virtual Project Manager 3)

Once virtual teams have been formed, the manager must move to ensure
that necessary interdependencies occur. Political awareness represents the
manager's abilities to read members' emotions and understand power
structures. Managers' who are able to maneuver in these difficult waters
are more likely to gain the necessary cooperation from members. Those
who are not, fail. The following excerpt details the problems associated
with gaining availability and commitment from virtual team resources.

Working virtually can get irritating. I've worked in companies
where ... I've tracked somebody down, and said, "Come and sit with
me for ten minutes." I went into their office, and shut the door, and
said, "We need to discuss this. This is getting to be critical." But, in
this virtual world, – telephone calls – we could never get hold of the
person. We'd leave message after message, and never get called back.
We'd send e-mails. Never get returns. And, when we finally talked to
the person they said, "I get four to five hundred e-mails a day. I'm
lucky if I read half of them, and respond to a third of them. I get
another hundred phone calls a day. If you don't catch me live I won't
return your call." (E-learn Virtual Project Manager 4)

Managing personal emotions (e.g., frustration, anxiety, surprise, fear,
skepticism, etc.) is the final tactic noted under developing a comprehensive
understanding of situations. This tactic represents manager's abilities to
recognize their emotional states and the resulting consequences.
Goleman's (1998) work on emotional intelligence concludes that self-
awareness is the first step toward controlling harmful impulses and
actions. Only after we become aware of these emotions can we move
toward social awareness and relationship management.

Virtual project managers must understand their emotions. Left
unchecked these sentiments impact their ability to facilitate cooperative
performances. Self-control, trustworthiness, conscientiousness, adaptability, and innovation help managers move virtual teams from independence
to interdependence and lead to the development of team synergies.
Without self-regulation managers are left unable to control destructive

emotions and teams fail. The following excerpts represent the destructive emotions often accompanying virtual teamwork.

> We now have a new technology manager ... but the client is still getting more frustrated. The last meeting that we had with them, they were yelling and screaming. ... The head of IT is retiring in a month. And, he wants this issue to be resolved. ... This is so frustrating for me. (E-learn Virtual Project Manager 11)

> There just was nobody else there to share information with, or to ... you know, vent about the situation. I couldn't put it in perspective. So, as the day went on, the more calls that I got from customers, the more frustrated I became, and the more I was just feeling like ... you know, I'm not good at my job. I can't solve these problems. You know, our product is terrible. It's not working. We're never gonna get this fixed. You know, it all kind of snowballed ... you know, for the whole day. And, it just made me feel very negative. (E-Learn Virtual Project Manager 21)

Successful virtual project managers master personal competencies and rely upon social and emotional skills to develop and nurture instrumental relationships. These instrumental relationships moderate cooperation in situations where critical resources are not readily available or committed. Tactics noted under social competence include: building rapport with members, cultivating and maintaining informal networks, seeking out new mutually beneficial relations, and making and maintaining personal friendships. Project managers who enhance virtual cooperation attempt to ingratiate themselves to others. They embrace the value of being likeable and make efforts to ensure critical resources look upon them with favor. The following excerpt describes one project manager's strategy to build rapport.

> Ask personal things about them. For example, I know all about her husband. I know about her two sons ... and where they each work. ... I remember those things. It's really good to start an e-mail that way ... How's so-and-so? ... It really helps. It ensures that they feel friendly with you. They feel a tie with you. ... Some sense of loyalty is created. (E-learn Virtual Project Manager 8)

Socially competent managers spend extra time cultivating and maintaining relationships with others. They rely upon both preexisting and newly formed relationships to gain availability and commitment from critical resources. Immediate access describes direct interaction with instrumental resources. Moderated access refers to instrumental relationships, which are facilitated by trusted resources. The following excerpt depicts the ease associated with direct access to critical resources.

I get very good information at the source: what content is in development; what the time-frame is for getting it released; whether we have plans to develop content in this area. Things like that. So, I'll contact Dublin directly to get that information. In this case, I did get hold of the direct manager for content development over in Dublin. (E-learn Virtual Project Manager 15)

Although cooperation is enhanced by the immediate availability of critical resources, resources must demonstrate the knowledge, skill, and ability necessary to engage in interdependent performance. According to the data, those supportive behaviors include competence, empathy, and facilitation. Availability is not enough. The above excerpt continues:

And, that's where the process broke down. ... He told me it was going to be available for another customer on this date ... So, I added a week to that. I said to my customer, "I expect it to be available by this date," which was probably the first week in March, something like that. It didn't happen. (E-learn Virtual Project Manager 15)

The art of networking facilitates the development of human and social capital, which is critical to virtual cooperation. Networking, however, is inhibited by the lack of awareness regarding responsibility and accountability. The following is one virtual project manager's response to the question: what do you need to be more effective?

I need a point of reference. I need to know who to call. Who to get answers from. The rest ... I can figure it on my own. I really ... we really need some processes in place. We need to be able to ... pick up a book, and go through the index, and find out who to call when we have a question. ... Who can we call? Who do we send an e-mail to? ... Not just send an e-mail in to a general mailbox. We need someone that can help us out here. And, I'm not talking about Tech Support. (E-learn Virtual Project Manager 17)

Virtual project managers exhibiting an overreliance on organization-based processes fail. Those who are successful rely upon relationships instead. They use formal and informal networks to discover individual resources willing and capable of completing interdependent objectives. If instrumental relationships do not avail, they enlist the aid of champions – advocates willing support their cause. Virtual project managers with high emotional intelligence fostered alliances that served to enhance formal and informal networks. The follow excerpt illustrates one project manager's journey to find a champion.

> I feel better because I have a contact over in Dublin [Ireland] now. Dublin is a huge place. I've never been there. I don't know what it looks like. I can't visualize it. And, I know there are five hundred people over there. Well, now I have one person to funnel it [questions] through. He directs me to the appropriate people. So, I have … an informal contact. It [the relationship] wasn't the result of an existing process. It was something that I informally set up because he was able to get me some answers. (E-learn Virtual Project Manager 11)

Although locating and commandeering the right resources can prove daunting and iterative, the successful managers are the ones who work at finding them. With diligence they find others willing to help.

> It didn't surprise me that they [expert resource] wouldn't just instantly drop everything and answer me. My next thought was I needed someone at the corporate location to help me rally these people together in some way. But, I didn't know exactly how to go about it. [One of the company administrators] helped me quite a bit. She … was happy to try and help … and amplified my request. … She honed in on a couple of different groups … and steered me in the right direction. (E-learn Virtual Project Manager 22)

Virtual teamwork research has grappled with the idea of controlling individual performances. However, it has been largely found that such control is difficult, at best, to do virtually. Instead, successful virtual project managers enlist tactics that foster a desire and willingness to help. Creating a sense of personal connection with critical resources enhances loyalty and commitment. Management behaviors that enlist empathy enable critical resources to place themselves in the project manager's shoes. As a result, they understand others' perspectives and are more apt to act in a manner that supports them. The following excerpt demonstrates the frustration and need to develop competencies that foster empathy.

> They don't understand what we do. They don't understand what happens when they don't deliver. They don't understand the pain that their lack of

responsibility causes to the field. I think if they had a better sense of that, they might try a little harder to meet their deadlines, build a quality product, and do thorough testing. (E-learn Virtual Project Manager 13)

In the absence of a relationship, managers should work to ensure that critical resources understand their plight. Imparting this knowledge has the potential to sway support efforts. Notwithstanding, building bonds is critical to attaining support in situations where help is otherwise unavailable. The development and utilization of these networks develop synergies that span beyond the immediate reach of the individuals involved.

Contingency approach to virtual cooperation

Developing guidelines are not in themselves enough to enhance virtual cooperation. We must explore when and how to enlist tactics that lead to effectiveness. This study proposes tactics for building virtual cooperation established in accordance with the level of virtuality. Three such levels or phases resulted from an analysis of data: immediate availability, informal moderated availability, and formal moderated availability (Figure 4.2). Immediate availability occurs when critical resources are available and respond as such. This leads to the prompt determination of resource competence, empathy, and facilitation. If these competencies were found to exist, cooperation ensued. Meyerson, Weick, and Kramer (1996) refer to the uninhibited completion of this Phase 1 as "swift trust." Swift trust is defined as ...

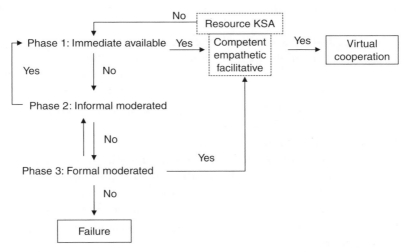

Figure 4.2 Varying phases of virtuality dependent upon perceived resource availability and commitment

Moderated availability comes about when critical resources are not readily attainable and swift trust fails. Panteli (2004) describes this phenomenon in terms of degrees of virtual presence. Availability of virtual team members is portrayed in accordance with three dimensions: (1) present availability, (2) absent unavailability, and (3) silenced availability. Present availability results when critical resources respond to inquires. Absent unavailability results when critical resources respond that they will be unwilling or unable to offer support. Finally, silenced availability results when critical resources do not respond and their status cannot be ascertained.

Tactics associated with moderating availability are necessary when critical resources are (1) absent and unavailable, or (2) silent and perceived as available. Reliance on moderated availability requires managers to determine if situations warrant informal or formal intervention. Phase 2, informal moderation enlists the aid of social capital. Here managers rely upon established relationships to nudge availability from reluctant resources. They also use these social and relational networks to discover substitute resources. Multiple enumerations at this level are often required before adequate resource(s) can be commandeered. If Phase 2 tactics fail, efforts must progress to Phase 3. Formal moderation relies upon preestablished rules of engagement, hierarchical structures, and other organization-based control mechanisms to force availability of critical resources. If successful, these tactics result in both availability and compliance. However, data strongly suggests Phase 3 be enlisted as a last result as these tactics tend to alienate resources, hinder the development of human and social capital, and "burn bridges."

This phased approach to building virtual cooperation is contingent upon perceived availability and commitment on the part of critical resources. Therefore, tactics should be enlisted based upon the level of perceived virtuality. Phase 1, immediate availability, suggests that tactics focus on ensuring critical resource competence, empathy, and facilitation. Phase 2, informal mediation, presumes managers have viable social and relational networks upon which to rely. Thus, tactics associated with developing, maintaining, and utilizing relationships are paramount. Phase 3, formal mediation, results when moderating resources are unwilling or unable to assist. These situations require tactics associated with finding and connecting to networks that can force compliance or avail the necessary human and social capital to complete performance objectives.

Implications for research and practice

This research offers a number of significant contributions. First, the proposed contingency approach to building virtual cooperation illuminates the need for further study on how and when to enlist tactics for enhancing cooperation. Subsequent research efforts should research this contingency approach to increase our knowledge of the tactics and the impact of virtuality on virtual team performances. Additional effort should also be placed in validating and further defining the tactics. Finally, added benefit would be gained from understanding how these efforts impact both efficiencies and effectiveness of resource mobilization.

Further, the research proposes a modification of Hackman's (1983) model of group effectiveness to include the attainment of human resources prior to group synergy and process criteria of effectiveness. Additional research should help distinguish the impact of both tangible and intangible resources to virtual team effectiveness. These efforts will lead to additional understanding regarding the significance of (1) social and relational networks, (2) organization-based control mechanisms, and (3) advocacy, to name a few. This would, in turn, further our understanding of the impact of tactics beyond trust and control. Finally, additional work is needed to help ascertain virtuality and its impact on varying measures of performance (satisfaction, output, interdependence, etc.).

While existing research provides some indication as to the best practices associated with virtual team effectiveness (Jarman, 2005; Lee-Kelley, Crossman, and Cannings, 2004; Lurey and Raisinghani, 2001), it does not provide immediate guidelines for implementing those behaviors within virtual contexts. The results of this study will help practitioners to understand phased approaches to gaining critical support resources, specific tactics to enhance interdependent performance, the value of developing and utilizing support networks, and the preparation of individuals, teams, and organizations to support virtual teamwork.

Practitioners must understand and begin implementing tactics for enhancing virtual cooperation if virtual teams are to be successful. This will involve finding, commandeering and facilitating interaction among members whose roles are critical to performance objectives. The task of forming virtual teams is often daunting and will require tactics for ensuring critical resources are available, accountable, and responsive. These tactics, in turn, will be contingent upon the manager's assessment of the situation and their ability to develop and utilize human and social capital. Finally, if organizations are to continue to embrace virtual teamwork they must prepare their employees for virtuality. This means training individuals on models of virtual team effectiveness, ensuring virtual members are adequately motivated to engage in interdependent performances, and creating organizational cultures and structures, which facilitate virtual teamwork.

Conclusion

Research associated with understanding virtual team effectiveness is needed (Furst, Blackburn, and Rosen, 1999). Gaps addressed within this chapter include understanding the impact of virtuality, the perceived availability or commitment of expert resources, on tactics for enhancing virtual cooperation. Particular emphasis is placed on tactics beyond trust. This contingency approach highlights the need for competent, empathetic, and facilitative support resources; social and relational networks; and at times organization-based control mechanisms to help ensure availability, accountability, and responsiveness of critical team member resources.

The following is a first-person description of virtual project manager behaviors that have been found to enhance virtual cooperation. Use swift trust when possible. Remember, other forms of trust can be developed over time. So ingratiate yourself to others. It will eventually work in your favor. Develop interpersonal meaningful relationships based on intimate connections. Implore other sensitivities. Be sure others understand your plight. You will find they may be willing to help. Continuously develop and hone your personal and professional networks. Expand your networks by establishing linkages with outside contacts. Do not just rely on those you know personally. Rely on those deemed reliable. Understand the myriad of alternative resources, which could help in the completion of objectives. Be clear on your options (i.e., primary, secondary, and tertiary) and exercise them wisely. Understand your organization's structure and culture. Discover how to use departmentalization, procedures, and other formalized rules of engagement to your advantage. Seek out and develop champions to support your causes. Promote win–win solutions. Finally, locating and commandeering the right resources can prove daunting and iterative. With diligence you will find a champion willing to rally your cause.

References

Bettenhausen, K.L. (1991) Five Years of Group Research: What We Have Learned and What Needs to be Addressed, *Journal of Management*, 17, 345–381.

Biocca, F., and Delaney, B. (1995) "Immersive Virtual Reality Technology", in F. Biocca, and M.R. Levy (Eds), *Communication in the Age of Virtual Reality*, pp. 57–124. Lawrence Erlbaum: Hillsdale, NJ.

Bordia, P. (1997) Face-to-face Versus Computer-mediated Communication: A Synthesis of the Experimental Literature, *The Journal of Business Communication*, 34, 99–120.

Boyatzis, R.E. (1998) *Transforming Qualitative Information: Thematic Analysis and Code Development*, Sage: Thousand Oaks, CA.

Bunderson, J.S. (2003) Recognizing and Utilizing Expertise in Work Groups: A Status Characteristics Perspective, *Administrative Science Quarterly*, 48(4), 557–591.

Corpola, N.W., Hiltz, S.R., and Rotter, N.G. (2004) Building Trust in Virtual Teams, *IEEE Transactions on Professional Communication*, 47(2), 95–104.

Creswell, J. (1998) *Qualitative Inquiry and Research Design: Choosing Among Five Traditions*, Sage: London, New Delhi, Thousand Oaks, CA.

Daft, R., and Lengel, R. (1986) Organizational Information Requirements, Media Richness, and Structural Design, *Management Science*, 32, 554–572.

Daft, R.L. (2005) *The Leadership Experience*, 3rd edn, Thomson South-Western: Mason, OH.

Das, T.K., and Teng, B. (1998) Between Trust and Control: Developing Confidence in Partner Cooperation in Alliances, *Academy of Management Review*, 23, 491–512.

Dougherty, D. (1992) Interpretive Barriers to Successful Product Innovation in Large Firms, *Organization Science*, 3, 179–202.

Eisenhardt, K.M. (1989) Agency Theory. An Assessment and Review, *Academy of Management Review*, 14, 57–74.

Elron, E., and Vigoda, E. (2003) "Influence and Political Processes in Virtual Teams," in C.B. Gibsonand S.G. Cohen (Eds), *Virtual Teams that Work: Creating Conditions for Virtual Team Effectiveness*, pp. 317–334. John Wiley: San Francisco, CA.

Furst, S., Blackburn, R., and Rosen, B. (1999) Virtual Team Effectiveness: A Proposed Research Agenda, *Info Systems Journal*, 9, 249–269.

Gaertner, S.L., Mann, J., Murrel, A., and Dovidio, J.F. (1989) Reducing Intergroup Bias: The Benefits of Recategorization, *Journal of Personality and Social Psychology*, 57, 239–249.

Gallivan, M.J. (2001) Striking the Balance Between Trust and Control in Virtual Organizations: A Content Analysis of Open Source Software Case Studies, *Information Systems Journal*, 11(4), 277–304.

Goleman, D. (1998) *Working with Emotional Intelligence*, Bantam Books: New York.

Guzzo, R.A., and Dickson, M.W. (1996) Teams in Organization: Recent Research on Performance and Effectiveness, *Annual Review of Psychology*, 47, 307–338.

Hackman, J.R. (1983) *A Normative Model of Work Team Effectiveness*, Yale School of Organization and Management, Research Program on Groups Effectiveness: New Haven, CT.

Hammer, M. and Champy, J. (1993) *Reengineering the Corporation*, Harper Business: New York.

Handy, C. (1995) Trust and the Virtual Organization, *Harvard Business Review*, May–June, 41–50.

Hollenbeck, J.R., Ilgen, D.R., Sego, D.J., Hedlund, J., Major, D.A., and Phillips, J. (1995) Multilevel Theory of Team Decision Making: Decision Performance in Teams Incorporating Distributed Expertise, *Journal of Applied Psychology*, 80(2), 292–316.

Jarman, R. (2005) When Success Isn't Everything – Case Studies of Two Virtual Teams, *Group Decision and Negotiation*, 14, 333–354.

Jarvenpaa, S.L., and Leidner, D.E. (1999) Communication and Trust in Global Virtual Teams, *Organization Science*, 10(6), 791–815.

Jones, T., and Bowie, N.E. (1998) Moral Hazards on the Road to the "Virtual" Corporation, *Business Ethics Quarterly*, 8(2), 273–292.

Kahn, W.A. (1992) To Be Fully There: Psychological Presence at Work, *Human Relations*, 45(4), 321–349.

Lawler, E. (1986) *High-Involvement Management. Participative Strategies for Improving Organization Performance*, Jossey-Bass: San Francisco.

Lee-Kelley, L., Crossman, A., and Cannings, A. (2004) A Social Interaction Approach to Managing the "Invisibles" of Virtual Teams, *Industrial Management and Data Systems*, 104(8), 650–657.

Lipnack, J., and Stamps, J. (1997) *Virtual Teams: Reaching Across Space, Time, and Organizations with Technology*, John Wiley: New York.

Littlepage, G., Robison, W., and Reddington, K. (1997) Effects of Task Experience and Group Experience on Group Performance, Member Ability, and Recognition of Expertise, *Organizational Behavior and Human Decision Processes*, 69(2), 133–147.

Lombard, M., and Ditton, T. (1997) At the Heart of it All: The Concept of Presence, *Journal of Computer-Mediated Communications*, 3(2). Available: http://jcmc.indiana.edu/vol3/issue2/lombard.html

Lurey, J.S., and Raisinghani, M.S. (2001) An Empirical Study of Best Practices in Virtual Teams, *Information and Management*, 38, 523–544.

McClelland, D.C., and Daily, C. (1972) *Improving Officer Selection for the Foreign Service*, Mcber: Boston.

McGrath, J.E. (1984) *Groups: Interaction and Performance*, Prentice Hall: Englewood Cliffs, NJ.

Meyerson, S., Weick, K.E., and Kramer, R.M. (1996) "Swift Trust and Temporary Groups," in R.M. Kramer and T.R. Tyler (Eds), *Trust in Organizations: Frontiers of Theory and Research*, Sage: Thousand Oaks, CA.

Motowidlo, S. (1992) Studies of the Structured Behavior Interview, *Journal of Applied Psychology*, 77(4), 571–587.

Nemeth, C.J. (1993) "Dissent, Group Process, and Creativity," in E.J. Lawler and B. Markovsky (Eds), *Social Psychology of Groups: A Reader*, pp. 107–126, JAI Press: Greenwich, CT.

O'Leary, M., Orlikowski, W., and Yates, J. (2002) "Distributed Work over the Centuries: Trust and Control in the Hudson's Bay Company, 1670–1826," in P.J. Hinds and S. Kiesler (Eds), *Distributed Work*, MIT Press: Cambridge, MA.

Panteli, N. (2004) Discursive Articulations of Presence in Virtual Organizing, *Information and Organization*, 14, 59–81.

Panteli, N., and Duncan, E. (2004) Trust and Temporary Virtual Teams: Alternative Explanations and Dramaturgical Relationships, *Information Technology and People*, 17(2), 423–441.

Ragin, C.C. (1987) *The Comparative Method: Moving beyond Qualitative and Quantitative Strategies*, University of California Press.

Ronan W.W., and Latham, G.P. (1974) The Reliability and Validity of Critical Incident Technique: A Closer Look, *Studies in Personnel Psychology*, 6, 53–64.

Short, J., Williams, E., and Christie, B. (1976) *The Social Psychology of Telecommunications*, Wiley: London.

Steuer, J.S. (1992) Defining Virtual Reality: Dimensions Determining Telepresence, *Journal of Communications*, 42(4), 73–93.

Stewart, D.D., and Stasser, G. (1995) Expert Role Assignment and Information Sampling during Collective Recall and Decision Making, *Journal of Personality and Social Psychology*, 69(4), 619–628.

Strauss, A.L., and Corbin, J. (1990) *Basics of Qualitative Research: Grounded Theory Procedures and Techniques*, Sage: Newbury Park, CA.

Tusi, A.S., Egan, T.D., and O'Reilly, C.A., III. (1992) Being Different: Relational Demography and Organizational Attachment, *Administrative Science Quarterly*, 37, 549–579.

Watson, W.E., Kuman, K., and Michaelson, L. (1993) Cultural Diversity's Impact on Interaction Process and Performance: Comparing Homogeneous and Diverse Task Groups, *Academy of Management Journal*, 36, 590–602.

Weems-Landingham, V. (2004) The Role of Project Manager and Team Member Knowledge, Skills and Abilities in Virtual Team effectiveness, *ProQuest Dissertations and Theses* (Doctoral dissertation, Case Western Reserve University, May).

Yamagishi, T., and Cook, K. (1993) Generalized Exchange and Social Dilemmas, *Social Science Quarterly*, 54(4), 235–248.

Yin, R.K. (1994) *Case Study Research: Design and Methods,* Sage: Thousand Oaks, CA.

CHAPTER 5

Virtuality in organizational team environments: Concept, measurement, and effects in the context of sustainable management

C. Schmidt, B.K. Temple, A. McCready, J. Newman, and S.C. Kinzler

Introduction

The phenomenon of "virtuality" is well known in our occupational and private life, but remains rather unexplored. It is arguable what it comprises, what sort of effects it has at different levels and how one should deal with the new complexities associated with it. It is also an issue for organizational research investigating forms of virtual collaboration and work organization such as virtual teams (VTs). This chapter provides a quantifiable approach to virtuality in organizational team environments. It follows the interest in virtuality and its relation to dimensions of context, attitude, management, and team performance at the economic, social, and psychological level. The notion of VTs and a classification scheme as part of a broader framework are presented to distinguish different types and degrees of virtuality (DoV) in team environments. In addition, the chapter includes the methodology, the research framework, and design, as well as results of the quantitative and qualitative empirical phases. By integrating sociological/organizational views, relations between virtual, economical, social, psychological, contextual, and managerial forces in the VT environment are investigated. Several conclusions are highlighted in regard to theory and practical implications for the managerial level striving to combine strategic aims of sustainable social and psychological performance and operational daily business in VTs. We find that virtuality does not significantly relate to economic effectiveness but to additional dimensions that display a team's social and psychological efficiency at the individual and the team level. These comprise team-related orientation, motivation, and identity/identification. Given a noticeably low level of orientation in all virtualized teams and low identity/identification in lower levels of virtualization, we identify practical indications to support these attitudes in order to enhance the performance of teams in the virtual.

Virtuality: a pervasive mystery

"Virtuality" is assumed to have an increasing impact not only on our private, but also our occupational lives (Menzies, 1999). The term is often associated with the rapid development of information and communication technologies (ICTs) over the last years. Global markets are fuelled increasingly by innovation cycles and developments in ICTs so that collaboration is possible without having to meet partners face-to-face. In parallel, the supply of bandwidth and advanced conferencing or shared application tools is increasing at decreasing cost (Panteli and Dawson, 2001). According to Aichele (2006), this has brought about an all-embracing change of wide scope that is often described as the second industrial revolution. Yet, it is agreed that the development of the information society also brings along danger, which is as prevalent as it is unexplored. ICT development has to be questioned according to its societal acceptance and effects. Although virtuality seems to be a salient issue to be taken into account when conducting research on organizational work groups, studies rarely provide clear descriptions of the characteristics of the teams under their investigation (Dubé and Paré, 2004). A review of VT-related managerial, organizational, sociological, and psychological literature reflected heterogeneous approaches to the terms "virtuality," "virtual teams," and "degree of virtuality." Additionally, classifications vary and a few studies provide a quantifiable analysis of the effects of working vir- tually on the involved individuals and social systems. This constitutes a need for further research because it is known that economic issues are not the only factors expressing the vital states of organizations and their members. Nieder (1984) states that a "more healthy" organization distin- guishes itself from a "more ill" one by a better balance between economic effectiveness and social efficiency. Little attention is paid to this aspect, especially in VT-related publications, although underestimation or mis- management of "soft" key figures is known to contribute to negative effects at various levels, not only harming project success (Lee-Kelley,

Crossman, and Cannings, 2004), but also the organizational culture (Scholz, 2000a; Türk, 1976). This research study is directed at examining this issue in more detail, influenced by an approach first suggested by Türk (1976). It was chosen because recent VT-related literature highlighted the less viable role of direct, interpersonal supervision in VTs (Kirkman et al., 2004; Bell and Kozlowski, 2002). Additionally, the omission of analyzing and measuring behavioral, psychosocial outcomes in regard to the performance of VTs is noted (Zhang, Fjermestad, and Tremaine, 2005; Martins, Gilson, and Travis Maynard, 2004). Türk (1976) integrates direct, interactional, and indirect structural strategies and furthermore enables a systematic access to the explanation of the development of problems in organizational structures. The theoretical foundations are described in the following section.

Türk's social system organization: mechanisms and problems

Türk (1976) presumes that the action of a person within the organization as a social system is determined by processes in the dimensions of orientation (O), motivation (M), and identity/identification (I). In regard to a team context, orientation involves knowing where to find the resources needed to fulfill one's task. Motivation embraces the intrinsic and extrinsic dimension. Greene and Lepper (1974) describe intrinsic motivation as doing what one wants, while extrinsic motivation refers to doing something in order to get something in return (Reiss, 2005, pp. 4f). Identity in the team environment means the identification with the task, the team and the involved organizations. The direct or indirect impact of O, M, and I influences an individual's behavior. Mismanagement in the areas of O, M, and I relates to symptoms of dysfunctional patterns reflected in the behavior and perception of individuals. When dysfunctional states are shared by individuals they threaten all organizational levels and are characterized by pathological cultures. Scholz (2000b, p. 779) describes culture as the implicit awareness of a business, which accrues from the behavior of the members of the organization and, in return, governs the behavior of individuals. Thus, dysfunctional cultures are ones that contribute to psychic and social costs, which are borne by both individual employees and organizations (Scholz, 2000a; Bruch and Kuhnert, 1994; Türk, 1976). Türk (1976) characterizes three types of costs: dominance, psychic, and social costs. Dominance costs affect the organization and are reflected in increased managerial or technical effort to maintain a certain performance level or loss of yield caused by deficiencies in terms of fluctuation, absenteeism or poor quality of goods and decisions due to information scarcity. Psychic costs are borne by the individual and embrace frustration, fear, feelings of inferiority, and higher individual effort or constraint to overcome motivation loss. Social costs refer to those efforts at the expense of an employee in terms of his socio-emotional relations to others.

VTs in the literature: the double-edged sword

Various benefits are associated with VT work, for example, time advantages and reduction of travel and transaction cost, as described in Konradt and Hertel (2002), Lipnack and Stamps (2000), and Duarte and Snyder (2001). Nevertheless, the gradual workplace virtualization and dispersed collaboration harbours problems (Eichmann and Hermann, 2004). Recent studies on VTs reported information suppression (Hollingshead, 2003), alienation from organizations (Griffith, Sawyer, and Neale, 2003), stress indicators such as information overload (Haywood, 1998), role overload, and ambiguity, which were often observed with low individual commitment, absenteeism, and social loafing (Jarvenpaa and Leidner, 1999). Konradt and Hertel (2002) identify a lack of social integration/group cohesion in VTs. This harbours a risk of poor performance, since other studies identified a positive relation between group cohesion and group performance (Kelly, 2003; Mullen and Cooper, 1994). Unlike conventional working environments, where poor leadership is a major cause of stress (Kelloway et al., 2004), VT studies lack models that concretize what constitutes poor leadership and attitudinal outcomes in the virtual. This opens up a vast area of research, but is a problem for both research and practice, where the use of techniques developed for traditional settings may not be appropriate to virtual environments (Kuruppuarachchi, 2006). As the negative issues mentioned can be viewed as symptoms of pathological patterns in the tradition of Türk (1976), this study strives to investigate their antecedents in relation to the conceptual construct of "virtuality." This is viewed as important, because it seems reasonable to assume that virtuality has a certain impact on antecedents of noticeable deficiencies, which itself contributes to a pathological culture in social systems, and produces hidden costs that mediate economic performance. Lee-Kelley, Crossman, and Cannings (2004) note a risk in overlooking human psychological needs and behaviour in search for project team success.

Research problems and questions

Given the lack of knowledge about patterns and measuring mechanisms in forms of virtual collaboration, especially in VT research (Stevenson and Weis McGrath, 2004) and "little current theory to guide research on the leadership and management of virtual teams" (Bell and Kozlowski, 2002, p. 15), the need for further research in the area of virtuality is obvious. In view of the previous section, the following research questions (RQs) can be established:

RQ 1: How can VT environments be described and classified?

RQ 2: How can relations between managerial, situational factors, and effects of working in VTs – especially in regard to social and psychological efficiency – be analyzed empirically?

RQ 3: What are the effects of working in virtual team environments?

    a. Are teams that are highly virtualized more economically effective than those less virtualized?

    b. Are teams that are highly virtualized more socially/psychologically efficient than those less virtualized?

    c. How do VT workers (members and managers) involved in differently virtualized teams perceive the managerial leadership forces in their respective team environments?

In order to answer these questions, we first establish the concept of VTs by examining the intersection of the domains of virtuality, team, and DoV. The next goal is to characterize virtuality and productive team performance at the economic, social, and individual level into a framework. Here, productivity is assumed to embrace economic, social, and psychological measurements of performance. The importance of social and psychological factors in consideration of productive group output is stressed in Halfhill et al. (2005) and Furst, Blackburn, and Rosen (1999). By integrating the variables of orientation (O), motivation (M) in its intrinsic and extrinsic dimensions, as well as identity/identification (I) into the research framework of this study, the analysis strives for a scalable perspective that acknowledges both the organization and the team as social systems made up of individuals in the tradition of Türk (1976). The concept offers a pertinent starting point for a quantifiable analysis of VT environments via integrating nonpersonal indirect and direct managerial leadership forces as part of the social systemic organizational context. On the basis of the framework, we explore how virtualization relates to a team's performance at the economic, the social, and the psychological level. In this context, the multimethod approach and findings of the empirical phases are presented in view of the RQs.

Aspects of virtuality

Concepts and characteristics

Theory misses a common definition of the terms "virtuality" and "virtualization." While some contributions point at the Latin term "virtus" (Engl.: "virtue, bravery") with the stem "vir" (Engl.: "man") (Konradt and Hertel, 2002; Pindl, 2002; Lipnack and Stamps, 2000), they either lack or vary in detailed descriptions.

There is a missing link between the linguistic roots and today's perception of "virtual" as something that has "the effect, but not the form" (Birchall and Lyons, 1995, p. 18). One link is provided by John Duns Scotus, a Scottish Franciscan friar in late scholasticism, as one of the earliest to use the expression "virtualiter" to describe the possibility of existence as opposed to "realiter," the reality of existence (Diemers, 2002; Dichanz, 2001).

In view of Sandbothe (2001), "virtual" first describes the spectrum of all alternative concepts of one's future that individuals have and out of which individual identity constitutes itself. Second, it means an artificial space of new potential, which is made up of digital processed data. It provides space for individuals to develop new identities as versions of themselves. Thiedeke (2001) characterizes virtuality as a space in which alternatives of the real world are reflected. Scholz (2000a, pp. 328f.) describes virtual as the nature of an object, which is not existent in reality, but in potential. Virtuality specifies a concrete object by four characteristics. Constitutive characteristics are those shared by both the real object and its virtual pendant, whereas physical attributes refer to those elements lost when a real object becomes virtualized. Added qualifications relate to essential knowledge required for realizing a virtual state for an object and added values are described as those advantageous effects evolving out of the loss of certain physical attributes.

The process perspective: virtualization

Thiedeke (2001) describes virtualization as a process of shifting the boundaries of the valid reality into potentiality and possibility. Mowshowitz (1986) and Dollhausen (2001) view it as a further division of labor supported by computational technology. Working places are decoupled from boundaries of space and time.

In order to implement virtuality based on a mental abstract model, Thiedeke (2001) identifies two techniques: staging and simulation. Staging, or displaying, means to artificially bring about a situation of perception that is not present in an individual's everyday experience. As an example, staging is associated with arts delivering insight into other realities or imaginations that display alternatives of reality. Simulation refers to the reproduction of realities primarily achieved through computer technology.

"Virtuality" seems to characterize a state within the process of virtualization that starts when humans model abstract alternatives of real objects. This process is closely connected both to technology and human beings. Technology is both an enabler for human beings to realize virtuality and a means to access and perceive it.

Virtuality in working groups

Groups or teams (these terms are used synonymously in the following) are described as two or more individuals who directly interact interdependently within a certain time-frame (Rosenstiel, 1995; Gebert and Rosenstiel, 1981). Group communication toward accomplishing a common purpose is predominantly carried out face-to-face (Guzzo and Dickson, 1996; McGrath, 1984; Alioth, 1980).

Given the previously explained foundations, a team can be assumed to enter the virtual, when its interaction is digitally represented to a certain extent. The more frequently a co-located situation with synchronous interaction and communication channels is simulated via ICT, the more virtually its members operate. Interaction, in our perspective, comprises formal, task-related, and informal, interpersonal/social information and communication exchange.

It seems reasonable to assume that virtuality occurs in different degrees and constitutes multiple configurations of organizational design in the hybrid workplace somewhere in between traditional and fully virtual environments.

Hybrid teams

While Palmer and Speier (1997) describe VTs as intraorganizational groups, the dominant opinion is that VTs also comprise interorganizational collaborations, for example, virtual organizations or virtual enterprises (Mowshowitz, 2002; Tjortjis et al., 2002; Travica, 1997; Davidow and Malone, 1992).

It is recognized that the term is as a genus itself for different varieties of virtualized groups and that various hybrid forms, between the fully co-located and fully virtualized team, occur in industrial and educational practice (Chudoba et al., 2005; Griffith, Sawyer, and Neale, 2003; Griffith and Neale, 2001; Wong and Burton, 2000). Kirkman and Mathieu (2005, p. 703) state that many teams "fall between these extremes and occupy middle ranges on a continuum of virtuality."

According to our concepts of the conventional team on the one hand and the fully virtual team on the other, a wide range in the middle is left out. Table 5.1 shows that this gap is filled by the conceptual construct "hybrid" or "virtualized" team.

Hybrid teams are part of a complex spectrum of possibilities between completely virtual and completely traditional. In an effort to at least partially characterize and classify these teams we have defined the DoVs. It is viewed as important because virtuality is recognized as a potential characteristic of all teams (Martins, Gilson, and Travis Maynard, 2004; Griffith, Sawyer, and Neale, 2003). Therefore the next section highlights approaches to DoVs.

Degree of virtuality (DoV) in hybrid teams: quantity and quality

Besides variables that are also used to classify traditional team varieties, the question remains as to how to characterize, quantify and measure the

Table 5.1 Conventional, hybrid, and virtual teams

| | | Virtual | |
Team type	Conventional/ Traditional	Hybrid/virtualized	Fully virtual
Definition:		• Two or more individuals:	
	• in direct face-to-face interaction	• in mixed interaction/ communication • with the possibility to cross distance/time	• in interaction through digital, (a)synchronous ICTs • with the possibility to cross distance/time
		• over a period of time • with role differentiation • and common norms • perceiving themselves as being a group/team • attempting to achieve an organizational task	
	• with absence of digital ICTs in communication/ interaction	• with presence of (non)digital ICTs and face-to-face interaction	• with absence of nondigital communication/ face-to-face interaction

DoV to differentiate teams in the hybrid space. While several contributions associate virtuality and its degree with geographic dispersion (Staples and Cameron, 2005; Walther and Bunz, 2005; Lipnack and Stamps, 2000), critics acknowledge that teams may well be highly virtualized when not operating over huge borders of time and space (Kirkman and Mathieu, 2005). Others discuss virtuality as a composition of different dimensions. Chudoba et al. (2005) introduce three dimensions of virtuality comprising team distribution, workplace mobility and variety of practices. Others share the view that technology mediation is one indicator and dimension characteristic of the DoV. The application and usage of digital ICTs not only enables workers to cooperate synchronously and asynchronously (Pauleen, 2003), it also makes a team virtual to different extents. Bell and Kozlowski (2002) highlight the absence of face-to-face interaction between team members as the key factor making a team virtual. ICTs enable the digital representation of real, interactive face-to-face situations in which team members communicate at a certain frequency and exchange different formal, task-related, and informal, interpersonal/social contents. In the view of Kirkman and Mathieu (2005), virtuality embraces reliance on ICT, informational value, and synchronicity. A less virtualized team is characterized by a high frequency of usage of virtual tools, low synchronicity, and low informational value. Dubé and Paré (2004) underpin the reliance of ICT as a key factor of team virtuality and additionally view both ICT availability and the members' proficiency in ICT as additional characteristics that to different degrees are shared by all VTs. By aggregating the concepts and dropping those dimensions that are not necessarily characteristic of teams that are virtualized, we propose two dimensions of the DoV for empirical analysis. These include a quantitative dimension (to what extent is face-to-face interaction digitally represented) and a qualitative dimension (to what extent are formal, task-related and informal, person-related contents exchanged). The following section highlights the operationalization of this assumption as part of the methodology.

Methodology

In order to find answers to the RQs, this study combines deductive, positivistic, and inductive-phenomenological elements, and can be characterized as a multimethod approach following Saunders, Lewis, and Thornhill (2000). RQ 1, with respect to describing and classifying virtuality in teams, has already been discussed in the Section "Virtuality in working groups". With respect to RQ 2, the following section describes how we relate our definition of the DoV to the framework of this study. Subsequently, the design of the quantitative and qualitative empirical phases and the approaches to the data analysis are highlighted.

Research framework

The framework comprises the dimensions attitude, context, management/ leadership, and performance, each subdivided according to the organizational, team, and individual level (see Figure 5.1).

"Context" is reflected by a set of situational variables, part of which the DoV forms, in its two perspectives (Figure 5.2).

The qualitative DoV comprises two items, namely frequency of exchange of formal and informal content. The quantitative DoV is approached by generating the weighted mean value of the communication mechanisms. The more synchronous a mechanism is and the more frequently it is used, the higher the weight and the specific quantitative DoV. Table 5.2 displays the weighting scheme for the DoV calculation in the quantitative dimension.

The values are normalized to achieve scores between 0 and 1. Respondents scoring values within $0.1 \leq x < 0.5$ would accordingly be characterized with a low DoV, while values within $0.5 \leq x \leq 1$ indicate a high DoV. It has to be noted that digitality in the quantitative dimension does not increase but is either achieved or not. Although the ratio of digital and nondigital opens up further interesting questions and options to classify teams in the virtual, it exceeds the scope of this study and shall serve as a stimulus for others. Nevertheless it is acknowledged that teams also use traditional analogue devices in the hybrid by additional calculation of a degree of traditionality or nonvirtuality (DoNV) similarly to the DoV. Within the social entity "team," every member is associated with a specific DoV according to the quantity and quality of digitally represented interaction with other team members that is carried out. A VT is not marked with a static DoV per se. Dahme and Raeithel (1997) state that virtuality is an introversive form of reality, which is connected to the individual persons acting in an environment in a particular way.

The dimension "performance" includes measurements of economic effectiveness at the organizational level and indicators of social and psychological efficiency. The view is expanded by the dimension "attitude" measuring the current, team-related states of orientation (O), motivation (M), and identity/identification (I), as well as enduring states that are acknowledged as influential forces on current attitudinal perceptions.

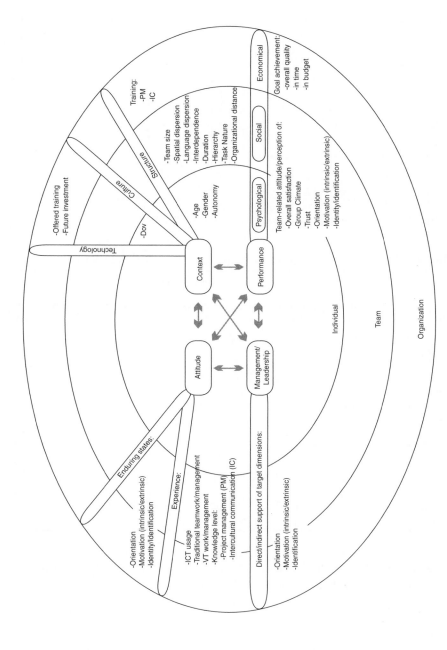

Figure 5.1 Research framework

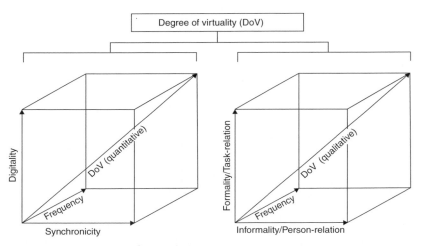

Figure 5.2 Dimensions of virtuality in team environments

Table 5.2 Exemplary DoV-weighting scheme (quantitative dimension)

	Frequency scale/(weight)						
Channel	Never (0)	Very rarely (1)	Rarely (2)	Occasionally (3)	Frequently (4)	Very frequently (5)	Channel weight
E-Mail	0	1	2	3	4	5	0.1
Internet (team publication)	0	1	2	3	4	5	0.1
Intranet (team publication)	0	1	2	3	4	5	0.1
Team-related news/ discussion groups	0	1	2	3	4	5	0.1
Shared applications	0	1	2	3	4	5	0.1
Audio conferencing/VoIP	0	1	2	3	4	5	0.2
Video conferencing	0	1	2	3	4	5	0.3
Chat/IM	0	1	2	3	4	5	0.2
Shared calendaring software	0	1	2	3	4	5	0.2
Project management systems	0	1	2	3	4	5	0.2

"Management/leadership" measures the aggregated indirect or direct levels of support of the dimensions O, M, and I.

Research design

The framework elements were designed into a questionnaire. Subsequent to a pretest, the bilingual online survey in English and German was conducted from December 2005 to June 2006 (Phase I) and delivered to a database of 159 respondents. Additional semi-structured interviews (Phase II) with five practitioners were conducted in December 2006. This was done to approach the research aim with multimethods (quantitative and qualitative) in order to enable both a triangulation of findings and a deeper penetration of the subject. Themes evolved out of the RQs and findings from Phase I and included: their perceptions on the virtualized team environment, (dis-)advantages, objectives, and the understanding of productive performance. In addition, the perception of effects of virtuality on the workplace and their (self-) management, identified problems and how to solve them, and the perception of O, M, and I were of interest.

Analysis of data

In light of RQ 2, the deductive part of the research included the establishment and testing of working hypotheses (see Section "Test of hypotheses") based upon theoretical suggestions from the literature on how to support the dimensions of O, M, and I as dependent variables. Given the aim of finding out how the suggestions are reflected in the data and the ordinal, metric nature of the scales, hypotheses were tested by calculating construct relations with Spearman's Rho (SR) (Schlittgen, 2000). The reliability of the scales used in Phase I was assessed with a calculation of Cronbach's Alpha (α). This forms the basis for the further explorative, inductive part of RQ 3. The findings of Phases I and II round up the chapter and supplement a triangulated perspective in light of each RQ and further inductive exploration of theoretical and practical implications.

Findings

Test of hypotheses

Having described virtuality and teams in organizational environments in regard to RQ 1 (see Sections "Virtuality in working groups" and "Methodology"), RQ 2 included the establishment of a research framework that integrated the findings from RQ 1 and the theory following Türk (1976) (see Section "Research framework"). Subsequently, working hypotheses were established to deductively test how theory is reflected by the data. Table 5.3 summarizes the test results and especially highlights those hypotheses that are significantly supported in both the manager and nonmanagement perspective at a confidence level of 1 percent ($p < 0.01$).

Table 5.3 Overview of significant results (deductive phase)

H	Description	Significance (both groups)	SR (Members/ $n = 60$)	SR (Managers/ $n = 99$)
	Dimension: Orientation			
H1 (a)	The setting of individual goals is positively related to the perception of team-related orientation at the individual level.	X	0.360**	0.424**
H1 (b)	The setting of individual goals is positively related to the perception of team-related orientation at the team level.	–	0.280*	0.355**
H2 (a)	The setting of team goals is positively related to the perception of team-related orientation at the individual level.	X	0.357**	0.406**
H2 (b)	The setting of team goals is positively related to the perception of team-related orientation at the team level.	–	0.290*	0.284**
H3 (a)	The communication of expectations concerning the team is positively related to the perception of team-related orientation at the individual level.	X	0.426**	0.485**
H3 (b)	The communication of expectations concerning the team is positively related to the perception of team-related orientation at the team level.	–	0.269*	0.232**
H4 (a)	The assignment of tasks and responsibilities is positively related to the perception of team-related orientation at the individual level.	X	0.437**	0.442**
H4 (b)	The assignment of tasks and responsibilities is positively related to the perception of team-related orientation at the team level.	X	0.411**	0.311**
H5 (a)	Individual role awareness is positively related to the perception of team-related orientation at the individual level.	X	0.532**	0.322**
H5 (b)	Individual role awareness is positively related to the perception of team-related orientation at the team level.	X	0.535**	0.381**
H6 (a)	The awareness of team values is positively related to the perception of team-related orientation at the individual level.	X	0.538**	0.286**
H6 (b)	The awareness of team values is positively related to the perception of team-related orientation at the team level.	X	0.451**	0.325**
H7 (a)	The awareness of binding norms is positively related to the perception of team-related orientation at the individual level.	X	0.436**	0.269**
H7 (b)	The awareness of binding norms is positively related to the perception of team-related orientation at the team level.	–	0.244	0.273**

Continued

Table 5.3 Continued

H	Description	Significance (both groups)	SR (Members/ $n = 60$)	SR (Managers/ $n = 99$)
	Dimension: Motivation			
H8 (a)	The individual decision freedom is positively related to the perception of team-related intrinsic motivation at the individual level.	X	0.493**	0.258**
H8 (b)	The individual decision freedom is positively related to the perception of team-related intrinsic motivation at the team level.	–	0.501**	0.145
H9 (a)	The individual freedom of time management is positively related to the perception of team-related intrinsic motivation at the individual level.	–	0.177	0.156
H9 (b)	The individual freedom of time management is positively related to the perception of team-related intrinsic motivation at the team level.	–	0.166	0.121
H10 (a)	The freedom to choose communication channels at the individual level is positively related to the perception of team-related intrinsic motivation at the individual level.	–	0.453**	0.58
H10 (b)	The freedom to choose communication channels at the individual level is positively related to the perception of team-related intrinsic motivation at the team level.	–	0.386**	0.137
H11	The application of reward systems is positively related to the degree of traditionality in virtualized teams.	–	0.276	0.198*
H12 (a)	The application of reward systems is positively related to the perception of team-related extrinsic motivation at the individual level.	X	0.362**	0.488**
H12 (b)	The application of reward systems is positively related to the perception of team-related extrinsic motivation at the team level.	–	0.280*	0.387**
	Identity/Identification			
H13 (a)	The individual role awareness is positively related to identity/identification with the team at the individual level.	–	0.448**	0.209*
H13 (b)	The individual role awareness is positively related to identity/identification with the team at the team level.	X	0.338**	0.330**
H14 (a)	The decision freedom at the individual level is positively related to identity/identification with the team at the individual level.	–	0.430**	0.258*

Continued

Table 5.3 Continued

H	Description	Significance (both groups)	SR (Members/ $n = 60$)	SR (Managers/ $n = 99$)
H14 (b)	The decision freedom at the individual level is positively related to identity/ identification with the team at the team level.	–	0.355**	0.167
H15 (a)	The perception of a normative framework is positively related to identity/identification with the team at the individual level.	–	0.326*	0.157
H15 (b)	The perception of a normative framework is positively related to identity/ identification with the team at the team level.	–	0.331**	0.117

**p<0.01
*p<0.05

The hypotheses were developed to examine the difference between the views at the individual level (a) and the team level (b). We will now consider these in respect of O, M, and I.

Orientation

At the individual level there is support for assuming that the setting of individual goals (H1), team goals (H2), communication of expectations to the team (H3), and the awareness of binding norms (H7) positively relate to the perception of orientation. Additional influences at both the individual and group level are identified in the clear assignment of tasks/responsibilities (H4), individual role awareness (H5), and the awareness of team values (H6).

Motivation

At the individual level, there seems to be a positive relation between the decision freedom at the individual level and the indicated intrinsic motivation (H8), as well as between reward systems and extrinsic motivation (H12). The individual freedom to choose one's communication channels significantly relates to intrinsic motivation at both levels within the member perspective (H10), but is not reflected by managers. Interestingly, no relation to intrinsic motivation was identified for the freedom of time management as expressed in H9.

This raised the question if VT managers should be less involved in regulating the usage of tools but therefore be more involved in time management by setting timely goals, which in return support orientation. This constituted an additional interview theme with the focus to explore how time management and the freedom to choose communication tools is arranged and perceived by the interviewees (see Section "Phase II").

Identity/identification

Individual role awareness (H13) and decision freedom (H14) at the individual level show a significant relation to identification with the team at both levels in the perspective of members. Members also reflect a support for H15 in terms of a positive relation between the perception of a normative framework and the shared group identity.

Overall, the results of the deductive part showed several strong consistencies between theoretical assumptions and their reflection in the data.

Reliability analysis

Subsequent to having examined predictions on the theoretical basis of the framework, Cronbach's Alpha-values (α) for the scales established in Phase I (see Figure 5.1) were calculated. Table 5.4 summarizes the results for the measured multidimensional constructs.

In regard to Cronbach's Alpha, values over 0.8 are postulated for non-explorative studies (Bortz and Döring, 2002, pp. 198f.), while König (2001, p. 139) describes that values over 0.4 are generally acknowledged as acceptable when measuring constructs over two or three indicators. Given the explorative nature of this part of the study and the fact that the minimum value is exceeded by all displayed scales, an adequate reliability can be assumed.

Inductive findings

With further interest in perceived effects at different levels in the virtualized team environment, three subquestions were formulated. These are treated successively in the following section as part of the inductive findings of Phase I. In what follows, the findings from Phase II are highlighted in regard to the underlying themes.

Table 5.4 Results of reliability analysis

Framework dimension	Scale	No of items	α
Context	Autonomy	3	0.757
	Hierarchy	2	0.538
	Isolation/boundary	3	0.597
	Proximity/time dispersion	5	0.814
	Language dispersion	2	0.731
	DoV (quantitative)	10	0.834
	DoV (qualitative)	3	0.511
	DoNV	8	0.667
Performance (economical)	Economic effectiveness	2	0.743
(social)	Group climate	2	0.815
	Trust	2	0.708
	Orientation (team)	5	0.865
	Motivation (intrinsic/team)	3	0.752
	Motivation (extrinsic/team)	2	0.782
	Identity/identification (team)	3	0.781
(psychological)	Orientation (individual)	5	0.833
	Motivation (intrinsic/individual)	3	0.723
	Motivation (extrinsic/individual)	2	0.715
	Identity/identification (individual)	3	0.844
Management/leadership (member perspective)	Orientation-supportive	9	0.844
	Motivation-supportive	3	0.426
	Identity-supportive	2	0.525
Management/leadership (manager perspective)	Orientation-supportive	9	0.833
	Motivation-supportive	2	0.612
	Identity-supportive	2	0.473

Phase I

The sample of Phase I reflects the assumed diversity and pervasiveness of virtuality in business practice as recognized by Martins, Gilson, and Travis Maynard (2004) and Griffith, Sawyer, and Neale (2003). In fact, synchronous applications were comparatively likely used as compared with asynchronous methods such as e-Mail, internet and intranet. An overall trend of further investment into ICT is noticeable. Within the group of managers, 47 percent score a high DoV ($x \geq 0.5$) as opposed to 25 percent within the group of nonmanagement. The majority of respondents were located in Germany (46.5 percent), followed by the United States (15.7 percent) and the United Kingdom (10 percent). While large enterprises are represented at 57.2 percent, 42.8 percent account to SMEs. The majority of respondents belong to noneducational sectors (67.3 percent), of which 17 percent are in manufacturing.

The thrust of RQ 3 (a) was to ask if highly virtualized teams are more economically effective than those less virtualized. The DoV in its qualitative and quantitative perspective shows no significant relation to economic effectiveness. On the contrary, highly significant relationships at the 1-per cent confidence level were identified for attitudes at the individual level. These comprise orientation (SR = 0.250), intrinsic motivation (SR = 0.289), and identity/identification (SR = 0.257). At the team level, orientation (SR = 0.258), group climate (SR = 0.298), and trust (SR = 0.240) reflect positive relations to economic effectiveness. Indirect and direct support of orientation and identity/identification also reflect a statistical relation to the economic effectiveness in the manager and member perspective. As a result, the answer to RQ 3 (a) can be proposed as follows:

> *P1. The degree of virtuality is not positively related to economic effectiveness of a team's output. There is no statistical evidence to assume that highly virtualized teams are more economically effective than those less virtualized.*

Instead, positive relations between the managerial support and perceptions of O, M, and I are identified. Thus, social and psychological dimensions are salient prerequisites for achieving economical success in VT environments. O, M, and I not only significantly relate to economical effectiveness, but their relation is also noticeably stronger than other factors, that have been recently discussed in the context of VT management as targets of leadership and indicators of noneconomical performance, for example, trust (Jarvenpaa and Leidner, 1999).

RQ 3 (b) reflected the interest in finding out if the DoV positively relates to indicators of social and psychological efficiency. The correlation analysis showed that – assuming a confidence level of 1 percent – the quantitative DoV significantly relates to extrinsic motivation (SR = 0.242) and identity/identification (SR = 0.212) at the individual level. At the team level, identified relations comprise intrinsic (SR = 0.203) and extrinsic (SR = 0.257) motivation. At the individual level, the qualitative DoV shows significant relations with intrinsic motivation (SR = 0.348) and identity/identification (SR = 0.330). At the team level significant relations are identified with intrinsic (SR = 0.301) and extrinsic (SR = 0.218) motivation, as well as identity/identification (SR = 0.291). For better readability, the significant results are summarized in Table 5.5.

At first sight it would seem reasonable to assume that the DoV, in its qualitative and quantitative dimensions, positively relates to motivation and identity/identification as indicators for social and psychological efficiency. This, though, has to be put into perspective with the findings of

Table 5.5 Overview of significant relations between DoV and attitudes (individual and team level)

Performance level	Individual				Team			
Attitude		Motivation		Identity/		Motivation		Identity/
DoV	Orientation	intrinsic	extrinsic	identification	Orientation	intrinsic	extrinsic	identification
Quantitative	–	–	X	X	–	X	X	–
Qualitative	–	X	–	X	–	X	X	X

the subsequent question. RQ 3 (c) aimed at finding out how members and managers in different DoVs perceive the applied managerial forces supporting O, M, and I at the individual and the team level. The influence and support of motivation is indicated at a higher level by managers with a higher DoV. This is underpinned by a significant relation between the DoV and the level of perceived motivation support (SR = 0.211) at the 5-percent confidence level. The influence on the remaining attitudes is not indicated differently. No significant, positive relations between the DoV and the level of support of the remaining attitudes are identified.

In light of RQ 3 (b) and (c) this shows that managerial support of attitudes, except for motivation as indicated by managers, is largely independent of the DoV. Although positively related to economic effectiveness (see RQ 3 (a)), there is no increase in the quality of perception or the level of support of orientation with increasing DoVs. With regard to identity/identification the expected trend of a positive relation between the DoV and individual identification with team-related dimensions as well as the group identity is reflected. On that basis, the following propositions can be established:

P2. All virtualized/hybrid teams are characterized by a low level of social and psychological efficiency in the indicating dimension of orientation at both the individual and the team level. There is no statistical evidence for a positive relation between the DoV and the level of perceived managerial support of orientation.

P3. There is evidence that managers are aware of and adjust to the needs of the virtual environment in the dimension of motivation toward social and psychological efficiency. This is reflected statistically by a positive relation between the quantitative DoV and the level of perceived managerial support of motivation in the group of managers, as well as increasing perceptions of motivation at the individual level.

P4. There is a positive relation between the qualitative and quantitative DoV and identity/identification, with team factors as one indicator for psychological efficiency. There is no statistical evidence for a positive relation between the DoV and the level of perceived managerial support of identity.

In light of RQ 3 (b) and (c), several problems are evident. Besides motivation, managerial support is not increased to meet the needs of the virtual environment toward achieving more social and psychological efficiency as prerequisites for economic success. For practitioners the question arises as to how to overcome the need of creating identity in less virtualized environments and how to create more orientation in the virtual (see Section "Implications for practice").

Phase II

The semi-structured interviews examined issues arising from Phase I in more detail. The findings of the themes (see Section "Research design") are described in the following.

Approximately equal numbers of managers and nonmanagers enable a balanced explorative insight into two perspectives of VT practice. Phase II reflects that VTs appear in different shapes.

The first impressions gained from the interviewees were of low involvement, loss of time, and increased effort for coordination. Strong motivation to follow economic objectives with the implementation of VT work is identified. These include the saving of resources in regard to time and the ability to deploy skills and knowledge, which are not in-house, fast. Similarly, interviewees do not associate social or individual factors with the notion of productivity. One respondent explicitly doubts that work is carried out more effectively by teams just because of the fact that they are operating virtually. This supports the first proposition derived from Phase I (see Section "Phase I").

The majority of respondents considered the disadvantages of VT work to comprise intrapersonal (less involvement with the team and the task, isolation) and interpersonal aspects (reduced quality of conversation, reduced ability for adequate reaction and judgment) aspects. On the contrary, advantages such as another mention of saving resources and fast reaction to needs by choosing the right people for the job, are rather associated with the organization. Remote home workers describe effects of virtuality on their workplace more positively than respondents sharing an office situation with others. Thus, the comfortable environment without disturbances or stress caused by traveling is mentioned.

All respondents describe the effects of virtuality on their senior manage-ment and their self-management. While only negative aspects, such as more time-consuming effort for coordination, are noticed at the superior level, remote workers report a positive effect on their self-management. The blurred boundaries between work and family life are not perceived negatively, but positively by offering more flexibility with less (group) pressure.

Managers indicate that the usage of communication tools is not regulated by applying strict guidelines, which echoes the statistical rec-ommendation of less regulation discovered in Phase I (see Section "Test of hypotheses").

Respondents describe several problems. Cultural problems include misunderstandings in regard to commitment to meet appointments and adequacy of responding to requests in time. Technical problems include missing voice tracks in videoconferences or total connection breakdowns. Group and process problems comprise a lack of transparency about the availability of others and of progress, as well as social loafing and low perceived commitment/seriousness. The consequences that were men-tioned include negative aspects at the individual level, such as loss of time due to higher effort for coordination and in overcoming misunderstand-ings, frustration, and lowered team feeling/identification. Overcoming the problems, especially cultural ones, is described to be nearly if not fully impossible by a majority of the interviewees. Problem-solving strategies included traditional methods (milestones, delivery dates, appointment of discussion leaders in conferencing situations, dissemina-tion of protocols).

Lastly, themes aimed at exploring identify the effects and perceptions in regard to the attitudes of O, M, and I. Three respondents describe a positive orientation within their team environment that they associate with clarity of roles and goals in alignment with the strategic goal framework of the organization. Two comments highlighted the importance of achieving ori-entation in both traditional and virtual settings and view it as one's own responsibility. Nevertheless, negative aspects included the availability of others. Remote home workers clearly indicate a positive and higher work motivation in comparison to the remaining respondents, who describe their motivation as rather neutral and dependent on the task or topic.

In regard to identity/identification, three respondents, of which two work from home, indicate positive effects. The virtual environment enables individuals that are restricted to being at home for various reasons to participate in work life. In addition, higher identification with the orga-nization is reported by another respondent working from home. Distance and anonymity were described positively, because one can focus more on the task and detach more quickly from negative group situations. Negative comments include a full loss or a lowered team feeling, involvement and identification with the team and the task. Given the strong indicated reliance on asynchronous channels within the interview sample, Proposition 4 is neither supported nor rejected.

Conclusion

Having provided an approach to investigate virtuality in organizational team environments and its influences on economical, social, and psychological performance, several conclusions and implications can be drawn. These are highlighted in the following, according to their nature.

Implications for theory

In view of RQ 1, prerequisites for examining the effects of virtuality on the organizational team output were established. This included descriptions of the terms virtuality, virtualization, and VT. Three types of teams – conventional, hybrid and fully virtual groups – were identified and characterized. In order to classify hybrid and fully virtual teams, the importance of the DoV was highlighted in the context of other approaches and variables. As a basis for empirical analysis, our methodological approaches to managing and monitoring psychosocial performance with the dimensions of O, M, and I in the sociological systemic tradition of Türk (1976) were highlighted. Subsequently, the DoV was quantified by introducing a weighting scheme. This formed part of establishing and modeling a research framework with regard to RQ 2. The framework included a classification scheme for VTs, with additional contextual variables: indirect and direct managerial forces, as well as economic, social, and psychological team performance measures. The framework was modeled into a questionnaire for an online survey (Phase I). Subsequently, semi-structured interviews (Phase II) were conducted in order to enable both a triangulation of the findings discovered in Phase I and an exploration of additional themes with a focus on the multilevel effects of virtuality.

The deductive part of the study confirmed many of the hypotheses and constitutes a basis for practical implications on how to enhance O, M, and I (see Section "Implications for practice"). The reliability of the scales provided a pertinent basis for the subsequent inductive analysis in regard to effects of virtuality displayed by RQs 3 a–c.

Phases I and II underpin the assumption that virtuality is not significantly related to economic effectiveness (Proposition 1), but relates to indicators of social and psychological efficiency as displayed in the propositions. Positive effects are identified in the dimension of motivation but are associated with an increase in the support of motivation in higher DoVs (Proposition 3). Orientation seems to be low in all virtualized teams (Proposition 2). Although identity/identification is positively related to the DoV (Proposition 4), the general level of virtuality in the sample shows that this effect is not exploited to its full potential.

Overall, the results emphasize the importance of considering virtuality as well as social and psychological efficiency in team research and practice. Teams might achieve goals from the organizational point of view, but several significant relations at the team and individual level, which influence performance, were highlighted in ways relevant to team success. In particular, virtuality was found to modulate economic success. From the authors' point of view, several dysfunctional or negative aspects mentioned in relation to VT work already reflect symptoms of pathologies and noneconomical costs. As an example, timely advantages associated with faster project cycles by working virtually are questionable and are not supported by this study. Instead, more effort and time-consuming activities are reported, which reflect the existence of dominance cost in the virtual (see Section "Türk's social system organization: mechanisms and problems"). In addition Phase II reflected psychological costs, like isolation and frustration.

Our research showed that the identified increase in time-consuming activities in VTs contradicts the advantages that are associated with themselves (Konradt and Hertel, 2002), as well as those with teams in the traditional sense (Rosenstiel, 2000). This provides evidence that there is a need for further studies, since the validity of traditional theory in light of the construct "virtuality" appears to be limited.

This study furthermore provided an insight into identifiable facets of virtuality with a thrust to investigate its effects in organizational teams. The assumption that virtuality has different degrees (quantitatively and qualitatively) enabled a quantifiable and systematic approach to characterizing and distinguishing those team structures assumed to be prevailing in practice. There is a noticeable need for further theoretical and practical knowledge in order to actively enhance the ability to anticipate factors that might be threatening at the individual, the team, and the organizational level in the context of virtuality. Nevertheless, several indications for practice could be discovered from the results of this study. These are summarized in the following.

Implications for practice

Although we note a trend toward further investment into advanced ICTs, the domain of low DoVs that is characterized by a high usage of asynchronous tools still seems to be the prevalent level of virtuality in the hybrid teamspace. In our study, virtualization has been associated with problems in the dimensions of orientation and (team) identity/identification. For practitioners the question arises how to solve these problems. Given the complex nature of virtuality and teams, this study in a comparatively new and unexplored field can only be regarded as indicative. Nevertheless, in view of the strategic pyramid as described by Hollensen (2001, p. 18) several practical implications are offered by highlighting key performance indicators and activities to combine daily business in alignment with strategic social and psychological goals at the managerial level.

The deductive part of this study (see Section "Test of hypotheses") introduced ways to monitor and maintain or enhance social and psychological efficiency, with a focus on O, M, and I at the individual and the team level. These can be applied by both managers and members, who should be encouraged to demand or push forward clarity in the following dimensions.

Orientation can be enhanced for the individual and the team by setting goals at the individual (H1) and the team level (H2). That includes the communication of expectations concerning the team (H3), as well as the assignment of tasks and responsibilities (H4) and raising the awareness to individual roles (H5) and team values (H6). In addition, the awareness of binding norms as expressed by members supports individual orientation (H7 (a)). Phase II included additional practical experiences to enhance the orientation for oneself and others. When sending asynchronous group messages, the sender should clearly indicate if a request is desired, from whom and within what time. Here, one should be aware of the written word, the need for clear expression, and consider the longer response time when writing e-mails to recipients in other time zones. When using asynchronous platforms, regular maintenance, update, and a clear structure of information are mentioned. Daily or weekly status reports shared with superiors and members help in synchronizing the asynchronous activities of the team members. Prior to interacting synchronously in conferencing situations, interviewees highlighted the usability of double-checking via phone, the appointment of responsible persons for leading a discussion, with the need for clear contents, and acknowledged the value of discussion protocols. Generally, a group plan displaying the goal, the team structure, team milestones, members, and their availabilities and responsibilities, as well as rules of the game should be established. A print or electronic version of a team roadmap gives the team a visible shape.

Besides the level of challenge of, or excitement toward, a task, stimuli for individual motivation can be identified in both perspectives by more decision freedom in the intrinsic (H8), as well as the application of reward systems in the extrinsic dimension (H12). Out of the member perspective, the freedom to choose communication channels (H10) is added to enhance intrinsic motivation.

Identity/identification, in terms of current team-related states, is enhanced by the level of individual role awareness (H13) that also enhances orientation. Besides intrinsic motivation, the decision freedom at the individual level (H14) is pertinent to enhance identity/identification. In addition, the creation of a normative framework (H15) should be pursued, which is underpinned by postulations for rules of the game as reflected in Phase II. The most binding form would refer to a contract highlighting consequences in the case of noncompliance to agreed procedures and indicators for progress performance. Virtual interaction does not substitute personal contact. Participants support this by reporting a desire and a need for personal contact. Meetings, at least in the beginning phase or even more regularly, are viewed as necessary. In view of identity/identification, one should strive for high DoV environments with more frequent usage of synchronous, advanced tools and more frequent informal and formal content exchange. This should happen within a given set of tools, allowing members freedom to choose the suitable one. There is statistical evidence that members who can chose tools and channels themselves to a greater extent feel more intrinsically motivated than those having to follow strict guidelines. That way, effort for planning and controlling is reduced and resources are liberated to enable a stronger focus on other responsibilities. In addition, managers can play a more active role in the process of the member's time management. This is pertinent to support orientation (reduction of complexity) and there is no statistical evidence for a threatening effect to intrinsic motivation.

Overall, this study reflected that virtuality is a pervasive factor, which here has been investigated in the context of teams. Essentially, the approaches and findings of this study do not claim to be exhaustive. It is hoped that a fruitful and helpful basis for further penetration of the subject is provided.

References

Aichele, C. (2006) *Intelligentes Projektmanagement* [Intelligent Project Management], Kohlhammer: Stuttgart.

Alioth, A. (1980) *Entwicklung und Einführung alternativer Arbeitsformen.* [Development and Implementation of Alternative Working Structures], *Schriften zur Arbeitspsychologie XXVII*, Huber: Bern.

Bell, B.S., and Kozlowski, S.W.J. (2002) A Typology of Virtual Teams. Implications for Effective Leadership, *Group and Organization Management*, 27(1), 14–49.

Birchall, D., and Lyons, L. (1995) *Creating Tomorrows Organization. Unlocking the Benefits of Future Work*, Pitman: London.

Bortz, J., and Döring, N. (2002) *Forschungsmethoden und Evaluation für Human- und Sozialwissenschaftler* [Research Methods and Evaluation for Human and Social Scientists], 3rd edn, Springer: Berlin.

Bruch, H., and Kuhnert, B. (1994) Projekte als Kernelement einer ganzheitlichen Flexibilisierungsstrategie [Projects as a Core Element of an Integrated Strategy of Flexibilization], *Zeitschrift für Arbeitsforschung, Arbeitsgestaltung und Arbeitspolitik*, 3(3), 220–237.

Chudoba, K.M., Wynn, E., Lu, M., and Watson-Manheim, M.B. (2005) How Virtual are We? Measuring Virtuality and Understanding its Impact in a Global Organization, *Information Systems Journal*, 15(4), 279–306.

Dahme, C., and Raeithel, A. (1997) Ein tätigkeitstheoretischer Ansatz zur Entwicklung von brauchbarer Software [An Activity-Theoretical Approach to Developing Usable Software], *Informatik-Spektrum*, 20, 5–12.

Davidow, W.H., and Malone, S. (1992) *The Virtual Corporation. Structuring and Revitalising the Corporation for the 21st Century*, Harper Business: New York.

Dichanz, H. (2001) Zur Historie von Virtualität und Virtualisierung [About the History of Virtuality and Virtualization], *DIE Zeitschrift für Erwachsenenbildung*, 3, 40–41.

Diemers, D. (2002) *Die virtuelle Triade. Cyberspace, Maschinenmensch und künstliche Intelligenz* [The Virtual Triade. Cyberspace, Machine Humans and Artificial Intelligence], Haupt: Bern.

Dollhausen, K. (2001) Zur Virtualisierung von Organisationen [About the Virtualization of Organizations], *DIE Zeitschrift für Erwachsenenbildung*, 3, 35–37.

Duarte, D.L., and Snyder, N.T. (2001) *Mastering Virtual Teams: Strategies, Tools and Techniques that Succeed*, 2nd edn, Jossey-Bass: San Francisco.

Dubé, L., and Paré, G. (2004) "The Multi-faceted Nature of Virtual Teams," in D.J. Pauleen (Ed.), *Virtual Teams: Projects, Protocols and Processes*, Idea Group: Hershey, pp. 1–39.

Eichmann, H., and Hermann, C. (2004) Umbruch der Erwerbsarbeit-Dimensionen von Entgrenzung der Arbeit [Change in Gainful Employment-Dimensions of the Dissolution of Work Boundaries], *EAP-Diskussionspapier I*.

Furst, S., Blackburn, R., and Rosen, B. (1999) Virtual Team Effectiveness: A Proposed Research Agenda, *Information Systems Journal*, 9, 249–269.

Gebert, D., and Rosenstiel, L.v. (1981) *Organisationspsychologie: Person und Organisation* [Organizational Psychology: Person and Organization], Kohlhammer: Stuttgart.

Greene, D., and Lepper, M.R. (1974) How to Turn Play into Work, *Psychology Today*, 8, 49–54.

Griffith, T.L., Sawyer, J.E., and Neale, M.A. (2003) Virtualness and Knowledge in Teams: Managing the Love Triangle of Organizations, Individuals, and Information Technology, *MIS Quarterly*, 27, 265–287.

Griffith, T.L., and Neale, M.A. (2001) Information Processing in Traditional, Hybrid, and Virtual Teams: From Nascent Knowledge to Transactive Memory, *Research in Organizational Behaviour*, 23, 379–421.

Guzzo, R., and Dickson, M.W. (1996) Teams in Organizations: Recent Research on Performance and Effectiveness, *Annual Review of Psychology*, 47, 307–338.

Halfhill, T., Sundstrom, E., Lahner, J., Calderone, W., and Nielsen, T. (2005) Group Personality Composition and Group Effectiveness: An Integrative Review of Empirical Research, *Small Group Research*, 36(1), 83–105.

Haywood, M. (1998) *Managing Virtual Teams: Practical Techniques for High-Technology Project Managers*, Artech House: Norwood, London.

Hollensen, S. (2001) *Global Marketing. A Market Responsive Approach*, 2nd edn, Pearson Education: Harlow.

Hollingshead, A.B. (2003) "Communication Technologies, the Internet, and Group Rresearch," in M.A. Hogg and R. Scott Tindale (Eds), *Blackwell Handbook of Social Psychology: Group Processes*, Blackwell: Oxford, pp. 557–573.

Jarvenpaa, S.L., and Leidner, D.E. (1999) Communication and Trust in Global Virtual Teams, *Organization Science*, 10(6), 791–815.

Kelloway, E.K., Sivanathan, N., Francis, L., and Barling, J. (2004) "Poor Leadership," in J. Barling, E.K. Kelloway, and M.R. Frone

(Eds), *Handbook of Work Stress*, Sage: Thousand Oaks, CA, pp. 89–112.

Kelly, J.R. (2003) "Mood and Emotion in groups," in M.A. Hogg and R. Scott Tindale (Eds), *Blackwell Handbook of Social Psychology: Group Processes*, Blackwell: Oxford, pp. 164–181.

Kirkman, B.L., and Mathieu, J.E. (2005) The Dimensions and Antecedents of Team Virtuality, *Journal of Management*, 31(5), 700–718.

Kirkman, B.L., Rosen, B., Tesluk, P., and Gibson, C. (2004) The Impact of Team Empowerment on Virtual Team Performance: The Moderating Role of Face-to-face Interaction, *Academy of Management Journal*, 47(2), 175–192.

König, T. (2001) *Nutzensegmentierung und alternative Segmentierungsansätze: eine vergleichende Gegenüberstellung im Handelsmarketing* [Segmentation of Benefits and Alternative Approaches to Segmentation: A Comparative Study in Retail Marketing], DUV/Gabler Edition Wissenschaft Wiesbaden.

Konradt, U., and Hertel, G. (2002) *Management Virtueller Teams* [Management of Virtual Teams], Beltz: Weinheim, Basel.

Kuruppuarachchi, P. (2006) Managing Virtual Project Teams: How to Maximize Performance, *Handbook of Business Strategy*, 7(1), 71–78.

Lee-Kelley, L., Crossman, A., and Cannings, A. (2004) A Social Interaction Approach to Managing the "Invisibles" of Virtual Teams, *Industrial Management and Data Systems*, 104(8), 650–657.

Lipnack, J., and Stamps, J. (2000) *Virtual Teams: People Working across Boundaries with Technology*, John Wiley: New York.

Martins, L., Gilson, L.L., and Travis Maynard, M. (2004) Virtual Teams: What Do We Know and Where Do We Go from Here?, *Journal of Management*, 30(6), 805–835.

McGrath, J.E. (1984) *Groups: Interaction and Performance*, Prentice Hall: Englewood Cliffs, NJ.

Menzies, H. (1999) Digital Networks: The Medium of Globalization, and the Message, *Canadian Journal of Communication*, 24(40), online. Available: http://www.cjc-online.ca/viewarticle.php?id=548 (accessed: 27.04.2007)

Mowshowitz, A. (1986) Social Dimensions of Office Automation, *Advances in Computers*, 25, 335–404.

Mowshowitz, A. (2002) *Virtual Organization: Toward a Theory of Societal Transformation Stimulated by Information Technology*, Quorum Books: Westport, CT.

Mullen, B., and Cooper, C. (1994) The Relation Between Group Cohesiveness and Performance: An Integration, *Psychological Bulletin*, 115, 210–227.

Nieder, P. (1984) *Die "Gesunde" Organisation: Ein Weg zu mehr "Gesundheit"* [The "Healthy" Organization: A Way to More "Health"], Wilfer: Spardorf.

Palmer, J.W., and Speier, C. (1997) "A Typology of Virtual Organizations: An Empirical Study," in J. Gupta (Ed.), *Proceedings of AIS 1997*, online. Available: http://virtualni-organizace.xf.cz/virtual_organizations.htm (accessed: 15.04.2007)

Panteli, N., and Dawson, P. (2001) Video Conferencing Systems: Changing Patterns of Business Communication, *New Technology, Work and Employment*, 11(2), 88–99.

Pauleen, D.J. (2003) Leadership in a Global Virtual Team: An Action Learning Approach, *Leadership and Organizational Development Journal*, 24(3), 153–162.

Pindl, T. (2002) *Führen und Coachen von virtuellen Netzwerken– unabhängig von Ort und Zeit* [Leading and Coaching of Virtual Networks – Independent from Location and Time], Deutscher Wirtschaftsdienst: Cologne.

Reiss, S. (2005) Extrinsic and Intrinsic Motivation at 30. Unresolved Scientific Issues, *The Behavior Analyst*, 28(1), 1–14.

Rosenstiel, L.v. (1995) "Kommunikation und Führung in Arbeitsgruppen" [Communication and Leadership in Working Groups], in H. Schuler (Ed.), *Lehrbuch der Organisationspsychologie*, Huber: Bern, pp. 321–351.

Rosenstiel, L.v. (2000) *Grundlagen der Organisationspsychologie* [Foundations of Organizational Psychology], 4th edn, Schäffer-Poeschel: Stuttgart.

Sandbothe, M. (2001) Das Reale im Virtuellen und das Virtuelle im Realen entdecken! [Discovering the Real in the Virtual and the Virtual in the Real!], *DIE Zeitschrift für Erwachsenenbildung*, 3, 17–20.

Saunders, M.N.K., Lewis, P., and Thornhill, A. (2000) *Research Methods for Business Students*, 2nd edn, Pearson Education: Harlow.

Schlittgen, R. (2000) *Einführung in die Statistik: Analyse und Modellierung von Daten* [Introduction to Statistics: Analysis and Modelling of Data], 9th edn, Oldenbourg: Munich.

Scholz, C. (2000a) *Strategische Organisation-Multiperspektivität und Virtualität* [Strategic Organization – Multiple Perspectives and Virtuality], 2nd rev. edn, Moderne Industrie: Landsberg/Lech.

Scholz, C. (2000b) *Personalmanagement: informationsorientierte und verhaltenstheoretische Grundlagen* [Human Resource Management: Information-Oriented and Behavior Theoretic Foundations], 5th rev. edn, Vahlen: Munich.

Staples, D.S., and Cameron, A.F. (2005) The Effect of Task Design, Team Characteristics, Organizational Context and Team Processes on the Performance and Attitudes of Virtual Team Members, *Proceedings of HICSS'05* – Track 1, 52a.

Stevenson, W., and Weis McGrath, E. (2004) Differences between On-site and Off-site Teams: Manager Perceptions, *Team Performance Management*, 10(5), 127–132.

Thiedeke, U. (2001) Fakten, Fakten, Fakten – Was ist und wozu brauchen wir Virtualität [Facts, Facts, Facts – What is Virtuality and What Do We Need it for], *DIE Zeitschrift für Erwachsenenbildung*, 3, 21–24.

Tjortjis, C., Dafoulas, G., Layzell, P.J., and Macaulay, L.A. (2002) A Model for Selecting CSCW Technologies for Distributed Software Maintenance Teams in Virtual Organisations, *Proceedings of COMPSAC 2002*, 1104–1108.

Travica, B. (1997) The Design of the Virtual Organization: A Research Model, *Proceedings of AIS 1997*, online. Available: http://home.cc. umanitoba.ca/~btravica/pub_frameset.html (accessed: 06.04.2007)

Türk, K. (1976) *Grundlagen einer Pathologie der Organisation* [Foundations of a Pathology of an Organization], Enke: Stuttgart.

Walther, J.B., and Bunz, U. (2005) The Rules of Virtual Groups: Trust, Liking, and Performance in Computer-mediated Communication, *The Journal of Communication*, 55(4), 828–846.

Wong, S.S., and Burton, R.M. (2000) Virtual Teams: What are their Characteristics, and Impact on Team Performance?, *Computational Mathematical Organization Theory*, 11, 339–360.

Zhang, S., Fjermestad, J., and Tremaine, M. (2005) Leadership Styles in Virtual Team Context: Limitations, Solutions and Propositions, *Proceedings of HICSS'05* – Track 1, 48c.

CHAPTER 6

Regulated and emergent identifications: the case of a virtual organization

Lin Yan

Introduction

The past decade saw the emergence and proliferation of virtual organizations. With various names and labels,[1] virtual organizations are distinguishable from "conventional" co-located organizational forms in three aspects – the geographic dispersion of members, their shared goals and interdependence, and their reliance on electronic means (e.g., e-mail, fax, phone, video conference) for most of their communication and coordination (Martins, Gilson, and Maynard, 2004; Powell, Piccoli, and Ives, 2004). Research on virtual organizations so far may be broadly summarized along three related themes – the characteristics of mediated communications (Sproull and Kiesler, 1986; DeSanctis and Monge, 1999; Kiesler and Cummings, 2002; Gibson and Cohen, 2003); the mutual knowledge problem (Cramton, 2001); and the social relations over distance (Jarvenpaa and Leidner, 1999; Ariss, Nykodym, and Cole-Laramore, 2002; Gibson and Manuel, 2003; Feng, Lazar, and Preece, 2004).

Particularly along the last theme, it was often argued that it is difficult to achieve social cohesion in virtual organizations. Interpersonal trust, for instance, was found to be "swift," but transitory and vulnerable (Jarvenpaa and Leidner, 1999; Zolin et al., 2004); inappropriate attribution is more likely to occur when individuals find personal rather than situational faults (Cramton and Orvis, 2003); conflicts seem inevitable and more frequent (Hinds and Bailey, 2003; Griffith, Mannix, and Neale, 2003), coupled with slow discovery of coordination problems (Gibson and Cohen, 2003); and inaccuracy in detecting feeling and thoughts over distance, and in responding passionately toward others' distress (Feng, Lazar, and Preece, 2004).

Despite these difficulties, it has been argued that shared goals and understanding among distributed members are paramount in binding the organization together across distance, functions, and social and cultural backgrounds (Hinds and Weisband, 2003; Gibson and Cohen, 2003). Organizational identification (or OI), broadly defined as an individual's sense of belonging to the organization, is therefore important in linking distributed members together. As with social relations in general, however, it has been noted that OI is difficult to develop in virtual organizations (Wiesenfield, Raghuram, and Garud, 1999).

In this chapter, I venture to explore this "difficult" issue of OI in a virtual organization. I will do so from a communication and practice perspective that takes OI as an ongoing process, as this perspective complements the current focus in the literature that defines OI broadly as an individual quality. I will set out by reviewing the literature on OI in virtual organizations, followed by reporting a longitudinal case study in a virtual consulting firm. After discussing the findings, I will revisit the notions of OI and shared understanding in virtual organizations, and outline directions for further research.

Organizational identification in virtual organizations

Organizational identification is generally conceptualized as an individual's connection to his/her organization – the bond that generates a sense of belonging and oneness (Mael and Ashforth, 1992; Dutton, Dukerich, and Harquail, 1994; van Dick et al., 2004). The connotation of OI is broadly twofold. At the individual level OI can be seen as a reflection of individual identity. The perceived link with one's organization reflects individuals' conceptualizations of who they are (Karreman and Alvesson, 2001). In addition, OI also refers to the link itself, namely, to what extent individuals feel attached to the organization. In this chapter, I will focus on the latter, as a major concern for managing virtual organizations is to connect individuals with the organization. It is at this collective level that virtual organizations face the particular challenge of geographical dispersion and lack of face-to-face "rich" communications (Daft and Lengel, 1984; Sproull and Kiesler, 1986; Cramton, 2001). In this section, I will briefly review the literature on OI as the link between individuals and organizations.

Conceptualization of organizational identification

The concept of OI has evolved over time, particularly with the recent adoption of social identity theory (SIT). Early conceptualizations of OI may be traced to Foote (1951), Brown (1969), Patchen (1970), and Cheney (1983; Cheney and Tompkins, 1987). Foote (1951) argued that individuals identify with other "fellows in groups," with this self-categorization motivating them to act on behalf of the group or organization. Brown (1969) emphasized the reactive role played by individuals and contended that identification was "a self-defining response, set in a specific relationship". He highlighted the interaction between individual identity and its context – as an individual defines (at least part of) his/her identity according to self-categorization in relation to the organization, the organization is able to shape individuals' beliefs. Further studies indicated that OI is embedded in individuals' perception of the attractiveness of the organization, the consistency between organizational and individual goals, and the resulting sense of loyalty (e.g., Patchen, 1970; Lee, 1971; Schneider, Hall, and Nygren, 1971; Rotondi, 1975).

More recent studies on OI drew upon SIT (Tajfel, 1981). In addition to the notion of self-categorization in early studies, the adaptation of SIT emphasized the importance of self-esteem in individuals' self-identification. We categorize ourselves so that we can compare ourselves more favorably against others. When group membership enhances self-esteem, individuals are more likely to associate themselves with the group, and develop a sense of "belongingness" (e.g., Ashforth and Mael, 1989; Mael and Ashforth, 1992; Dutton, Dukerich, and Harquail, 1994; Pratt, 1998; van Dick et al., 2004). The essence of this later conceptualization is mainly twofold. First, in line with earlier conceptualizations, it emphasizes that individuals internalize, thus "share," the values and characteristics that they believe to be central to their organization. Second, the social identity highlights how comparison results in positive self-esteem when individuals are more likely to feel attached to their organization. In other words, while the first element refers to individuals' need for affiliation, the second adds the issue of self-esteem.

Through categorizing oneself as a member of an organization, and comparing oneself with out-group members, OI, according to SIT, would influence individuals along three dimensions: cognitive, in "the knowledge that one belongs to a group"; evaluative, in that "the notion of the group may have a positive or negative value connotation"; and emotional, in that emotions, either positive or negative (love or hatred, like or dislike), "may be directed toward one's own group and toward others which stand in certain relation to it" (Tajfel, 1981, p. 229).[2] What is highlighted in the social identity approach is the distinction between in-group and out-group. The notion of OI is also extended beyond a cognitive state to include evaluative and emotional components, such as positive evaluation and affection toward one's group members, and negative evaluation, indifference, even resentment, toward out-groups.

Organizational identification in virtual organizations

It is acknowledged that Organizational Identification is important in virtual organizations. Given geographic dispersion, virtual organizations cannot rely on direct control and coordination, but need to bind the organization through shared values and norms (Wiesenfield et al., 1999; 2001; Fiol and O'Connor, 2005; Hinds and Mortensen, 2005). Wiesenfield, Raghuram, and Garud (2001, p. 778), for instance, maintained that the lack of physical co-location in virtual organizations makes OI particularly important, as OI "presents the social and psychological tie binding employees and the organization." Organizational identification is thus seen to moderate the often difficult social relations in virtual organizations, such as the transitory and fragile trust (Jarvenpaa and Leidner, 1999), the easy occurrence of conflicts (Hinds and Bailey, 2003; Griffith, Mannix, and Neale, 2003), and inappropriate attribution (Cramton and Orvis, 2003). The "cohesion-building consequences" of identification was seen as a major remedy to reduce physical contact and troublesome social relations over distance (Fiol and O'Connor, 2005; Hinds and Mortensen, 2005; Vora and Kostova, 2007).

The literature on OI in virtual organizations may be broadly divided into those at the organizational level, and those at the individual level. At the organizational level, there are mainly two themes. First, most studies emphasized its importance. Due to the lack of physical boundaries of the organization, identification is not only desirable, but serves as a fundamental tie between individuals and their organization (Wiesenfield, Raghuram, and Garud, 1999; 2001; Fiol and O'Connor, 2005). From a managerial perspective, it is also argued that OI in virtual organizations complements, and sometimes replaces direct coordination and control, such as formalization and centralization (DeSanctis and Monge, 1999). Second, shared goals and understanding are often noted as the core of OI in virtual organizations. Given the lack of physical co-location in virtual organizations, it is noted that physical "cues," such as the unique architecture of the company building and uniforms, contribute little to OI. Instead, the literature reiterates the centrality of shared goals and understanding (Hinds and Kiesler, 2002; Gibson and Cohen, 2003). It is OI that promotes a sense of "togetherness" in virtual organizations, despite the lack of physical proximity and shared context (Pratt, 2000; Fiol and O'Connor, 2005).

At the individual level, it has been noted that OI in virtual organizations addresses individuals' needs for affiliation, self-esteem, and uncertainty reduction. First, Wiesenfield, Raghuram, and Garud (2001) found that the need for affiliation was significantly correlated with individuals' OI. In order to "feel connected," individuals "reach out" to categorize themselves in relation to others and the organization as a whole. Second, in line with SIT, the need for positive self-esteem was found to be important in shaping individuals' attachment to their virtual organizations. Positive social relations, particularly with key members of the organization (e.g., coworkers, supervisors, top management), were found to generate a sense of well-being, which in turn enhances self-esteem and reinforces OI (ibid.). In addition, Fiol and O'Connor (2005) noted that OI also helped to reduce individuals' sense of uncertainty in virtual organizations. Given the lack of physical co-location, it is more difficult for individuals to check their perceptions against others'. This lack of reference may result in a sense of ambiguity and uncertainty. Organizational identification provides a reference point, where individuals can compare their values and perceptions with the "core" values of the organization. Agreement, even only superficial, reduces the sense of ambiguity and uncertainty – the third reason why OI is important for individuals.

In summary, the literature highlights the importance of OI. Organizational identification has been noted as necessary and desirable in virtual organizations, for both management and individuals. The current understanding, however, also leaves some key questions unanswered, or rather unasked. In particular, how do individuals develop OI? The recognition that OI reduces uncertainty, enhances self-esteem, and fosters affiliation answered the "why" question, but leaves the "how" to be explored. In a similar vein, how do organizations establish, maintain, and monitor individuals' OI in a virtual setting where direct supervision is largely absent? It seems that OI, as the link between individuals and organizations, may have a broader connotation. In addition to being an end result or desirable quality, it is perhaps worthwhile to explore its development process. Instead of taking it as a noun, OI may also be seen as a verb that connotes actions and dynamics. Indeed, it was not until the adaptation of SITs that OI focused on individual quality. A process view was implicit in earlier work on OI. To explore the dynamics of OI, I will revisit some of the earlier studies from a communication perspective, together with reviewing recent work in the virtual organization literature that echoed this perspective.

Communication, practices, and organizational identification

As noted by Edwards (2005), one influential but less-known and early scholar on OI was Cheney (Cheney, 1983; Cheney and Tompkins, 1987). From a communication and discourse perspective, Cheney defined OI not so much as self-identity or self-perception, but as "a process by which individuals link themselves to elements in the social scene" (Cheney, 1983, p. 342). Organizational identification was not only the "symbolic linkage" between individuals and the organization, but also the underpinning "development and maintenance" process that substantiates individuals' perceived "sameness" with others and with the organization (ibid., p. 5). In order to depict this process, Cheney drew heavily upon Burke (1937; 1969) who argued that persuasion is inherent in the process of organizing, achieved via "administrative rhetoric." Language and discourse were therefore central to Cheney's process view of OI, as they "classify, divide and separate" social groups (Cheney, 1983, p. 145).

Related to the emphasis on language and discourse, Cheney's work also centered on action. Contrary to the social identity perspective, he emphasized the active role played by individuals in communicating and negotiating identification. As he noted, "in response to the divisions of society, a person *acts* to identify" (1987, p. 145, emphasis in original). For Cheney, OI did not only indicate the link between individuals and organizations, but also the actions of linking. As he remarked: " [i]t is important to highlight that identifications function both as terms of *description* and as terms of *action* … to answer the question 'Who are they?' but also address the issue 'How should I act toward them?' " (Cheney and Tompkins, 1987, p. 3, emphasis in original).

Cheney's emphasis on communication and action seems to be particularly inspiring for studying OI in virtual organizations, as communications, mediated via technologies, play a central role in defining the boundary of virtual organizations, in the daily work practices, and in binding the dispersed members together (e.g., DeSanctis and Monge, 1999; Cramton, 2001; Hinds and Bailey, 2003; Hertel, Geister, and Konradt, 2005). In virtual organizations, therefore, Cheney's "action" of identification is perhaps best explored in these technology-mediated communications. A similar emphasis on communication and action was also put forward by a recent study on virtual organizing, in what was described as a "knowing-in-practice" view (Orlikowski, 2002).

Drawing upon contemporary sociological and anthropological work (Giddens, 1984; Lave, 1998; Hutchins 1991; 1995; Suchman 1987),

Orlikowski (2002) contended that recurrent practices and routines bear significant meanings that are not articulated but enacted and improvised in these practices and routines. The starting point of Orlikowski's thesis was that individuals act knowledgeably, that is, they have the ability to act purposively and reflexively, continually and routinely in monitoring the ongoing flow of actions. As a routine part of everyday activities, our knowledge of *how to do* lies precisely in our action of *doing*. For example, we can only say we know how to dance the waltz, when we are able to move (hopefully gracefully) around. Tacit knowledge, such as that of social relations, is dependent on human agency, generated and sustained in our actions. The knowledge of dancing the waltz starts when we make the first step with the first note of the music, and ends as we resume a standing posture when the music dies. We do not "possess" the "knowledge" of dancing unless we are in the actions of doing so.

This shift from "knowledge" to "knowing," noted Orlikowski (2002, p. 51), has "substantial conceptual implications." Knowing is transformed from a stable state – of affairs to an enacted, ongoing accomplishment bounded by context, and sustained by repeated reoccurrence over time and across contexts. This "in-the-moment" nature of knowing highlights two issue in knowing-in-practice, that practices (the actions of knowing) in one context cannot be "transferred" to another; and that our "taken-for-granted" knowledge is subject to ongoing reflection, revision, and improvisation.

Both Cheney and Orlikowski highlighted communication and action. While Cheney focused on OI as both an outcome and a process of actions, Orlikowski's thesis illuminated the meaningfulness of routines and practices. Drawing upon both perspectives, our "knowledge" of our link with the organization is drawn upon, reflected, modified or reinforced in our ongoing "knowing" of the organization and its members; the answer to Cheney's question of "How should I act toward them?" indeed lies in "acting toward them," in the ongoing communications and interactions between dispersed members. It is with this practice-based view in which I set out to explore OI as a dynamic process that is embedded, enacted, and reflected in communication practices in a virtual organization.

Research setting and methods

ABC is a small firm specialized in management consulting. Its main services covered "strategic development and deployment," "operational effectiveness," and "emotional alignment." ABC first set up a "central office" in London. As the co-owners were located in the Netherlands and

Italy, local offices were soon set up in both countries. This was quickly followed by entry into Germany, Lithuania, Canada, China, the US, and other countries. Around three years after its establishment, ABC had become an international organization with offices, associates, and affiliates covering 18 countries.

ABC had a small, but highly experienced team. The "network" consisted of 53 members, with a "core team" of 16. Compared to leading multinational consulting firms, ABC saw its competitive advantage precisely in its small size. Instead of having a "pyramid," hierarchical structure usually found in large consulting firms, ABC's organizational structure was flatter, with most employees at the senior levels as "partners," "senior consultants," or "consultant." Most of the ABC members had international experience, with 84 percent (36 out of 53) being bilingual or multilingual.

This study was conducted over a period of 14 months in ABC. I started data collection with participant observation. My role as a researcher was known to the "gate-keeper," while, for other members of the organization, I took a covert role as a part-time IT consultant. Broad access was granted from the start, including access to the intranet, conference calls, company documents, newsletters, and group e-mails. After the initial observation at their central office in London, I surveyed the organization on their use of information technology in their daily work. This was followed by a round of interviews to all key members concerning their communications with others. The survey and interviews served as a good introduction to my further involvement in the organization. I was then able to highlight my previous experience in management consulting, and participated in their international projects, thus turning my role from an external IT consultant at the London "central office" into a member of the consultants. This led to the carbon copying of individual correspondence to me, which illuminated a different perspective from that known to London.

Most of my participation with the dispersed members was via computer-mediated communications. This "virtual" participation contributed to the majority of the fieldwork data on "who," "what," "when," and "how." When there was good rapport with the members, and sufficient observational data to crystallize a pattern of their communication practices, another round of interviews were conducted with all participants to explore the "why" question concerning their connections with the organization. These interviews typically lasted around one hour to 90 minutes, and were conducted over the phone, in English. All interviews were transcribed.

Guided by the principles of Grounded Theory (Glaser and Strauss, 1967; Glaser, 1992), data collection, and data analysis were conducted iteratively. While there was little reflection and deliberate theorizing at the early stage of data collection, the balance shifted significantly toward analysis at the later stage. My preliminary findings were shared with the participants in two ways – formally, in the interim and final reports submitted to all members of the organization, and informally, in seeking comments on my draft reports, and in the everyday "chats" with them, often one-to-one, over the phone or via e-mails. Both proved to be valuable in "elaborating and sharpening interpretation and yielding additional insights" (Orlikowski and Baroudi, 1991). Following the process of "describing, classifying, and connecting," a case description was first written up to highlight the most significant "storyline" (Taylor and Bogdan, 1998). In what follows, I report the findings on their communication practices, and OI in this case.

Communication practices in ABC

Like most consulting firms, ABC's work is organized around projects. In particular, international projects that involve members in multiple countries are important. The communications practices in ABC can be broadly divided into three categories – off-project (general) communications, on-project communications, and extensions of on-project communications.

Off-project communications

The use of an intranet, monthly conference calls, and monthly newsletters were set up by the "central office" in London for ongoing, off-project communications. Shortly after the London office was set up, its manager Mary saw the need in providing a comprehensive knowledge database for all members. An intranet was then set up. It included a large amount of information, from detailed project "manuals," the individuals' backgrounds and expertise, to an expanding database of "case studies" that aimed to document all completed projects. Mary, in the "central office," wished to see the intranet as providing the "weapons to fight," giving ABC members all necessary information for the initiation, implementation, and reflection of projects. With a similar aim of connecting the dispersed members, Mary initiated two other communication channels – a monthly global conference call and a monthly newsletter.

While the individual members appreciated Mary's effort in establishing and maintaining a range of communication channels, their practices of using these seemed to contradict their apparent acceptance. For instance, while they praised the comprehensiveness of the intranet, they also believed that "less is more," that some of the intranet's content was no more than "information" that had to be used "creatively," and that it dragged the organization backward from a "customer-driven" organization to a "content-driven" one. The London office's request for updating case studies for the intranet also met considerable resistance. While Mary in London saw this as important in providing up-do-date information, and therefore a necessary obligation for all, the members saw it more as an administrative burden. A member in the UK, for instance, commented during an interview:

> I'm not very good at doing the case studies, (laugh) I know that. At the moment, all my incentive is that Vale (*Mary's assistant*) makes me a nice cup of tea, and keeps staring at me every five minutes. (laugh) … Suggestions for that? Well, have something simple, tick boxes, what I call "one, two, three, and done" sort of thing. (Kate, UK)

Co-located in the same office with Mary and Vale, Kate was the only person who could be motivated "by making her a nice cup of tea and being stared at." To connect other members, London had to rely on mediated communications, equally without much success, as Mary remarked:

> We send them e-mails, or call them if desperate, but they don't get back to us. They say they're busy, and the project is already done. They would be happy to talk about it if others are interested, but ask them to write it down … well, they're busy. (Mary, "Central Office")

Similarly, the members were reluctant to participate in the conference calls, and saw the hour-long call each month as having "limited value." In interviews, they complained about the lack of "results" from conference calls. "Getting together on the phone and have nothing in common to say is not-value-for time. There's too much passiveness in the telephone conferences" (Horst, Germany).

In contrast, the monthly newsletter had a better reception, but its success was attributed to the flexibility the members had in engaging, or disengaging, with it.

> The newsletters are good for updating things, I think. … One thing is that you can control the input, you can talk about your project. And you know, each of us would talk about our own project for hours,

non-stop, till the audience is bored to death. (laugh) But the other good thing is that you can control the output. If something isn't relevant to you, skip it, so you have your own version of the news, so to speak. (Paola, Italy)

On-project communications

In contrast to the "orderly" and structured communications (that Mary would like to see) for off-project practices, on-project communications were more "chaotic," emergent, and centered on the needs for each project. There were several "gangs" in ABC, organized around the members' professional knowledge. The "overlaps in what we do" was often cited to be central in distinguishing a "gang member" from an outsider. As project needs arose, these "gangs" were constructed and reconstructed. In what follows, I will summarize the work practices in ABC's on-project communications. These can be broadly categorized as identifying one's gang members, standardizing practices (from Mary), and coordinating through project activities. Table 6.1 below lists some examples.

To identify a potential "gang member" for forthcoming projects, the individuals relied on intermediaries, both technical and social. Group

Table 6.1 On-project communication practices

Identifying one's "little gang"	I think that (reading the newsletters) is hugely beneficial, in that, you can identify your own "gang," but also keep your ears open for something else.
	[w]hen someone has done a project, it's very likely that it's not there (on the intranet). But still, you know someone must have done this sort of thing before. Then, I'll tap into my relations, and ask one or more people that (who) I know…
Standardization	"service manual" made available to all participants via intranet and group communications
	The execution of these manuals depended on individual members' expertise and approach
	[w]e use similar steps, hum, procedures, but do different things, solve different problems.
Coordinating through projects	I think you only know someone through working with them. After two or three projects, you know your partners inside out.
	I think it's the project itself, the deadlines, the feedback from the client. We had to keep the conversation going to solve this and that problem. And you grab whatever means you have to do it, telephone, e-mail, text.
	We worked toward deadlines, got client feedback periodically, and that set the, hum, the pace of communications.

communications, the intranet, conference calls, and newsletters, as mentioned earlier, were their technical intermediaries in connecting with the distant colleagues. As noted, they used these *selectively*. In addition, they used social intermediaries, in their words, to "tap into relations," in identifying others with whom they would like to establish connections. For instance, a member recalled his first collaboration with others:

> Well, that was back in 2001 … Well, to tell a long story short: I was looking for someone to work in Holland on this project. So I happened to say this to an old friend, he's also a consultant, and he recommended me to Ronald. That's how it all started, with ABC. (Roland, Sweden)

In addition to trusting someone on the basis of "also (being) a consultant," the members demonstrated a clear preference for "close recommendations," namely, being recommended by members already in their "gang," particularly those they had worked with on previous projects. Shared experience was considered to generate a reliable connection, as the same member explained:

> I think you only know someone through working with them. After two or three projects, you know your partners inside out. What they're good at, what they can contribute. In (the) future, you pick up those experiences and contact them for help. Now that you have done projects together, you know them. (Roland, Sweden)

Project coordination, in most cases, seemed to split between two different but intertwining approaches, with preplanned "steps and procedures," coupled with the recognition that all participants in a project were autonomous and able to "do things differently." Initially, the project "gang" members usually followed a set of standardized procedures set up by the "owner," or initiator, of the project. These procedures, usually documented in manuals, were distributed at the outset of international projects and made available on ABC's intranet. They provided detailed descriptions of the objective, theoretical framework, empirical case studies, and analytical tools surrounding the service. All ABC members participating in international projects were expected to follow the manuals closely.

Here, Mary in London again aspired to play an important role. ABC had a "duo-leader" system – one "project owner" who usually was the initiator of the project and provided the contents of the service manuals, and one "project manager" whose responsibility was to oversee its progress. Mary served as the default project manager. It was therefore her responsibility to provide support for documentation and funding, and to facilitate on-project communications. In addition to utilizing the intranet, Mary also insisted on the "proper use of e-mails" for ongoing projects, as she commented during an interview:

> Because we're in so many countries, we use e-mails a lot. But I find them a bit difficult … for example, I find myself being copied in a lot of e-mails about the projects; some of them, perhaps 50%, don't have much to do with us in London. But on the other hand, I do miss out some important updates; somehow they don't come to me. I suspect it's not very different for others. So I thought we should have a (sort of) standard of using e-mails, especially for ongoing projects, as part of project management. (Mary, "Central Office")

As reflected in the comment, Mary was often left out from "gang" members' interactions. The reason for this was because they believed that standardization, and Mary's support, were only helpful up to a point. The similarity between their services, and the necessity for standardization, "ends very soon when you talk to the real person."

> To the members, standardization should soon be followed by customization. As most of the "steps and procedures" were reflexive, requiring self-assessment by clients, the outcomes of these standard-ized tools were usually diverse. The ABC members would then rely on their own expertise in guiding clients and dealing with emergent requests. A consultant's ability to handle individual requests beyond the service manual, it was believed, was the benchmark to distinguish "the best from the rest." Working on collaborative projects, therefore, was both collective and individual. As a member remarked: "[w]e use similar steps, hum, procedures, but do different things, solve different problems." (Mechtild, the Netherlands)

Accordingly, centralized coordination was "weak" for on-project practices. The pace, means, and contents of these communications were largely unstructured and unplanned to accommodate deadlines and emergencies. Among project team members, it was the requirements of projects that prompted and sustained their communications. When difficulties arose, the communications not only accelerated in pace, but also expanded into various media. E-mail, telephone calls, conference calls, international mobile texting, online bulletin boards were just a few examples of what they used to "solve this and that problem." When required by the project, they would "grab whatever means we had." It is perhaps worth noting that there was little deliberate effort to articulate, regulate, or strengthen the identification as "gang" members. Most communications were task-focused, while the members seemed to have a clear sense of their "gang" membership.

Extension of on-project communications

"Catching up," follow-up communications with previous collaborators, was another key work practice in ABC. These "catching-ups" were irregular. The individuals did not seem to follow a plan on why and when to interact with others. These interactions, like the on-project practices, were task-oriented. Most "catching up" started with an exchange of information on individual projects, and ended with new ideas for future collaboration. For instance, a member commented on the usefulness of this "exchange of information once in a while": "It normally starts from some exchange of information, for example, Kate's last project … We chatted about these, and said 'hey, they have something similar' … so we decided to have some synergy" (Roland, Sweden).

Again, shared experience was regarded as important. Not only did it generate new projects, it was also thought to accumulate goodwill between the members. As noted earlier, it was believed that past collaboration was a most reliable way of knowing one's colleagues, which in turn became useful in their identification of potential "gang members" for forthcoming projects.

In summary, through "off-project," "on-project" communications, and "catching up," ABC sustained and developed its successful business in a globally distributed environment. If these practices are to be categorized further, they can be broadly divided into two kinds – those planned and structured, mainly from the "central office," and those emergent but goal-oriented that resulted in connecting the dispersed members. From a communication practice perspective, while the first category indicated regulated OI, the second category illuminated an emergent OI that was subject to ongoing negotiations and renegotiations. In the next section, I will build on this categorization of practices, and revisit OI.

Organizational identification in the case

A communication and practice perspective helped to illuminate the variety of identifications in the case. There are, broadly speaking, two kinds of

OIs in the case – one proposed and managed, hereafter termed regulated identification, and one which emerged ad hoc via project-based communications, termed emergent identification. While the former was mostly a "top-down" effort to regulate members' identification with the organization, the latter was "bottom-up," developed among the members, and with fuzzy boundaries. In this section, I will first illustrate these two kinds of identifications found in the case, then revisit the related issue of "shared understanding" in conceptualizing OI.

Regulated and emergent organizational identification

The attempt to regulate OI was exhibited in Mary's practices in establishing and maintaining the off-project communication channels, her advocating for their use, and the high level of standardization Mary aimed to achieve on-project communications. The regulated identification Mary sought to achieve was mainly threefold, concerning its foci (or target), content, and power relation.

First, Mary sought to recognize London as the center of the organization. Several practices were set up to assert London's centrality. It was expected that, as a result, the dispersed members would see London as representing the organization as a whole, and develop a sense of belongingness and membership toward London. As noted, this management of identification foci did not generate the expected result. Instead, identification with one another, not with London, turned out to be stronger. Second, in addition to regulating with "whom" the members should identify, Mary also attempted to specify "what" should be the content of their identification. London would like to assert itself as the center of information, communication, and coordination. This was reflected in her belief that London should provide all members with the "weapons to fight," her implicit request to be copied in project e-mails, and her assertion as "project manager." Finally, related to the foci and content of this regulated identification, it may be argued that Mary's practices also attempted to regulate the underlying power relation between London and the dispersed members – by claiming centrality of the organization, and regulating all key work and communication practices, Mary was expressing and reinforcing the authority she would like London to have.

To Mary, ABC was not a collection of largely self-governed professional experts, assembled and reassembled according to project needs, but an organization with structure and hierarchy. These regulations of identification foci, content, and power relation were mutually reinforcing. Through asserting London's centrality, Mary was in a legitimate position to regulate the content of identification, and in asserting London's power, while these regulating practices and assertion of power in turn reinforced the sense that London should be the center.

It is perhaps worth noting that regulating work practices, thus regulating members' identification, was a legitimate part of Mary's job. Given the geographic dispersion and professional specialization, ABC specifically set up a "central office" to undertake the coordination and regulation role. But as noted earlier, the regulated identification Mary attempted was accompanied by resistance. London's standardization effort met with inactive use of the intranet, reluctance in updating its content and passivity in participating in global conference calls. An exception was the monthly newsletters, but it was because the members found it to be less regulated. In a similar vein, Mary's on-project coordination was seen as secondary to self-coordination among the members. Contrary to Mary's aspiration to identify London as the center, they identified more and communicated more freely with one another than with London, and largely saw the authority London tried to assert as an unnecessary administrative burden. Unlike their relations with London, among the members, there was a stronger sense of connection, membership, and belongingness.

Emergent identification in ABC seemed to have two features. First, it was mainly task-oriented and project-based. The aim of initial communications was to identify potential team members, to coordinate practices during project to ensure its implementation, and to provide follow-up communications aimed at generating future projects. Unlike the implicit power relations in the regulated identification, emergent identification focused on tasks, rather than social relations. A sense of "gang" membership, *emerged* as a consequence of these task-oriented communications. Second, this membership was not fixed, nor exclusive, but somewhat fluctuating, according to the project orientation. Varying across projects, the "gangs" were assembled and reassembled, and the "gang" membership negotiated and renegotiated. While this may reflect Rousseau's (1998) notion of "situated identification," when individuals are playing their organizational roles, there was also a "deep structure identification," as all members, regardless of their current project teams, emphasized their identity as "being a consultant." Assembling project teams was seen as reflecting the professional value of consulting, resulting in both a reluctance and resistance toward central control. What was underlying the emergent identification in the case was the intertwining of both "situated identification," based on task needs, and "deep structure identification," based on shared values and norms. It is perhaps worth noting that this "deep structure identification" was not achieved through regulation at particularly the organizational level, but was enacted, reflected, and improvised in the members' practices of working around projects.

Comparing regulated and emergent identifications, the case indicated that regulated identification was much "weaker." Not only did Mary fail to achieve the coordination she hoped for, but, in a sense, it was her effort in regulating the members' identification that undermined the members' sense of connection and membership in relation to London. The members failed to understand the necessity of standardizing procedure and formalizing communications, resulting in resistance rather than identification. The emergent identification, though seemingly "loose," served as a stronger bond among the members. The question that then arises is "why?" – why was this "loose" emergent identification more efficient in binding the members than the well-articulated and managed regulated identification? With this question in mind, I revisit the issue of "shared understanding."

Organizational identification and shared understanding

It has been acknowledged that "shared understanding" is essential in generating and sustaining organizational identification in virtual organizations (e.g., Cramton, 2001; Hinds and Weisband, 2003; Gibson and Cohen, 2003). The distinction between regulated and emergent identifications in the case enabled further consideration of shared understanding, mainly along two themes; whether shared understanding can be achieved via regulating identification, and, in the case of emergent identification, how shared understanding is articulated and negotiated.

Can shared understanding be achieved via regulated identification? The ABC case provided little support. Despite Mary's effort in standardization, formalization, and centralization, her role and authority as the "center" was challenged in practice. It is worth noting that all the members understood Mary's intention, but they discounted it. The lack of common understanding was not due to variations in understandings, but to the members' purposeful negotiation, reluctance, and resentment. This raises the issue that the goal of management is not necessarily shared by others. While this may sound a mere reiteration of well-established theories on power in organizations (e.g., Pfeffer, 1992; Knight and Willmott, 1999), it perhaps highlights the over-emphasis on shared understanding in the virtual organization literature. Given the lack of direct control and coordination in virtual settings, there is a common assumption in the literature that "common ground" is essential in linking the dispersed members (e.g., Cramton, 2001; Hinds and Bailey, 2003; Gibson and Cohen, 2003). While this is valid, this case shed further light in illustrating that "shared understanding" is negotiated, subject to resistance and power struggles, rather than articulated, managed, let alone imposed. It further indicates that there is a politics underlying shared understanding. When identification is imposed from "above," the attempt to regulate shared understanding undermines the "togetherness" of the organization.

In contrast, emergent identification in the case reflected and reinforced shared understanding, particularly that reflecting the shared norms and values. The focus on projects, the ongoing reconfiguration of project teams, the emphasis on autonomy, the resistance to central control, and the respect for professional expertise all reflected the shared values of "being a consultant." Unlike in regulated identification, these values were neither explicitly stated, nor embedded in organizational policies or procedures. Instead, shared understanding rooted in these values was enacted and articulated in ongoing interactions. It was through their practices of identifying "gang" members, coordinating on projects, and "catching up" that the members appreciated, practiced, and negotiated these values of expertise-orientation, project-focus, and respect for autonomy.

Contrasting between the regulated and emergent identifications in the case, it may be argued that shared understanding is more likely to be achieved in the ongoing work practices that reflect and enact shared values, than through structures, rules, and regulations. This indicates that a practice or communication perspective has much to offer in exploring OI. Organizational identification, in addition to being an individual quality, a cognitive state, or a desirable outcome, can be seen as enacted, negotiated, and constructed in ongoing interactions. Individual members can and do play an active role in negotiating their connections with the organization through ongoing interactions that fostered emergent identification. A practice lens opens new perspectives in organizational studies (e.g., Orlikowski, 2002; Whittington, 2006), and, in this case, in exploring OI in virtual organizations. Detecting the unarticulated meanings of ongoing interactions, it may be argued, would also provide a useful perspective in understanding social relations over distance in other virtual settings (e.g., Yan and Panteli, 2006; Panteli et al., 2007) and in "actual" co-located settings (e.g., Faraj and Xiao, 2006); and indeed the interplay between the virtual and the actual (Robey, Schwaig, and Lin, 2003).

Conclusion

This study contributes to the discussion on virtual organizations in three respects. First, it examined a central, but less explored, topic on virtual organizations – how is a geographically dispersed organization bound together? This longitudinal case study provided rich data in further understanding OI in a knowledge-intensive organization. Second, this study explored the *process* of OI from a new practice and communication perspective. This approach reflects early studies on OI, and echoes an emergent and new perspective in organizational studies. Through this study, some dynamism is added to the current conceptualization of OI in virtual organizations, by recognizing individuals' active role in organizations and the increasing importance individuals assume in today's "knowledge-intensive" organizations. Introducing this perspective to OI in virtual organization was the second contribution that I sought to make. The third contribution is the distinction between regulated and emergent identifications, and the related rethinking of shared understanding. The contrast between regulated and emergent identifications indicates that shared understanding in virtual organizations should have its boundaries. While regulated identification does not always reinforce shared understanding (for example, not in this case), emergent identification, featuring "fuzzy boundaries" and ongoing unstructured negotiation may generate, sustain, and reinforce a shared understanding that is "unarticulated."

Implications for theory and practice

The distinction between regulated and emergent identifications has significant implications. For academic research, this study raises the issue of measurement. While the use of scales has been well established in measuring OI (e.g., Brown, 1969; Hall et al., 1971; Cheney, 1983; Mael and Ashforth, 1992), the emergent nature of OI revealed in this study suggests that identification is more dynamic than could be captured and reduced in scales. The ongoing negotiation between members indicated that their identification continues to change, from time to time, from context to context (in this case, across different projects). A longitudinal approach seems to be more fruitful in observing and recording the emergence of OI and its changes. In addition, this study indicated that OI is not value-free. Its measurement, therefore, calls for examination from multiple perspectives. There could be substantial differences between the perceptions of the "management" and the members, between members, and between the same members in different settings. In seemingly routine practices, individuals signal, interpret and negotiate their social relations with others. To "capture" this, a more ethnographic approach, such as case studies, may help to shed more light on OI than surveys and questionnaires.

For managers, the distinction between emergent and regulated identifications emphasized the "bottom-up" approach in managing virtual organizations. In contrast to the difficulties in defining and implementing regulated identification, emergent identification was more rooted and successful in binding the dispersed individuals together. This further confirms the suggestions in the literature that formalization and centralization need to be complemented by socialization. Meanwhile, implementing regulated identification is not entirely redundant. This case study suggests that the "top-down" approach did not disappear, even in professional and dispersed organizations. I would therefore endorse a "portfolio" approach in managing virtual organizations, comprising both regulated and emergent identifications, with close attention being paid to emergent identification.

While this study might have served as a useful initial step, much more remains to be explored in future studies on OI in virtual organizations. In particular, it would be interesting to explore regulated and emergent identifications in more cases, and other settings. For instance, this case suggested that regulated identification was detrimental to shared understanding. Would there be contrasting cases where clear articulation and systematic regulation contribute to OI? The comparison between contradictory cases will help to understand the context of regulated identification – under what circumstances is it binding, under what circumstance it is not. Similarly, much needs to be done to explore emergent identification. With the new concept in mind, it would be important to investigate identification practices further. What practice(s) in particular enact shared understanding? Given the "slippery" nature of emergent identification, how does the (inevitable) variation among members influence their interactions, and their negotiation of identification? A key limitation of this study was that it was based on a single case. A longitudinal and grounded approach, as in this study, would be needed to explore further cases to refine these concepts. For now, it is perhaps appropriate to conclude that OI in virtual organizations is not only an appropriation of individual identity, as emphasized in the current literature, but also an ongoing negotiation process where individuals enact, appreciate, and improvise shared understanding in work and communication practices. Our quest to understand virtuality goes on. For now, this study highlights its social nature, as illustrated in emergent, ongoing, and political practices.

Acknowledgments

I would like to thank all members at ABC for their participation and support. I am also grateful to Niki Panteli and Mike Chiasson for their insightful comments on an earlier draft of this chapter.

Notes

1. Virtual organizations (e.g., Mowshowitz, 1997; 2002) are also known as virtual corporations (Griffith, Mannix, and Neale, 2003), (geographically) distributed organizations (Kelly and Jones, 2001), virtual work (Zolin et al., 2004), distributed work (Hinds and Kiesler, 2002), virtual working (Jackson, 1999), and on a more temporary "as needed" basis, (global) virtual teams (Powell, Piccoli, and Ives, 2004; Gibson and Cohen, 2003), distributed teams (Hinds and Bailey, 2003), and geographically distributed work groups (Armstrong and Cole, 2002).
2. Adding a behavioral component, this was extended to four dimensions in van Dick et al. (2004).

References

Ariss, S., Nykodym, N., and Cole-Laramore, A. (2002) Trust and Technology in Virtual Organization, *SAM Advanced Management Journal*, Autumn, 22–25.

Armstrong, D., and Cole, P. (2002) "Managing Distance and Differences in Geographically Distributed Work Groups," in P. Hindsand S. Kiesler (Eds), *Distributed Work*, MIT Press: Cambridge, MA.

Ashforth, B.W., and Mael, F. (1989) Social Identity Theory and Organization, *Academy of Management Review*, 14, 20–38.

Brown, M.E. (1969) Identification and Some Conditions of Organizational Involvement, *Administrative Science Quarterly*, 14, 346–355.

Burke, K. (1937) *Attitudes Toward History*, New Republic: New York.

Burke, K. (1969) *A Rhetoric of Motives*, University of California Press: Berkeley.

Cheney, G. (1983) The Rhetoric of Identification and the Study of Organizational Communication, *Quarterly Journal of Speech*, 69, 143–158.

Cheney, G., and Tompkins, P.K. (1987) Coming to Terms with Organizational Identification and Commitment, *Central States Speech Journal*, 38, 1–15.

Cramton, C. (2001) The Mutual Knowledge Problem and its Consequences for Dispersed Collaboration, *Organization Science*, 12(3), 346–371.

Cramton, C., and Orvis, K.L. (2003) "Overcoming Barriers to Information Sharing in Virtual Teams," in C. Gibson and S. Cohen (Eds) *Virtual Teams that Work: Creating Conditions for Virtual Team Effectiveness*, Jossey-Bass: San Francisco.

Daft, R., and Lengel, R. (1984) Information Richness: A New Approach to Managerial Behaviour and Organization Design, *Research on Organizational Behavior*, 6, 191–233.

DeSanctis, G., and Monge, P. (1999) Introduction to the Special Issue: Communication Processes for Virtual Organization, *Organization Science*, 10, 693–703.

Dutton, J.E., Dukerich, J.M., and Harquail, C.V. (1994) Organizational Images and Member Identification, *Administrative Science Quarterly*, 39, 239–263.

Edwards, M.R. (2005) Organizational Identification: A Conceptual and Operational Review, *International Journal of Management Review*, 7(4), 207–230.

Faraj, S., and Xiao, Y. (2006) Coordination in Fast-response Organizations, *Management Science*, 52(8), 1155–1169.

Feng, J., Lazar, J., and Preece, J. (2004) Empathy and Online Interpersonal Trust: A Fragile Relationship, *Behaviour & Information Technology*, 23(2), 97–106.

Fiol, C.M., and O'Connor, E.J. (2005) Identification in Face-to-face, Hybrid, and Pure Virtual Teams: Untangling the Contradictions, *Organization Science*, 16 (1), 19–32.

Foote, N.N. (1951) Identification as the Basis for a Theory of Motivation, *American Sociological Review*, 16, 14–21.

Gibson, C., and Cohen, S. (2003) *Virtual Teams that Work: Creating Conditions for Virtual Team Effectiveness*, Jossey-Bass: San Francisco.

Gibson, C., and Manuel, J. (2003) "Building Trust: Effective Multicultural Communication Processes in Virtual Teams," in C. Gibson and S. Cohen (Eds), *Virtual Teams that Work: Creating Conditions for Virtual Team Effectiveness*, Jossey-Bass: San Francisco.

Giddens, A. (1984) *The Constitution of Society: Outline of the Theory of Structuration*, University of California Press: Berkeley, CA.

Glaser, B. (1992) *Basics of Grounded Theory Analysis*, Sociology Press: Mill Valey, CA.

Glaser, B., and Strauss, A. (1967) *The Discovery of Grounded Theory*, Aldine: Chicago.

Griffith, T., Mannix, A., and Neale, M. (2003) "Conflict and Virtual Teams," in C. Gibson and S. Cohen (Eds), *Virtual Teams that Work: Creating Conditions for Virtual Team Effectiveness*, Jossey-Bass: San Francisco.

Hertel, G., Geister, S., and Konradt, U. (2005) Managing Virtual Teams: A Review of Current Empirical Research, *Human Resource Management Review*, 15(1), 69–95.

Hinds, P., and Kiesler, S. (2002) *Distributed Work*, MIT Press: Cambridge, MA.

Hinds, P., and Mortensen, M. (2005) Understanding Conflict in Geographically Distributed Teams: The Moderating Effects of Shared Identity, Shared Context, and Spontaneous Communication, *Organization Science*, 16(3), 290–307.

Hinds, P., and Weisband, S. (2003) "Knowledge Sharing and Shared Understanding in Virtual Teams," in C. Gibson and S. Cohen (Eds), *Virtual Teams that Work: Creating Conditions for Virtual Team Effectiveness*, Jossey-Bass: San Francisco, pp. 21–36.

Hinds, P.J., and Bailey, D.E. (2003) Out of Sight, Out of Sync: Understanding Conflict in Distributed Teams, *Organization Science*, 14(6), 615–632.

Hutchins, E. (1991) Organizing Work by Adaptation, *Organization Science*, 2, 14–39.

Hutchins, E. (1995) *Cognition in the Wild*, MIT Press: Cambridge, MA.

Jackson, P. (1999) *Virtual Working: Social and Organizational Dynamics*, Routledge: London.

Jarvenpaa, S., and Leidner, D. (1999) Communication and Trust in Global Virtual Teams, *Organization Science*, 10(6), 791–815.

Karreman, D., and Alvesson, M. (2001) Making Newsmakers: Conversational Identity at Work, *Organization Studies*, 22(1), 59–91.

Kelly, S., and Jones, M.R. (2001) Groupware and the Social Infrastructure of Communication, *Communications of the ACM*, 44(12), 77–79.

Kiesler, S., and Cummings, J.N. (2002) "What Do We Know about Proximity and Distance in Work Groups? A Legacy of Research," in P.J. Hinds and S. Kiesler (Eds), *Distributed Work*, MIT Press: Cambridge, MA, pp. 57–80.

Knight, D., and Willmott, H. (1999) *Management Lives: Power and Identity in Work Organizations*, Sage: London.

Lave, J. (1998) *Cognition in Practice*, Cambridge University Press: Cambridge.

Lee, S.M. (1971) An Empirical Analysis of Organisational Identification, *Academy of Management Journal*, 14, 213–226.

Mael, F.A., and Ashforth, B.E. (1992) Alumni and their Alma Mater; A Partial Test of a Reformulated Model of Organizational Identification, *Journal of Organizational Behaviour*, 13(2), 103–123.

Martins, L., Gilson, L.L., and Maynard, M.T. (2004) Virtual Teams: What Do We Know and Where Do We Go from Here?, *Journal of Management*, 30(6), 805–835.

Mowshowitz, A. (1997) Virtual Organizations, *Communications of the ACM*, 40(9), 30–37.

Mowshowitz, A. (2002) *Virtual Organization: Toward a Theory of Social Transformation Stimulated by Information Technology*, Quorum Books: Westport, CT.

Orlikowski, W. (2002) Knowing in Practice: Enacting a Collective Capability in Distributed Organizing, *Organization Science*, 13(3), 249–273.

Orlikowski, W., and Baroudi, J. (1991) Studying Information Technology in Organizations: Research Approaches and Assumptions, *Information Systems Research*, 2(1), 1–28.

Panteli, N., Chiasson, M., Yan, L., Papargyris A., and Poulymenakoy, A. (2007) Exploring Virtuality: Global and Local Dimensions, in IFIP 8.2/9.5 Edited Proceedings "Virtuality and Virtualization," 29–31 July, Portland, USA.

Patchen, M. (1970) *Participation, Achievement and Involvement in the Job*, Prentice Hall: Englewood Clifs, NJ.

Pfeffer, J. (1992) *Managing with Power: Politics and Influence in Organizations*, Harvard Business School Press: Boston.

Powell, A., Piccoli, G., and Ives, B. (2004) Virtual Teams: A Review of Current Literature and Directions for Future Research, *Database for Advances in Information Systems*, 35(1), 6–28.

Pratt, M.G. (1998) "To Be or Not to Be? Central Question in Organizational Identification," in D.A. Whetton and P.C. Godfrey (Eds), *Identity in Organizations: Building Theory Through Conversations*, Sage: London.

Pratt, M.G. (2000) The Good, the Bad, and the Ambivalent: Managing Identification among Amway Distributors, *Administrative Science Quarterly*, 45(3), 456–493.

Robey, D., Schwaig, K.S., and Lin, J. (2003) Intertwining Material and Virtual Work, *Information and Organization*, 13, 111–129.

Rotondi, T. (1975) Organizational Identification: Issues and Implications, *Organizational Behaviour and Human Performance*, 13, 95–109.

Rousseau, D.M. (1998) Why Workers Still Identify with Organizations, *Journal of Organizational Behaviour*, 19, 217–233.

Schneider, B., Hall, D.T., and Nygren, H.T. (1971) Self Image and Job Characteristics as Correlates of Changing Organizational Identification, *Human Relations*, 24, 397–416.

Sproull, L., and Kiesler, S. (1986) Reducing Social Context Cues: Electronic Mail in Organizational Communication, *Management Science*, 32(11), 1492–1512.

Suchman, L.A. (1987) *Plans and Situated Actions: The Problem of Human Machine Communication*, Cambridge University Press: Cambridge.

Tajfel, H. (1981) *Human Groups and Social Categories*, Cambridge University Press: Cambridge.

Taylor, S., and Bogdan, R. (1998) *Introduction to Qualitative Research Methods*, 3rd edn, Wiley: New York.

van Dick, R., Wagner, U., Stellmacher, J., and Christ, O. (2004) The Utility of a Broader Conceptualisation of Organizational Identification: Which Aspects Really Matter?, *Journal of Occupational and Organizational Psychology*, 77, 171–191.

Vora, D., and Kostova, T. (2007) A Model of Dual Organizational Identification in the Context of the Multinational Enterprise, *Journal of Organizational Behavior*, 28(3), 327–350.

Whittington, R. (2006) Completing the Practice Turn in Strategy Research, *Organization Studies*, 27(5), 613–634.

Wiesenfield, B.M., Raghuram, S., and Garud, R. (1999) Communication Patterns as Determinants of Organizational Identification in a Virtual Organization, *Organization Science*, 10(6), 777–790.

Wiesenfield, B.M., Raghuram, S., and Garud, R. (2001) Organizational Identification among Virtual Workers: The Role of Need for Affiliation and Perceived Work-based Social Support, *Journal of Management*, 27, 213–229.

Yan, L., and Panteli N. (2006) The Politics of Presence in Distributed Environments, ECIS 2007. Track: e-Work, 7–9 June 2007, Switzerland.

Zolin, R., Hinds, P., Fruchter, R., and Levitt, R. (2004) Interpersonal Trust in Cross-function, Geographically Distributed Work: A Longitudinal Study, *Information and Organization*, 14, 1–26.

CHAPTER 7

Reconciling visions and realities of virtual working: Findings from the UK chemicals industry

Paul Dunning-Lewis and
Maria Katsorchi-Hayes

Introduction

In this chapter we introduce and discuss the findings from a large, UK e-science research project. The GOLD project (Morris et al., 2004) built upon earlier e-science success but was unusual in being focused upon taking Grid computing beyond its use by scientists and academics and to explore its use for commercial ends. The intention was to focus upon the development, production, and marketing of specialty, high profit margin chemicals. In this industry sector an economic case could be made that "new ways of working based around dynamic virtual organizational structures" were needed.

The GOLD project was interdisciplinary with the research team consisting of computer scientists who were investigating the development of computer middleware, and chemists and chemical engineers looking at required R&D and manufacturing processes. The authors were involved as part of an investigation into the chemical companies' requirements and to raise awareness of the social implications of the use of any developed technologies. Findings confirm previous work on virtuality but also emphasize the importance of existing practices and norms in shaping the intended users' visions of "virtuality in practice."

In the initial stages of the project the meaning of virtuality was socially constructed among the project team, and heavily influenced by the technical team's view of what the technology would allow. These views of virtuality and of how the chemical companies might form virtual organizations relied upon the literature concerning virtual organizations, and were formed in isolation from any knowledge of existing work practices and attitudes toward technology in the UK chemicals sector. And in some cases the agenda was driven by what seemed most interesting to research. For example, at the start of the project there was an interest in enabling high security communication between anonymous parties. As the authors discussed those visions of virtual organizations and interactions among companies with the industrial partners, they were able to feed back to the technical teams a greater understanding of what might actually be acceptable, leading to changes in emphasis and intent. It was clear, for example, that there would never be any need for communication among anonymous participants and security requirements within the sector were lower than had been imagined or hoped for. Thus, the visions of virtuality that the technology would support were radically different at the end of the project from those at the start.

This does not simply illustrate better requirements engineering leading to a better "fit" between a technical artifact and the intended users. The artifacts in this case were middleware rather than end-user systems, and the end users would not interact with the developed software but with applications-level software employing the developed software and methods. The application software, and the users' uses of it, would nevertheless be constrained by the assumptions built into the developed middleware. Most important of these would be assumptions over what virtuality and virtual working might be.

Virtuality: meaning and "real" implications

Virtuality or places that humans have no actual ability for physical presence has always been an area of interest as Nguyen and Alexander (1996) explain:

> Despite the stubborn resistance of our limited physical bodies, we have long tried to explore, and set up as real, domains beyond our immediate senses. As a civilization, we have learned to live with many virtual realities. Think of the molecules and atoms of our physical and chemical structure. Think of the virtual reality of this pulsating universe measured in light years and sprinkled with black holes and supernovas. We have learned to find compelling the virtual reality of other people's suffering across oceans and time zones. Our TV screens display everyday the contemporality of all possible human experience. (pp. 100–101)

However, despite our familiarity with technologies such as television, terms such as virtuality, the virtual world, and the virtual organization are used loosely and variously in describing a wide range of complex interactions occurring where physical presence is impossible, restricted or deemed unnecessary and so presence is attempted by advanced information and communications technologies (ICTs). Definitions of the terms "virtual" and "virtuality," range from purely technical interpretations of the term to the more socially oriented. For example Schultze and Orlikowski (2001) discuss existing perceptions of virtuality by using the "metaphorical" elements in the definitions of virtual organizations as: platforms, spaces, bits, communities, and networks. They point out the linguistic ambiguity of each metaphor and the consequences it entails for researchers to adopt one metaphor over another.

Many authors have tried in vain to discover organizations that fit any pure definition of the "virtual organization." This is disappointing since virtual organizations, enabled through extensive use of new electronic technologies, are often justified on the basis of improving the efficiency and profitability of business operations. Efficiency arguments are supported by reductions in paperwork and the need for travel. Effectiveness, it is argued, will be achieved by promoting possibilities that were difficult if not impossible before. For example, virtual teams composed of experts from around the world, may be engaged continuously in a project while remaining in their home countries and never meeting in person. Why then are actual virtual organizations so elusive?

We suggest, first, that the consequences of virtual working are complex, having contradictory implications and different meanings across individuals in differing or even similar organizational contexts. The very same things that promise efficiency may inhibit acceptance; the distantiation in time and place that allows the virtual team from around the world to work together brings also a loss of the personal that engenders loss of trust and an unwillingness to work together. Thus, visions of the virtual organization are difficult to bring into existence. Second, we suggest that advocates of the virtual organization often fail to recognize that those they would convert to their vision are already working virtually to a great extent, and understand intuitively that working virtually must be integrated into existing organizational practices and take account of practical constraints.

Despite the increased hype in recent years concerning virtuality, there are accounts that urge us to examine the range of intended and unintended consequences of virtual work. Watson-Manheim, Chudoba, and Crowston (2005), for example, reflect on the concepts of continuity and discontinuity in virtual work environments and suggest that the implications from virtual technologies both facilitate and hinder people in day-to-day work practices. Woolgar condenses the learning from the ESRC project named "Virtual Society?" to produce insightful accounts on the nature of virtuality grounded, to a large extent, on empirical findings (Woolgar, 2002). Woolgar captures the essence of these studies by identifying what he defines as "five rules of virtuality," explaining that these rules are not to be followed in any deterministic sense but, quoting Garfinkel, as "aids to the sluggish imagination" (p. 14), and "in the face of determinative claims about the effects and impacts of any new technology that comes on stream, each of these rules provides a rule of thumb or slogan for evaluating these claims" (p. 14).

These rules are used here as a framework against which to present some of the findings of the GOLD study.

The uptake and use of the new technologies depends crucially on local social context

Woolgar (ibid.) refers to the adaptability of virtual technologies beyond their technical dimension and their relevance to the social context in which they are implemented. Technical capability is one aspect in the implementation of virtual technologies but not the only one, and cannot, by itself, provide an explanation for the use or nonuse of such technologies. A series of examples are discussed which put a cautionary note on the universalistic nature of current arguments about the use of virtual technologies (see Wyatt, Thomas, and Terranova, 2002; Liff, Steward, and Watts, 2002).

This message was strongly supported by the GOLD research, where, in the UK chemical industry, the particular and the local proved to be of prime importance. For example, the need for accountability over health and safety issues, even where the manufacturing takes place thousands of miles away, is done by another company working under different local laws, regulations, and expectations, is essential. As one manager told the researchers, he would never trust what his partners told him about safety in a manufacturing plant unless he had looked them in the eye and seen the plant for himself. No virtual presence or other form or interaction could substitute.

The fears and risks associated with new technologies are unevenly socially distributed

Our own research gave little insight into whether differences might exist between socially differentiated groups because the social differentiation between actors was narrow. All the participants in the GOLD research were of the professional managerial class, well informed and educated; in addition, their training as chemists and chemical engineers was common, despite their varied national roots. Furthermore, they were experienced within an industry that has and continues to undergo aggressive reshaping globally, so that they knew, and sometimes had already felt, the transformative effects of technological change.

What the GOLD study did find was that some expected differences between *technologically* differentiated groups did not occur. An example of this was that the technical teams, on learning that the managers made relatively little and unsophisticated use of IT, had come to the false conclusion that they were technologically backward; this would perhaps lead to difficulties in their understanding of virtuality and what might be achieved through the technology.

In fact, the GOLD study found that the managers had very little difficulty in working at a distance with parties they had no social interaction with; this is what they did routinely as their job and had done for many years. Those managers simply wanted to know if the technology might allow them to do it more easily and effectively.

Virtual technologies supplement rather than substitute for real activities

Woolgar (2002), aiming to criticize the extensive claims of substitution made by virtuality enthusiasts, provides evidence indicating that "old" nonvirtual practices often coexist with new, virtual practices. "The virtual thus sits alongside the real that, in much popular imagination, it is usually supposed to supplant" (p. 16).

Furthermore, new interactions may emerge that are the result of this novel mix between traditional and virtual; Woolgar cites corridor conversations initiated by "I've just sent you an e-mail" openers; other examples would be that electronic conferencing can allow "Shall we call in Fred and see what he thinks?" possibilities that don't exist in located meetings.

The empirical findings that suggest this rule for Woolgar are from domains such as education and social support, where virtual activities supplement rather than substitute existing learning and social support activities (Crook and Light, 2002; Nettleton et al., 2002). The GOLD research, taking place in a different, commercial domain, confirmed that managers could envision, without any apparent contradictions, the coexistence of old and new practices. An example would be the communication of intellectual property and commercially valuable process information. Currently, nondisclosure agreements are required before details of manufacturing procedures are discussed with potential partners, and sensitive documents are hand-delivered. We discovered that if new safeguards were implemented by the GOLD middleware (every access to the material and every stage of the transmission to be scrupulously audited, use of "your-eyes-only," nonforwardable or printable e-mails) there would be few concerns over the substitution of face-to-face completion of agreements and communication of documents with electronic, virtual equivalents. Yet, the very same managers who told us this insisted that before negotiations ever got to that stage, face-to-face meetings with potential partners were essential.

The more virtual, the more real

Woolgar (2002) suggests that virtual technologies frequently have subsequent "real" consequences on day-to-day practices, echoing previous concerns on the transformative claims of virtual technologies on eliminating the need for travel and face-to-face interactions, for example (Moss and Townsend, 2000). The emergence of teleworking, for example, may in fact increase the need of travel, since teleworkers, assisted by advanced communications technologies, are able to contact more customers and this increases the need for face-to-face visits. Other examples include the increase in phone calls and letter writing (Nettleton et al., 2002) and the unexpected increase in informal contacts arising through e-mail (Brown and Lightfoot, 2002).

We found no support for an increased use of virtual technologies and ways of working resulting in more "real" activity. A possible explanation lies in the particular nature of the specialty chemicals business; the number of companies able to produce any particular product is necessarily small due to the need for specialized equipment and skills in handling sometimes dangerous production processes. In this industry it seemed that new and virtual ways of working might alter the forms of interaction among existing companies, but was unlikely to generate an increase in the number of active parties or face-to-face contacts.

The more global, the more local

Drawing on the empirical work, including that of Hughes, Rouncefield, and Tolmie (2002), Woolgar (2002) suggests that it is frequently local efforts and existing ways of working that must be taken into account to make new technologies work at a global level. In the context of a retail bank, Hughes, Rouncefield, and Tolmie (2002) discovered that, contrary to existing arguments, instead of needing new skills and novel working practices to become a global or virtual organization, actors make great efforts to "fit" new technologies into their existing day-to-day work practices.

This was strongly confirmed by our discussions with chemical companies and their representatives. There was an overwhelming consensus that, given the tight margins and somewhat precarious survival of many firms, they could not gamble on substantially new practices emerging from new IT-driven initiatives. Only where it could be seen that new methods of working would give commercial benefits at low risk would new technology and corresponding practices be considered. And benefits could most easily be seen in the small, local tasks that needed to be done, such as the secure communication of sensitive documents and contracts. Suggestions of "broadcast tender invitations" and other substantial changes to the ways of conducting business were dismissed immediately.

Changing interpretations of the virtual

One of the most interesting results of the GOLD study was the insight gained into how the managers in the specialty and fine (S&F) chemicals industry operated in and understood their world, and how this led to changes in the GOLD team's visions of what virtual working in that industry might be like.

It has been said that it is very hard to remember what we once did not know, and, in most research projects, knowledge of how people's interpretation of "the problem" changed across time is lost. In the GOLD project, the authors were careful to record, wherever possible, the way in which the team's perceptions of requirements and the meaning of virtuality changed over the course of the project. In some cases the differences between ideas early in the project and later were quite marked, and this affected the technical artifacts. An interesting example was that only toward the end of the project, when demonstrations of the software were required, did it become obvious that explaining what was happening when a new business partner was being enrolled into the virtual organization was very difficult. The problem was overcome by use of additional software, to give a meta-level animated graphical display of what was happening in the virtual organization and the corresponding activities of the GOLD software. Only once this was working did the GOLD team realize such representations of the virtual would themselves be extremely useful to participants in virtual organizations. And the reason they now saw a use for such software was that their vision of virtual working in the industry had changed from that of a semi-automatic set of procedures to a complex and hard-to-understand set of changing interactions requiring human management and interventions.

Following some further explanation of the GOLD project, it is these changing visions of virtual working that we examine.

The GOLD project

The GOLD project was an Engineering and Physical Sciences Research Council (EPSRC) funded e-science project that aimed to develop Grid middleware as the enabling technology for dealing with trust, security, lifecycle, and information management in highly dynamic virtual organizations (VOs). It was therefore seen as creating technologies that would virtualize the nonvirtual.

The potential application domain for such technology-facilitated, interorganizational working is wide, for example, in construction, electronics, and the military sectors. The chosen area for the GOLD project was the production of S&F chemicals, which are produced in small quantities but which have a high price. In this sector the secrets of success lie in finding new but practical ways of manufacture, to quickly meet the unpredictable demand while adhering to very strict quality and delivery requirements. Trust and security impose very stringent requirements, and the sector could be seen as a critical case of virtual work.

There were also good reasons to believe that the S&F chemicals industry would benefit from new and agile ways of working. This is a sector where the UK has only a modest $9–12 billion share of a $250 billion global market. The nature of the products means that much legal paperwork has to be completed for every interorganizational collaboration, and health and safety authorities, customs, even the police, have to be aware of the movement of products between partners.

The traditional strengths for companies in this industry have been the protection of intellectual property (IP) knowledge, a skilled workforce, plant efficiency, and good reputation. In recent years, however, cheap labor and facilities in new economies have been used to reduce the overall price, so that production skill and efficiency have become less important as factors for success. There is, therefore, increased pressure upon all to innovate in order to maintain their competitive advantage through *business intensification*: the ability to commercialize innovations more quickly than competitors. Previous attempts at virtual working were claimed to have produced significant cost savings of 92 percent, with time to market reduced by 66 percent (Wright and Bramfitt, 1999; Wright, 2004). However, the previous attempts were not scalable. The information necessary to coordinate, manage, and control outsourced activities in remote locations proved too large, and the necessity for ad hoc reconfigurations in response to external events and the evolving state of each project was beyond the capability of existing software systems. Grid technologies were seen as the way to render this problem more tractable, offering sufficient and readily accessible processing power to participants, wherever located; the way is thus opened to transparent global interorganizational working, with outsourced R&D labs, safety assessments, chemical analysis, data analysis, pilot studies, manufacturing, marketing, and distribution. However, moving to such new ways of working would have considerable implications on an industry where health and safety records and intellectual property rights play such a large role.

An interdisciplinary approach

Within the GOLD project, there were three main groups, working on six work packages. The groups were:

1. The technical team of computer scientists and security experts who were creating the middleware and demonstrating its functionality. This work was the core of the GOLD project and would be the primary measure of success or failure of the whole project.
2. A smaller group, called here the chemical team, was concerned with the application of the middleware to chemicals production, demonstrating the usefulness of e-science outside the academic community to which applications had, until now, been directed.
3. The third and smallest group, the business team, was concerned with investigating the real-world opportunities and constraints of using the technology in a commercial setting. This group, based at the Management School at Lancaster University and to which the authors belonged, would feed back to the technical and chemicals teams relevant information gained from the S&F chemicals industry.

The work of the technical and chemicals teams has been reported in the relevant disciplinary journals.

The findings here stem from interviews undertaken with 24 organizations in the S&F chemicals sector. Access was gained either through direct contact or through a respected professional association. At least one of the business team was present at every interview; in some interviews members of the technical and chemicals teams were also present. Interviewees varied from chemists, engineers on site to R&D, operations, and/or IT managers and CEOs. The aim of the interviews was to understand the way in which business was conducted, the day-to-day activities of participants, and to discuss how virtuality might be implemented in a particular real-world setting. Interviews lasted between one and a half and three hours, were recorded with permission of the interviewees and later transcribed. The qualitative data analysis software Atlas was used to organize the themes emerging from the interviews.

Imagining the virtual

At the start of the research the technical team wished to pin down and define exactly what was meant by a "virtual organization" and how such an organizational form would operate in the chemicals industry. After all, they argued, how can we produce software if we do not know what it is?

Several weeks were spent collecting insights from the literature, seminars, and visits to knowledgeable academics and group discussions. Emerging from this was a vision of a virtual organization that could be most relevant to the chemicals industry and which the to-be-developed technology might facilitate. This was of the "highly dynamic virtual organization" swiftly formed and dissolved, in which companies might cooperate on a production project even while being competitors on other contracts.

Such dynamic virtual organizations would operate within a "common," secure virtual space, within which customers and suppliers of chemicals could log on, check prices of chemicals and initiate business-to-business collaborations. After the end of such collaborations the virtual organization would be terminated. During the relatively short life of such collaborations, information concerning patents, formulae, intellectual property rights, etc. would be freely exchanged in a technically "secured and trusted" way.

The role of managers in the new, virtual way of working would be to monitor and control the operation of each virtual collaboration. Workflow management facilities could assist with this, since every collaboration was seen to follow the same set of predefined activities.

This was the vision of the virtual by the GOLD team, enabled by the new computing and communications technologies they were constructing.

It was a credible vision well supported by the literature of virtual organizations and by real-world electronic business-to-business markets in other industries. While the technical teams carried out the preliminary work in creating the technology, the business team began their work of validating the vision and refining its fit to industry concerns.

Validating the vision

The GOLD project had from its outset the aim of providing practical benefit, and so the feasibility of all of the above was to be tested against the requirements of the industry. Because this was seen as a novel application of a new technology, conventional requirements engineering methods could not be used. Instead, a set of required business activities was identified through the use of soft systems modeling (Checkland, 1981; Lewis, 1994; Checkland and Poulter, 2006). It was believed that even though ideal virtual work was not present, there must be real-world equivalents already happening, albeit done in a nonvirtual way. Understanding how these activities were presently done would illuminate what would be required of the new applications that would be supported by the middleware. Second, it would be necessary to explore exactly how chemical companies operated with customers and suppliers, and what functionality they would most value. The soft-systems modeling (SSM)-activity models would provide a template for what it was thought ought to be done, provide an initial structure to our questioning and allow us to produce use-cases that would help define the detailed functionality of any eventual technologies.

Eighteen months after the start of the project, a further possibility for validation arose. The chemical engineering team were asked to consult with a group of companies forming a virtual project in R&D. Detailed records were kept of all meetings and events for this project, giving the opportunity for the chemicals team to compare predicted interactions with those occurring over the course of that project. This also produced use-cases that were grounded in real practice.

Perceptions of work practices versus actual practices

In this section we contrast two views of work practices and possible virtual forms of those practices. The first view presents the assumptions made by the GOLD project. It was upon these assumptions, and the vision of a

Table 7.1 Differing interpretations of elements of virtuality

	GOLD team	Managers and professionals in S&F chemicals industry
Pricing	Prices are public knowledge, key determinant of choice of partners	"Big Secret" of the industry, each price is negotiated and specific. Set down initially verbally, only later in confidential contracts
Trust	Trust was open to technical solutions of controlled communications and audit Trust invoked at discrete, temporary transaction level	Trust is at personal level, between individuals Contracts are formal arrangements of relationships that do not happen without trust; contractual penalties will never be needed Requiring long-term established relationships
Management	Managers seen as monitoring and controlling the operation of a virtual organization, which could be workflow-modeled Business interactions and activities required in development and production repeatable and can be defined in advance	Managers seen as attenuators of change Major role to establish and judge trusting business relationships Each relationship, project seen as idiosyncratically unique ICTs seen as having no inherent attraction but merely as possible facilitators to existing and continuing requirements
Locality	Being local is not a necessity in a virtual context	Locality of facilitating services important
Travel	Virtual presence leads to reduced need for travel	Essential to travel, especially when nurturing new collaborators

virtual organization allowed by those assumptions, that the middleware to assist virtual working was being created.

The second point of view encapsulates the interviewees' descriptions of working practices, their ways of interacting with customers and suppliers and their understanding of virtuality. Table 7.1 summarizes the key points of the discussion.

How do chemicals organizations really collaborate?

The GOLD study revealed that the ways in which chemicals organizations dealt with their customers and suppliers was deeply rooted in experiential and professional knowledge of the managers in each organization. Their perceptions of virtuality and plausible future patterns for work were closely related to context-specific characteristics of collaboration; the strongest of these in the S&F chemicals area were price, trust, the role of managers, locality, and need for travel. Each is briefly discussed below.

Price

Assumptions were made by the GOLD designers that S&F chemicals had a price, and that companies might publicly advertise the price they were willing to pay, or the price for which they were willing to sell. Based on this assumption, the early thinking of the GOLD team centered on the notion of a virtual organization dynamically formed as the result of price bids, where a party would require partners to supply services or chemical raw materials for the production of a specialty product. That need would be advertised and the companies replying with the lowest-priced bids would become partners in a short-term virtual company. The early ideas were extended to the possibility of a global and specialized electronic marketplace for chemicals. This meant that the early thinking about the technical architecture and about security requirements was centered on the vision of what a virtual organization might look like.

The interviews with managers soon revealed a far more complex process of pricing chemicals. As a commercial manager explained

> Price is the big secret of the industry. Many things indicate the final price of a chemical: who is the customer; what they want the chemical for; how much profit they will make. You do not go round telling people how much you paid for your raw materials or how much you are selling your products for. You are losing credibility in this way and get a bad reputation.

This was a revelation; this was a global industry where the majority of the products were custom-made. The "ideal" of a purely economical basis for virtual collaboration with customers and suppliers was simplistic and naive.

Trust

A further confusion arose from the technical team's understanding of trust. The literature of virtual organizations had identified trust as important, but the word was used for a considerable time before it was realized that subtly different interpretations were being used by GOLD members, and by the managers in the S&F chemicals industry.

Within the GOLD researchers there were differing meanings attached to trust by the computer scientists, security experts, and the business team. For the technical teams, trust had its roots in the technical considerations of communication theory, which emphasizes the extent to which an individual may believe that a received message comes from the claimed sender (encryption – authentication), and is the same message that was sent, and so it was not intercepted and tampered with by others. Trustworthiness is thus seen as a property of the technology.

For the business team of GOLD, trust was a perceived relationship between cooperating parties. Under this view then I might have every confidence in your message, that the message I receive is the one you sent, that no one intercepted, and even that it is factually true. But even then, I may not trust why you sent it. The GOLD team therefore early on began to differentiate between "trust" and "business trust."

The interviews with managers revealed further differences in the understanding of trust. Trust, as explained by many managers, in the everyday operations had largely a social rather than a technical dimension. Trust was repeatedly described as a relationship based on long-term knowledge of other individuals within the industry and personal judgments on the professional capabilities of others to perform. One CEO tried to explain the process he follows to trust others:

> I think if you know somebody a lot and you have an experiential relationship you can look at your experience and decide how many times has that person disappointed you. I think there is another level of trust when you are looking forward and people normally need to be able to codify the information you are giving them in their own matrix. So, I come along and say we need to work on this and this will make loads of money. Firstly, you will be thinking the issue of being credible in believing in this idea and, secondly, it is sharing the benefits of the credible, what evidence do I have for that? So I think there are a lot of value judgments that happen that are either made, or that are chucked away and destroyed because they are not credible; nothing to do with the purchase. Too good to be true or completely not understandable. ... Then it does not start. It is a complex issue.

And, the words of the vice president of a multinational petrochemicals organization emphasized the importance of knowledge and trust in specific individuals:

> In this industry, you deal with individuals. You have a long-term relationship that takes a long time to build; ten years at least I will say.

> We do not follow companies, we follow individuals. That means, if a trusted person moves from one organization to another we follow the person not the company.

Such a basis for collaboration is quite different from the purely technical and economic criteria for collaboration in the GOLD team's early vision of a virtual organization, where the rational economic manager would promiscuously rearrange relationships with whoever offered the most economic returns at that moment.

Managers and managing

The role of management was also very different from that which the GOLD team expected in a virtual environment, though it was some time before this was realized. Even two years into the project there was still discussion of workflow management being a core activity that the GOLD middleware would facilitate. Reliance on such software assumes that there is a given and predefined set of interactions to be carried out, with well-defined exchanges of information and identifiable triggers and signals for when an action can legitimately commence. The instantiation of this process and information model can then be monitored by software, and alerts produced when there is deviation from an expected sequence or, say, one process has finished but the next has not begun.

Managers in the S&F chemicals industries certainly did monitor progress and institute corrective actions. One manager expressed a robust view of what was required:

> And over the years, the one thing that you find out is that nothing happens unless you are persistently kicking arse and shaking people. And the whole world is the same. Our success, I suppose, is that because we get so frustrated at lack of action that we go out there (China) and kick arse. So we are pushing every day because unless you do …

However, all the managers saw their role as unpredictable and different in almost every situation. Managers described that the majority of their time was spent on negotiations, face-to-face communication, and making decisions based on their experience and personal judgment. This was perceived to be their job and the source of whether they were a good manager or not. Asking managers to have the role of monitoring and controlling the operation of a virtual organization was alien in the context of chemicals organization, and this dissonance between their experienced world and the vision behind some interpretations of virtual working could cause comments such as that given by one CEO, that: "Using new software to implement new ways of working is very stressful and you never get the job done. There is nothing relevant to the chemicals industry and we find the language alienating. New technologies will slow us down."

Locality

The importance placed on locality was expected to diminish through virtual collaborations, but managers reported that, even with the more global working practices, locality was still important. This was especially true in relation to facilitating services; in such things as legal disputes or dealing with local regulations it was important to work with local experts. It was not foreseen this would be any less true in future.

The creation and dissolution of contracts and contractual obligations was an area that the GOLD team's vision foresaw as easily benefiting from new methods. Boilerplate contracts could be rapidly created, automatically tailored to the circumstances, and then authorized virtually in order to speed up the process of creating new partnerships and operating arrangements. However, for the managers interviewed, a lack of assurances of safeguards and auditability convinced them that this would never work.

Travel

Travel was viewed as an essential part of their job. Despite the global nature of their organizations, managers repeatedly stressed the importance of meeting the people who they were dealing with, especially during initial collaboration. This was justified partly upon trust and partly by technical need.

Trust, we were told, was built upon face-to-face experience of the other party; once established then, as stated by one manager, other things might follow:

> For our key raw materials and key customers it all depends on face-to-face communication and building a relationship, both with suppliers and customers. At some point you are trying to establish the personal contact and once you establish that you can try to do it via telephone, e-mail, do videoconferencing, etc.

Even where trust was established travel was required because many of the collaborations that these companies were involved in centered on some unique and innovative production processes. As a result, there was the necessity to explain or interpret the underlying science or development process.

Conclusions

We have given in this chapter an overview of what was discovered when the GOLD project attempted to test out visions of virtuality against practice. The discussion is grounded in a single and somewhat specific context, that of the manufacture of S&F chemicals, and as such we cannot claim generality across different industrial sectors. The work does though provide support for previous authors' conclusions as demonstrated in respect to Woolgar's "rules" of virtuality. In particular it supports that understanding virtuality in contemporary organizations requires an understanding of the business context and norms of these organizations. It illustrates how those contexts and norms lead toward differing visions of the virtual. In the GOLD project, the two groups of researchers and managers were separated not merely by differing knowledge (though this was the case too) but also by different assumptions about how persons and organizations interact now and in the future. The lesson is not that good system development requires good requirements analysis, but that requirements sometimes do not exist; they are emergent properties of the dialogue between the parties. As such they will be born partly from past practice and partly from visions of what is technically possible and what is practically and culturally feasible.

This is most significant for considering future developments in the S&F chemicals industry when coupled with another finding from the GOLD project, namely that virtual working is more readily acceptable than might be supposed. For the managers in the project, the concepts themselves were not novel; the telephone, fax, and simple e-mail have allowed them to work globally for the last 30 years, frequently working with partners with limited contact and in different time zones. They could readily judge the potential usefulness of technical artifacts enabled by the GOLD middleware.

It would seem, therefore, that the route to novel virtual working practices, perhaps to virtual organizations becoming commonplace in S&F chemicals production, may lie not through immediate adoption. Already several attempts to establish business-to-business electronic markets have failed. Instead, it seems that where some new facility (be it secure document transmission, automatic audit trailing of messaging or whatever else the GOLD middleware enables) is useful it would be adopted. Gradually, and over time, this accretion of changed practices might move the industry toward something resembling the visions of virtuality in the literature. For the managers this would not be a sea change but merely an extension of current practice.

The findings of the GOLD project, we suggest, may be true of industries other than S&F chemicals. In construction, for example, many firms may come together for the lifetime of a specific project and there would seem to be similar advantages in newer ways of organizing those interactions. But the construction industry has its own ingrained traditions and practices that will not be abandoned overnight. While application-level offerings to that industry will be different to those in the S&F chemicals industry, what will be similar is the need to account for and incorporate existing ways of working and norms of behavior.

Finally, we may note that new, virtual forms of working appear to require social contextualism and tailored designs, perhaps knitted together by flexible middleware. It is unfortunate that these are becoming increasingly rare in commercial organizations due to the widespread use of standardized and un-customizable global solutions in the form of enterprise resource planning (ERP) software. An interesting future tension is thus suggested for the field of systems development.

References

Brown, S.D., and Lightfoot, G. (2002) "Presence, Absence and Accountability: E-mail and the Mediation of Organizational Memory," in S. Woolgar (Ed.), *Virtual Society? Technology, Cyberbole, Reality*, Oxford University Press: Oxford.

Checkland, P., and Poulter, J. (2006) *Learning for Action*, Wiley: Chichester.

Checkland, P.B. (1981) *Systems Thinking, Systems Practice*, Wiley: Chichester.

Crook, C., and Light, P. (2002) "Virtual Society and the Cultural Practice of Study," in S. Woolgar (Ed.), *Virtual Society? Technology, Cyberbole, Reality*, Oxford University Press: Oxford.

Hughes, J., Rouncefield, M., and Tolmie, P. (2002) "The Day-to Day Work of Standardization: A Sceptical Note on the Reliance on IT in a Retail Bank," in S. Woolgar (Ed.), *Virtual Society? Technology, Cyberbole, Reality*, Oxford University Press: Oxford.

Lewis, P. (1994) *Information-Systems Development; Systems Thinking in the Field of Information Systems*, Pitman: London.

Liff, S., Steward, F., and Watts, P. (2002) "New Public Places for Internet Access: Networks for Practice-Based Learning and Social Inclusion," in S. Woolgar (Ed.), *Virtual Society? Technology, Cyberbole, Reality*, Oxford University Press: Oxford.

Morris, A.J., Shrivastava, S., Wright, A.R., Ryan, P., Dunning-Lewis, P., and Martin, E. (2004) *Grid-Based Information Models to Support the Rapid Innovation of New High Value Added Chemicals*, EPSRC, UK.

Moss, M., and Townsend, A. (2000) "How Telecommunications Systems are Transforming Urban Spaces," in J.O. Wheeler, Y. Aoyama, and B.L. Warf (Eds), *Cities in the Telecommunications Age: The Fracturing of Geographies*, Routledge: New York.

Nettleton, S., Pleace, N., Burrrows, R., Muncer, S., and Loader, B. (2002) "The Reality of Virtual Social Support," in S. Woolgar (Ed.), *Virtual Society? Technology, Cyberbole, Reality*, Oxford University Press: Oxford.

Nguyen, D.T., and Alexander, J. (1996) "The Coming of Cyberspace Time and the End of the Polity," in R. Shields (Ed.), *Cultures of the Internet: Virtual Spaces, Real Histories, Living Bodies*, Sage: London.

Schultze, U., and Orlikowski, W.J. (2001) Metaphors of Virtuality: Shaping an Emergent Reality, *Information and Organization*, 11(1), 45–77.

Watson-Manheim, M.B., Chudoba, K.M., and Crowston, K. (2005) *The Paradox of Discontinuities and Continuities: Toward a More Comprehensive View of Virtuality*, http://crowston.syr.edu/papers/paradox2004.pdf (accessed: November 2006)

Woolgar, S. (2002) "Five Rules of Virtuality," in S. Woolgar (Ed.), *Virtual Society? Technology, Cyberbole, Reality*, Oxford University Press: Oxford, New York.

Woolgar, S. (Ed.) (2002) *Virtual Society? Technology, Cyberbole, Reality*, Oxford University Press: Oxford, New York.

Wright, A.R. (2004) Turning Virtual Development Methods into a Reality, Proceedings of BatchPro. Symposium on knowledge-driven batch processes, Poros, Greece.

Wright, A.R., and Bramfitt, V.J. (1999) *The Reality of Virtual Process Development*, Proceedings of EU99, Bern, Switzerland.

Wyatt, S., Thomas, G., and Terranova, T. (2002) "They Came, They Surfed, They Went Back to the Beach: Conceptualizing Use and Non-Use of the Internet," in S. Woolgar (Ed.), *Virtual Society? Technology, Cyberbole, Reality*, Oxford University Press: Oxford.

CHAPTER 8

Virtuality of teams: Extending boundaries and discontinuities

Keith Dixon and Niki Panteli

Introduction

The transformation of business and social lives continues as communication technology becomes ever more pervasive, opening up access to numerous "virtual spaces" from the many "real spaces" occupied by individuals – the home, the coffee shop, the airport, the train, etc. As anyplace-anytime portals into virtual space move a step closer, so the separation between real and virtual becomes increasingly blurred giving individuals a "social presence on a worldwide scale" (Turoff, 1997, p. 42). Communities established through face-to-face interactions in the real world migrate to the virtual as their increasingly mobile members move physically apart. Conversely, virtual communities and teams emerge through technology-mediated interactions around shared interests or common goals and go on to meet in the real world as their commitment to their shared purpose develops (Blanchard and Horan, 2000). The limitations of time and physical space are, therefore, blurred not by virtual space itself, but by the blurring of the separation between them.

While the pervasiveness of technology-mediated communication underpins this phenomenon, the effects ripple through the fabric of society. Early-stage research tended to revolve around technology, as the central driving force of these changes, and was predominantly in work settings, since organizations were the earliest adopters of the technology. This gave rise to concepts and strands of research at the individual (e.g., "telecommuting"), group (e.g., "virtual team"), and organizational levels (e.g., "virtual organizations") (Chudoba et al., 2005). With the growing adoption of the internet and World Wide Web, consideration is now being given to the effects of these technologies on society in the widest sense rather than just the narrow context of organizational life (Blanchard and

Horan, 2000). However, while perhaps there has been more research within the organizational context, it is nevertheless still relatively immature compared to other strands of organizational research. For example, by comparison, teams and teamwork in general have been studied for more than half a century, whereas the concept of virtual teams is little more than a decade old.

Unsurprisingly then, the study of virtual teams has been characterized by comparisons with so-called "traditional," co-located, or face-to-face teams, focusing on identifying and exploring the key differences and their effects (Powell, Piccoli, and Ives, 2004). Having yielded useful insights, the limitations of isolating characteristics in this way is now recognized (Griffith, Sawyer, and Neale, 2003) and some research has begun to shift from this perspective (Watson-Manheim, Chudoba, and Crowston, 2002). The wider societal-level adoption of technology is potentially playing a role in this as researchers recognize that with technology embedded in people's everyday lives, pure and isolated forms of virtual and traditional teams are no longer widely generalizable. With individuals using face-to-face and technology-mediated communication in conjunction with one another, there is a move toward understanding virtuality in teams as being defined by discontinuities; such discontinuities exist not just in terms of geography and time zones, but also in culture, work practices, organization, and technology (Chudoba et al., 2005) rather than in terms of the extent to which technology-mediated communication is used.

This chapter builds on this perspective, away from the micro-level issues of how individual interactions are undertaken toward a concept of virtuality based on the emergent effects on discontinuities within teams that arise as a result of the combination of face-to-face and technology-mediated interactions. In doing this, the aim is to look beyond the bridging of boundaries or discontinuities of space and time by technology-mediated communication and to identify and examine the nature of the discontinuities, and the wider and higher-level ripple effects of these changes. Building on the relative strength of the empirical research in the organizational context of virtual teams to anchor the development of further insights into boundaries and discontinuities, the chapter goes on to apply and develop these insights using data from a case study of an interorganizational "virtual centre of excellence." Having discussed the findings and the potential further development of these insights in the more general terms of virtuality in society as a whole, conclusions are drawn and the limitations and avenues for future research are outlined.

An emerging view of virtuality

Organizations have been adopting computer-based communication technology as part of their ongoing drive to improve their efficiency and effectiveness. The changes this has brought about have not only been significant for the organizations themselves, but also through their role in society, as a whole. More recently, the advent of the internet and the World Wide Web has meant that these effects on wider society have become more direct as organizations have emerged and developed, not only to interact directly with individuals as customers, but also to enable individuals themselves to interact in new ways beyond an organizational context. This has developed to a point where now the pervasive nature of these communication technologies and their adoption and adaptation by individuals in wider society is creating new and changed behaviors in the work environment. Although these more recent developments garner widespread academic and populist attention, the starting point is to examine virtuality in the organizational context. The aim in this section is to highlight and support the emergence of a concept that enables a shift away from technology-oriented perspectives toward their emergent effects and in the next section to move thinking forward by adopting it to reveal new insights about virtual teams.

A key driver for change in organizations is the pursuit of productivity as a basis for improved performance. Belief in the power of information technology to provide opportunities in this regard is central to its early adoption in organizations. Equally, the pursuit of productivity is also the basis for the shift toward the use of team structures. The nexus of these two trends, driven in particular by the rapidly expanding access to communication technology, was therefore the "virtual team."

Building on the concept of the team, a virtual team has quite simply been defined as a team whose interactions take place primarily using technology-mediated communication (Lipnack and Stamps, 1997). However, because teams are already somewhat elusive to define, the emergence of the virtual team led to renewed questions in a number of areas, particularly since early research attempted to build on the credibility of the existing team literature, making comparisons between virtual and such "traditional" teams. For example, some researchers defined virtual teams on a temporal dimension as being more transitory or temporary than "traditional" teams (Jarvenpaa, Knoll, and Leidner, 1998) and therefore embedded this assumption in their choice of research design, using students to form virtual teams for a short duration (Martins, Gilson, and Maynard, 2004). However, while this may be true in certain times and circumstances, the increasingly pervasive nature of communication technology has lead to its widespread adoption as an aspect of all organizational teams (Griffith, Sawyer, and Neale, 2003; Bell and Kozlowski, 2002).

This emerging reality is one in which face-to-face and technology-mediated communication are used not as substitutes, but rather in conjunction with one another. While perhaps this would not surprise pragmatists, it does demand a shift away from the still predominant research perspective that assumes a substitution by way of isolating and comparing characteristics of face-to-face communications with technology-mediated communications and virtual with "traditional" teams. This is more fundamental than some attempts to create typologies of virtual teams (Bell and Kozlowski, 2002) or other measures of "virtualness" (Griffith, Sawyer, and Neale, 2003) or dimensions of "team virtuality" (Kirkman and Mathieu, 2005) that, although recognizing the hybrid nature of most teams, still attempts to employ definitions based on the extent of use or support of communication technology. The shortcoming of these studies is that they do not adequately capture any of the complementarities that emerge in the combination of face-to-face and technology-mediated communications. In this regard we are dealing with a more complementary phenomenon rather than simply an extension of face-to-face teams.

Adopting a perspective of "virtuality in teams," as opposed to one of "virtual teams," involves shifts in two directions. The first is upward away from micro-level comparisons between technology-mediated and face-to-face interactions and the second is sideways away from comparing virtual and "traditional" teams. This approach recognizes that the growing use of technology-mediated interactions has not created predominantly purely virtual teams but rather a predominance of teams in which technology-mediated communication has a transformative effect (Chudoba et al., 2005; Hertel, Geister, and Konradt, 2005; Martins, Gilson, and Maynard, 2004). Severing this link, and thus adopting a concept of virtuality as a characteristic of a team, can provide a means by which the complementary contributions of combining face-to-face and technology-mediated communication can be recognized. In this way, research in virtuality can develop both theory and recommendations for practitioners that extend beyond the purely technology-oriented view.

Here, then, the proposal is to adopt a definition of virtuality that was initially put forward by Watson-Manheim, Chudoba, and Crowston (2002). Proposed, in the title of their paper as "a new way to understand virtual work" their framework used types of continuities and discontinuities to develop "a more precise understanding of the term 'virtual' " (ibid., p. 191).

Subsequently, they developed this into a definition of virtuality and applied it to create a "virtuality index" (Chudoba et al., 2005) to "assess how 'virtual' a given setting is," not according to the use of technology-mediated communications, but according to the extent of discontinuities within the teams. To do this they drew on the literature and "identified six discontinuities – geography, time zone, culture, work practices, organization and technology – that captured distinctive aspects of the virtual teaming environment" (ibid., p. 282). Accepting, then, that geography and time represent discontinuities commonly associated with this field of work, it is the aim here to look beyond them since we hold the view that it is by bridging these that other discontinuities become apparent. Thus, while there are clearly links across levels, it is the case, for example, that differences in culture or work practices may not represent a discontinuity between groups or individuals where little interdependency means there is not much need for interaction, or where the more significant discontinuity of space and time acts to obfuscate the effect. Thus, where face-to-face communication is supported by technology-mediated communication to provide a bridge across space and time, the behaviors associated with different cultures and work practices have the potential to emerge as significant discontinuities where interdependencies demand significant interaction.

In summary, by shifting the perspective to one in which the concept of virtuality is defined beyond the level of technology-mediated interactions, the effect is to focus on the changes that come about when face-to-face and technology-mediated modes of communication are combined. Existing research suggests the use of discontinuities as the basis for such a definition (Chudoba et al., 2005; Watson-Manheim, Chudoba, and Crowston, 2002). This provides a conceptual basis for looking beyond the direct effects of time and space commonly associated with the field to the effects of other higher-level discontinuities.

In the next section, we explore the nature of these higher-level discontinuities and develop some proposals for the development of this perspective, which we then examine in a case study.

Discontinuities, boundaries, and teams

To continue the thinking that has given rise to the concept of virtuality as defined by discontinuities, we first reflect on how they themselves have been defined in the context of teams. In doing so, this raises the question as to the nature of boundaries, by comparison, and in particular boundaries created through organizational structures, such as teams. This leads us to consider the implications for team boundaries, and the discontinuities they create, as a result of both the increasing team interdependencies, stemming from increasing task complexity and dynamism, and the emerging effects of individuals simultaneously participating in multiple teams, or "multiteaming," a phenomena increasing supported by pervasive technology-mediated communication. These issues are then examined in the next section using case study data as the basis of our contribution to the further development of the concept of virtuality in teams.

Watson-Manheim, Chudoba, and Crowston (2002) have defined discontinuities as "gaps or a lack of coherence in aspects of work, such as work setting, task, and relations with other workers and managers" (p. 193). This reflects dictionary definitions of discontinuity as "to cease to continue" and discontinuous as "separated" or "interrupted by intervening spaces" (Schwarz et al., 1988). The sense of the term clearly relies considerably by what is meant by continuity. Hence, in the absence of discontinuities, there is an endurance of state, stability, a consistency that makes for predictability; no factors that would introduce or foretell of limits. Equally, it can also be felt to be a somewhat "objective" term, with no suggestion as to a cause or purpose for such a separation or interruption, but rather simply that it exists.

Some authors have incorporated the concept of discontinuities into that of boundaries (Espinosa et al., 2003); however, others, taking a more philosophical view, define them as "semiotic," signaling the borders or limits that end or interrupt continuities (Shields, 2006). Further, boundaries in a social context tend to signal somewhat abstract, socially constructed limits rather than real physical ones, although as with the physical borders of countries and even the boundaries of organizations and organizational units, which may have people at different physical locations, there is often a spatial dimension involved. For example, in one study, it was found that geographically dispersed individuals were creating impressions of boundaries in the way they acted and interacted within a computer-mediated environment (Panteli, 2003). Thus, socially constructed boundaries themselves can induce a variety of discontinuities rather than simply signaling those that exist.

In their study, Chudoba et al. (2005) include organizational discontinuities in their definition of virtuality, and make clear their inclusion of both intra- and interorganizational discontinuities, while making no explicit reference to teams themselves in this context. Building on the view that explicitly constructed boundaries, of the nature that occur within organizational structures, both signal and create a range of discontinuities, they suggest these are equally applicable to teams as they are to functional departments. In this sense, team boundaries are defined – not to create discontinuities per se – but to achieve perceived productivity associated with the continuities represented within a team by cohesion and coherence. By definition, through the term "bounded," there is a suggestion that what is within the boundary is restricted (Schwarz et al., 1988) in some way. However, this does not imply the same level of restriction suggested by the term "barrier," where the implication is that a boundary or separation not only exists, but is actively enforced in some manner, physical or otherwise.

By contrast, another form of discontinuity that arises naturally in social networks occurs as a result of a group's dense network of strong social relationships, often referred to as a clique (Granovetter, 1973). Within the clique, there is continuity in the form of shared beliefs, norms, and understanding stemming from the strong relationships. However, by definition the severely limited external relationships give rise to what is referred to in an organizational context as "structural holes," acting "like insulators in an electric circuit" (Burt, 1997, p. 353). To some extent then, we can see existing approaches to teams and the focus on teambuilding as an effort to artificially create cliques, sometimes bypassing existing ones in the process, with a given shared purpose. Well-defined team boundaries, in signaling members and nonmembers, therefore defines the location in which the "structural holes" are "dug" and therefore discontinuities in culture, norms, and work practices are created.

Accordingly, boundaries can be considered to represent a higher-level abstract concept that, by signaling separation, gives rise to discontinuities. In this sense, boundaries can give rise to discontinuities that can reinforce or cut across "natural" discontinuities in social networks, making barriers either easier or more difficult to create and maintain. Thus, the wealth of literature on cross-functional teams highlights the efforts to create continuities within team boundaries that cut across the natural discontinuities that occur between individuals with different functional backgrounds. Both in this and the wider team literature, the focus remains on team cohesion as a driver of performance and hence, the importance of well-defined team boundaries. Arguably this equates to higher barriers (or wider structural holes) with greater levels of internal coherence and cohesion (continuities), which, because of the separation, also have a greater potential for divergence from those continuities outside of the boundary (i.e., greater levels of cultural and practice discontinuity).

Traditionally, it is the focus on maintaining stability, or continuity over time, which ultimately makes the survival of cliques and the success of teams unsustainable in dynamic environments. In all but extreme circumstances, previously assigned resources cannot achieve the central purpose that defines a team. This is in part due to the fact that efficiency and effectiveness at higher levels than the individual team dictate that there are both task and resource dependencies between a team and its environment.

The extent and nature of the tasks and resources that a team shares with other teams in its context influences the extent and nature of its interteam dependencies. The resulting dynamics of the interdependencies with other teams means they are unlikely to succumb to simple decision-making and therefore will require some form of interaction, if not negotiation, across the team boundaries to be resolved. This in turn will require some level of shared understanding of the external context and with the other teams in order to make efficient and effective trade-offs. The result is a complex nested problem since the resources and time required for such exchanges are also time-dependent and affect the effectiveness and efficiency of each team and the wider system to which they belong.

The implication is that while intrateam coherence and cohesion might be important for achieving performance at the team level, when placed in the context of higher-level goals and associated performance measures this is unlikely to be the case. The nature of the team boundary, rather than its existence, plays an important role in balancing intra- and interteam coherence and cohesion in the way it affects discontinuities that emerge in culture, norms, and the shared understanding that underpins work practices. Thus, the separation that leads to beneficial specialization and inward focus on learning through the closing of internal gaps in knowledge can also lead to an unhealthy (from a performance perspective) level of resistance to alternative knowledge sets, which by their nature stem from outside the boundary that has created the discontinuity. Such a challenge to continuity of culture, norms, shared understanding, and work practices within the team also represents the prospect of change or a temporal discontinuity. Arguably, the higher the barriers formed by team boundaries, the longer the internal stability, but the greater the potential divergence from other teams in the same environment and hence the increased temporal discontinuity, the greater the subsequent challenge of reintegrating the team with its context.

The twin trends toward more complex and equivocal tasks and specialized resources means that teams are increasingly interdependent, and for the purposes of efficiency, this growing band of individuals with specialist expertise must dynamically "multitask" and "multiteam," enabled by their communication technology (Chudoba et al., 2005), according to the changing needs of the tasks and teams. Both multitasking and multiteaming have implications for the boundaries associated with tasks and teams and the extent to which discontinuities are created (see Figure 8.1).

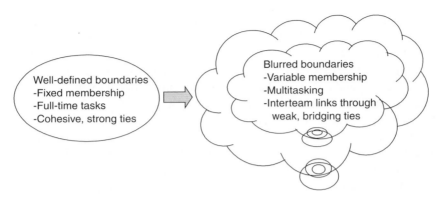

Figure 8.1 Multitasking and multiteaming effects on teams

Arguably, in some regards with teams sharing common team members, the boundary creates less of a discontinuity than in teams with different members. This could be through reduced identification with a particular team and hence perhaps lower intrateam cohesion at the expense of higher interteam cohesion. This not only affects performance but perhaps the measurement of performance. Multitasking and multiteaming helps balance efficiency and performance robustness in dynamic environments through the flexible sharing of expensive resources across teams rather than dedicating them to one. However, it also significantly complicates the task of attributing resource inputs and team outcomes in team-level analyses since the benefits accrue when looking across the teams sharing the resources.

At an individual level multitasking and multiteaming offer the potential to broaden the number and nature of boundary spanners improving the integration of interdependent teams. Conversely it increases the problem of relying on specialist resources that, when not identifying with and engaging with a team, become constraints either on the team itself or, as a result of boundary spanning role, on the relationships with other interdependent teams. So, while, for example, individuals who are central and identified closely with their team might also identify closely with the wider goals of those teams as a whole, because their team is central to the network of teams. However, success of the whole might be significantly affected by the majority of individuals in noncentral teams in the network, some of whom might also lie at the periphery of a number of such peripheral teams and be multiteaming between them. The limits to the benefits of multitasking and multiteaming are therefore likely to be approached as the complexity of team interdependencies stemming from task and resource dependencies increases. In this scenario, it can be anticipated that individuals might either revert to identifying only with a single team or with the organization as a whole. If generalized, this would result in an organization either of small teams operating independently without access to the resources they need, and with little regard to the wider organizational goals, or an organization with strong cohesion around a broad set of organizational goals, but with no means or ability to translate them into actions to achieve organizational goals.

Existing work at the team and sub-team level in the virtual team literature reflects aspects of these issues that suggest somewhat paradoxical strategies toward the partitioning of tasks across remote team members. On the one hand, analyses of micro-level interactions led some (Braha, 2002; Ramesh and Dennis, 2002) to suggest that technology-mediated interactions should be minimized by partitioning tasks such that the inter-dependencies requiring rich interactions are performed face-to-face. This reflects the research suggesting that technology-mediated communications are "lean" (Daft and Lengel, 1986), with a limited ability to transmit social cues and hence create the sense of social presence on which higher-level social relationships can be built (Sproull and Kiesler, 1986). As such, this appears to support a traditional approach to team-building, based on well-defined, spatial boundaries creating local cohesion ahead of overall team cohesion or, for larger tasks, intrateam cohesion over interteam cohesion. However, others advocate the opposite (Hertel, Konradt, and Orlikowski, 2004), arguing that by maximizing the technology-mediated interactions, capitalizing on phenomena such as "swift trust" (Jarvenpaa, Knoll, and Leidner, 1998), relationships and shared understanding can be built that are not constrained by spatially well-defined boundaries. In this case, it is argued that although such relationships may take longer to develop, this investment will pay back in terms of the flexibility, it responds to changes in the task more quickly than traditional teams.

Further, such insights can also be drawn from the organizational level, where an exploration of the structures adopted by incumbent firms in light of environmental change in the shape of the internet and World Wide Web (Siggelkow and Levinthal, 2003) also suggest similar and paradoxical approaches to the boundaries between existing businesses and the new internet and Web-based activities. On the one hand, where a firm's activities were identified as nondecomposable, a decentralized approach with the new activities being autonomous followed by subsequent reintegration was found to yield the highest long-term performance. However, on the other hand, where the firm's activities were decomposable, the creation of temporary "unnecessary" interdependencies yielded the best long-term performance.

The study of such paradoxes in management suggests that although thinking can be developed by keeping the opposing views separate, it is possible, as is the case here, to use a new perspective "to eliminate their opposition" (Poole and van de Ven, 1989, p. 565). Accordingly, we adopt a perspective of virtuality that enables face-to-face and technology-mediated interaction to be viewed as complementary, producing new effects in teams. The resulting concept of virtuality based on discontinuities helps draw our attention to these emergent effects of the combined use of face-to-face communications and technology-mediated communications, in particular their role in changing the nature of the discontinuities created by boundaries.

In the next section, the exploration of these insights in the context of data from a case study yields both illustrative examples of these insights and further suggestions as to the development of this thinking.

Case study of virtuality in teams: an interorganizational "virtual center of excellence"

Continuing with the organizational context of the team, we explore here a case study of a UK government-funded interorganizational "virtual center of excellence" to further develop insights into'the boundaries and discontinuities of virtuality beyond those of space and time. The benefit of choosing this context is the extent of virtual teamwork, which we can subsequently draw on and then further develop in the discussion of the findings.

Given the emphasis in this work on the importance of boundaries and context, we start by outlining the research setting and its boundaries before going on to briefly describe how the data was collected and the approach to its use in this chapter. Thus, despite the wider purpose of the research from which the data is drawn, we confine ourselves here to discussing the nature of the discontinuities and boundaries within the setting as a basis for revisiting virtuality in the broader discussion in the next section.

Research setting and approach

Initially selected as a case study setting to examine how virtuality in teams contributes value to organizations through the development of teamwork, the setting of a UK government-funded interorganizational entity, comprised of governmental, industrial, and academic partners, presented an opportunity to capture evidence on an early stage of interorganizational development. Set up to conduct research into a specific area of emerging technology, it formed part of a program described by the UK government as creating "virtual centers of excellence"; as such the particular organization studied is referred to here as "the VCE."

The fourth of four similar such organizations focused on different areas of research and technology, the VCE was part of a program created by one government department in response to a wider, longer-term government initiative to improve the exploitation of the broad-based research conducted within academic and commercial organizations. The VCE, while focusing on its own specific area of research and technology, also differed in one important way from the three other organizations in the program. In addition to undertaking research in its domain, it was also researching the needs and challenges of integrating its own research and the associated technology developments from it, into usable systems. The VCE therefore represented an opportunity to access not just an increasingly common form of interorganizational work and its embedded teams, but also those teams and sub-teams that formed within each of the partner organizations.

Funded for an initial three-year period, there was an option for this VCE to be extended to six years. The partnering nature of the program was emphasized by the requirement of participating consortium members to make "in kind" contributions up to the value of the government's funding. This could take a number of forms, from human resources in research or the management of it, to the use of specialist equipment such as simulators, software or demonstration equipment.

The government department running the program ran a bidding competition to select a primary commercial partner to establish and operate the VCE. Through this competition, which took some 18 months to complete, a number of consortia emerged and were reduced to shortlists of four and then two before final selection. Formally established in January 2005, with the signing of contracts with the prime contractor, it was not until September 2005 that the majority of the commercial and academic research providers had been contracted and begun work. The data collection, which began in June 2005 and continued for a year, covered this crucial stage of the VCE's development.

The strategy of the consortium winning the competition involved creating and developing a portfolio of research projects within an environment that both encouraged collaboration and proactively guided the direction of the research, where appropriate. Their aim was to use both routes to develop linkages between projects to create exploitable knowledge and technologies. The structure reflected this strategy with the portfolio of research activities, proposed by a mix of consortium members, academic

		Research teams						Integration team
		T1	T2	T3	T4	T5	T6	
Board and Management team members	Prime Dept 1							✓
	Prime Dept 2	✓	✓		✓			
	Prime Dept 3		✓					
	CM 1		✓					
	CM 2	✓			✓			
	CM 3					✓		
	CM 4						✓	✓
	CM 5							✓
Research providers only	Uni 1	✓	✓	✓	✓			
	Uni 2		✓	✓	✓	✓	✓	
	Uni 3	✓		✓				
	Uni 4						✓	✓
	OC 1		✓		✓			
	OC 2			✓				
	OC 3					✓		
	OC 4		✓					

Figure 8.2 Involvement of major participants in VCE virtual teams

Notes:
Prime dept: Major department within the prime contractor
    CM: Consortium member
    Uni: University research provider
    OC: Other commercial research provider

institutions, and other (nonconsortium member) commercial organizations, managed in six research teams (see Figure 8.2).

A further "integration" team was to create the environment for collaboration, by building the input and mechanisms for identifying and developing linkages between research activities, and by developing the understanding of how to integrate these types of technology. The seven members of the consortium that participated in the bid to operate the VCE each led one of the seven teams, and the individuals leading each team were also members of the VCE's management team. Leading the management team was an experienced technical director who, although independent of the consortium members, had a long career in the industry, supported by a program manager and an administrative staff. The management team, in turn, reported to a board, where a senior representative from each consortium member sat alongside two representatives from the UK government department funding the VCE. The VCE program manager was an employee of the prime contractor and was the only full-time member of the management team.

The data and analysis drawn on for this chapter formed only a part of the case study, whose broader aim lay in understanding the value of virtuality to organizations, and had employed an interpretivist approach using a number of frameworks to guide the work (Miles and Huberman, 1994). In accordance with this decision, qualitative data collection methods were used to analyze various data sources, including: documentation, both formal documentation, such as reports, and informal documentation, such as e-mail interactions; direct observation of formal monthly management meetings, quarterly board meetings, biannual team workshops, and various informal meetings, discussions, and conference calls; and semi-structured interviews. The informal meetings, discussions, semi-structured interviews, and e-mail interactions with participants presented opportunities to gather data on unobservable events, as well as to triangulate or sometimes explicitly validate evidence and our interpretations of it.

Our approach to the examination of the case study for this chapter, as with the purpose of case study itself, also reflected that favored by Miles and Huberman (1994). As such, we drew on the insights gained through our *a priori* thinking, in the form of the concept of virtuality defined by discontinuities, to structure our initial examination of the data. Then in an iterative process, the emerging results of the analysis were used to both inform and guide the ongoing thinking as further data was explored.

Findings

Using the insights from the perspective of virtuality in teams as discontinuities, the most immediate and noticeable results from the case study were the sheer complexity of the boundaries and discontinuities within the VCE. In addition to the extent of the organizational boundaries themselves, there were also familiar differences to be found between groups of organizations from governmental, academic, and industrial contexts, which could also be recognized as still higher-level discontinuities. This complexity is illustrated by the organizational level, with a formal picture of the VCE (see Figure 8.3) drawn from the formal contractual documentation identifying the nature of the participants. However, as the exploration moved through from the formal to the more informal data, it revealed just how incomplete and simplified even this picture was.

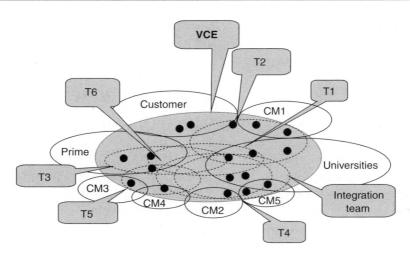

Figure 8.3 Illustration of top-level VCE complexity

Notes:
  CM: Consortium member
T1–7: VCE teams

Delving into this detail revealed for example, that both the UK government and the prime contractor, as major organizations, interacted in the VCE not through a single operational unit, but rather through a series of them. Each had a different role within their organization and the informal data revealed different perspectives, objectives, culture, etc. These were carried into their roles in the VCE. Although also spatially separate in most cases, it was the internal divisions and differing perspectives, which could often be attributed to differences in functional or role specialization, that created discontinuities. Drilling down to greater levels of detail it was evident, for example, that although engineers had shared perspectives and understanding at some levels, depending on their specialization, at further levels of detail these perspectives and understanding differed and represented a discontinuity. Thus, for example, the team leader of T1 informally described herself as being "on the same wavelength regarding complex systems" as another, informal, member of the management team. However, while she shared an understanding of the role of synthetic environments (complex computer simulations) "if not their exact nature" with another team leader, she did not agree with his perspective on a central concept within the VCE's research domain.

Equally, however, although in some cases member organizations were identified as separate entities, and therefore provided leaders for research teams, who participated in the management team and on the board, they were in three cases major operating divisions of the prime contractor, and, in two other cases, were partially owned or cofunded by the prime contractor. Further, these factors were dynamic despite the stability of the VCE structure itself. For example, during the first year of the VCE, one of the consortium members that had been partially owned by the prime contractor became fully owned, while yet another that had been partially owned by the prime contractor became independent.

These types of organizational histories and evolution also affected the extent of preexisting relationships that crossed organizational boundaries. Hence, for example, although the VCE technical director was independent, he had both worked for the government, in the predecessors to the department now funding the program, and through mergers and acquisitions, he now worked for companies that comprised elements of the prime contractor and other consortium members' businesses. Other individuals within the consortium member organizations had similar backgrounds. However, discontinuities were not confined to commercial organizations, with academics also reporting closer working relationships with those who they shared a history or particular expertise or interest, rather than those they shared a location; as one university professor put it: "I have more in common with [a group] in Cambridge than with [a group] who are just down the corridor."

In addition, evidence of the artificial creation of discontinuities through the imposition of boundaries in the form of the six research teams of the VCE structure were being recognized by the end of the first year, when a questionnaire reported the perception of links within and between team members:

T6 Leader: "most [researchers] have only identified opportunities [to link their work] with [tasks] in their [team]."

VCE Technical Director: "it's a reflection of the fact that they know only the [tasks] in their [teams] from the workshops."

T3 Leader: "Yes, we've been constraining ourselves to intra-[team] discussions."

The nature of the way in which research tasks were developed and defined in commercial contracts between the VCE and, in most cases, individuals rather than groups of research providers, appeared to reinforce these discontinuities. The T5 team leader commented, in answer to questions regarding the lack of interaction of some researchers within and across the research teams, that "it's not surprising, they've bid a piece of work and they're focused on delivering it, everything else is additional."

This represented a key concern for the VCE in that, while there were contracts that contained elements of predefined interaction on specific tasks between different organizations, the research nature of the work meant that there was considerable uncertainty as to how the tasks might develop, and which interactions among participants would be important. Inherently it was difficult to capture such issues in contracts and so flexibility was required on the part of those involved to be prepared to work to some extent outside of their contracts. While at a high level, the commercial or academic nature of the research providers had an effect on this, at a lower level the prior experience and therefore the relationships of groups and individuals with one another was apparent as a factor in mitigating the effects of discontinuities created by formal mechanisms such as contracts.

Turning to the individual level, the VCE provided considerable evidence of multitasking and multiteaming, with all but the program manager and a number of researchers having tasks and participation in VCE as just one part of their jobs. However, even in the case of the program manager and the researchers, the fact that their parent organizations had a distinct interest in their work meant that this created, at a minimum, an additional reporting task alongside that for the VCE itself. Multitasking, with potentially conflicting influences where it also represented multi-teaming, was therefore both a cause and a consequence of the complex boundaries and discontinuities represented by the level of virtuality in the VCE's teams. This manifested itself in slightly different forms depending, for example, on the extent to which the VCE was a "core" task perhaps among two or three others; a "near-core" task with less demanding time requirements; or a peripheral task requiring intermittent or low-levels of activity, for example mentoring or reviewing. From the team perspective, such multitasking of individuals altered the team boundary's effect through the nature of the discontinuity it created.

In addition to this was a temporal dimension. This stemmed from team members who began work before their contracts were in place or continued to interact with the VCE when they had, according to their contracts, completed it and were no longer officially part of the VCE. In some cases, such as in the instance of the T6 team lead, individuals also "rejoined" to undertake further tasks. Once again, although such changes are not unusual in organizations, technology-mediated communication can be seen, from this evidence, to affect them in such a way as to more fundamentally change our conception and understanding of a team's temporal boundaries. As such we now move on, in the next section, to discuss these illustrations and findings and the manner in which they extend our thinking on virtuality.

Discussion

Adopting the concept of discontinuities in our understanding of virtuality presented us with the opportunity to explore the nature of virtuality beyond those discontinuities most commonly associated with the term "virtual," that is, space and time. By choosing to undertake this exploration in an organizational context, we were able to draw on the literature from virtual team research, which is comparatively strong in this emerging field. Following this with an examination of data from a case study that features a complex interorganizational "virtual center of excellence" provided illustrative support of the insights into discontinuities, as well as suggesting further key considerations as regards this concept. To this extent, the VCE case study highlighted the manner in which the particularly pertinent discontinuity of the team boundary itself brought this into focus as central to the concept of virtuality in teams, and at the same time illustrates perhaps one of the potentially positive effects that virtuality offers to wider society.

The case study found that the multilevel nature of discontinuities within teams, and those induced by explicitly produced boundaries, is highly complex. Where team boundaries, or in a wider social context those of groups, might once have been well defined through physical presence in space and time, the lack of such an apparent continuity among members and clear discontinuity in space and time with nonmembers means that these boundaries signal and create intangible discontinuities. As such, these "boundary-induced" discontinuities can develop at a number of levels, interacting with one another and sometimes with discontinuities that have emerged, for example through differences in shared interests, in paradoxical ways. One effect of this, for example, is the situation where individuals, although physically present, interact with their co-located team colleagues as well as across space and time with colleagues in other teams. In this regard, the complexity of all of the teams' boundaries results in the development of much less abrupt discontinuities since greater interaction takes place across them. In the extreme, where the complexity is such that team boundaries have no affect on the behavior of individuals, that is, the formal structures are ignored, the vacuum is likely to be filled by the emergence of some form of informal group or team structure. Depending on the basis of this emergence, such a group or team's characteristics may provide a good fit with the short-term demands of its context. However, by definition some form of discontinuity with that context develops as the group emerges. Hence, just as with a formalized team, there will be a need to span this discontinuity if the group is to respond to contextual changes.

Accordingly, viewing the VCE case study, in terms of the discontinuities identified by Chudoba et al. (2005) as defining virtuality suggests that the level of complexity of these discontinuities adds a further dimension to the concept. In the VCE the complexity stems from both the sheer number of organizational units and subunits that the VCE brings together, and from the diverse range of interests, expertise, and cultures of each. While the former are apparent from the formal data, the latter are revealed through the informal data. This illustrates the discontinuities created not by boundaries but through the strength of relationships built through previous experiences working together or through social relationships beyond work. Based on these insights, we suggest that the complexity of discontinuities is an additional factor to consider with regard to virtuality.

The VCE study also provided evidence of multitasking and multiteaming on the part of most team members. While this provided a bridge between the VCE and their own organizations, through legitimized interaction, integration, and access to resources, the internal boundaries of the research teams in the VCE still created discontinuities resulting in limited links between them. This was highlighted by two situations in which a team of co-located individuals, belonging to a single organization, were simultaneously also participating in multiple VCE research teams of non-co-located individuals. This legitimated boundary spanning therefore stood in contrast to the discontinuities that otherwise existed and highlights the importance of considering not just the existence but also the nature and antecedents in the context of virtuality.

The complex and equivocal nature of the individual research tasks undertaken by the VCE were at cross-purposes with the broader VCE aim of integrating research outputs into exploitable systems. The emergent nature of the research tasks meant that, in contrast to traditional approaches to assembling systems, no definitive predetermined systems configuration or implementation plan could be created. As such, the emergent property of a team's tasks and the implications this had for resource requirements and dependencies can also be considered as a form of discontinuity; in this case one of continuity or stability from the past through the present to the future. In this sense the scale of the discontinuity is represented by the level of uncertainty that there is regarding the future.

In addition to the mitigating effects of multiteaming and multitasking on the discontinuities created by team boundaries, these also apply to the temporal boundaries of the team. Thus, individuals doing multiteaming or multitasking on preparatory work in advance of the "official" start of a team, or undertaking work after the "official" disbanding of a team or after the completion of their work on a team, are working across the discontinuities created by the team's temporal boundaries.

The value of persistent social relations is constrained by their accessibility. Hence, in the past, where teams have been co-located and lacked anytime access to their relationships, the potential benefits of such networks have been more limited. Even today, where teams tend to be more "traditional" than virtual, by not only being co-located but also having "full-time" resources focused on the activities of that one team, their access to virtual space enables them to appropriate resources by using their other relationships. However, further still, where a team is less "traditional" with team members multitasking and multiteaming, they are likely to have both wider and greater access to appropriate resources from those environments. The benefit this provides is a mechanism for creating greater interteam cohesion; however, it is also recognized that this can come at the expense of intrateam cohesion.

Finally, expanding this concept to a societal level, the extent to which the boundaries of otherwise closed cliques become more porous suggests that there is the potential for greater cohesion to be created at a societal level. However for some, the founding of this cohesion in virtual space may be viewed negatively, particularly if it is at the expense of cohesion of communities in real spaces. Perhaps then, just as the cost of wider interteam cohesion is less intrateam cohesion, so the cost of wider societal cohesion is less cohesion in local communities. Of course, the answer to the even wider philosophical question of whether this shift is good for society depends upon the level at which you choose to ask the question.

Conclusions

The central aim of this chapter was to further develop the concept of virtuality, looking beyond the bridging of the discontinuities of space and time, bringing into focus the higher-level discontinuities associated in particular with the shared understanding that emerges in work practices and culture within organizations in general, and, specifically here, within teams themselves. It is argued that the adoption of this emerging concept of virtuality, defined by discontinuities, is justified on the grounds of a need to shift the focus of research in the field away from perspectives that implicitly view face-to-face and technology-mediated communication as substitutes, and instead enable the potentially complementary and emergent effects of their combined use to be examined. The resulting insights offer further understanding and opportunities for building the concept of virtuality by drawing on the extensive work on social capital. In particular, this points to exploring "structural holes" (Burt, 2000) in social networks as "natural" sources of discontinuities in culture, norms, and practices but also to the role of boundaries in artificially inducing such discontinuities and "weak ties" (Granovetter, 1973) in bridging them. This further leads to insights into factors such as "multiteaming" and "multitasking," which, enabled by the combining of face-to-face and technology-mediated communication, affect the nature of and extent of the discontinuities induced by boundaries.

The use of case study data to further explore these insights contributes both illustrations and further development in specifically identifying that both discontinuity complexity and the temporal aspects of team membership boundaries also need to be considered as factors affecting virtuality.

Implications for theory and practice

The shift toward a definition of virtuality that is not based on the use of technology-mediated communication has major implications for the development of theory and practice in this field. By adopting such a concept based on discontinuities, this chapter has revealed the complex, multilevel nature of such discontinuities beyond those of space and time commonly associated with the field. This, coupled with the insights regarding the relationship between boundaries and discontinuities, the temporal dimensions of boundaries and the mitigating effects of multitasking and multiteaming on boundaries, provides a basis for further theoretical development. Promising approaches here are likely to include further exploration using structuration theory (Giddens, 1993), the concept of social capital (Nahapiet and Ghoshal, 1998), and actor-network theory (ANT) (Lee and Hassard, 1999).

The practical implications of these insights equally lie in the shift of practitioner focus in organizations from purely technology-based management interventions to the consideration of how face-to-face and technology-mediated interactions can be used to support organizational activities. In this regard, it highlights that there are limits to the benefits of team cohesion, and therefore team-building, particularly where flexibility of resources is needed among teams to respond effectively to an uncertain and dynamic context. More broadly, in society as a whole, the implications are that the bridging of space and time brings into sharp relief the cognitive discontinuities seen in differences in culture, beliefs, values, and understanding. While in some instances these discontinuities are aligned with underlying spatial discontinuities, the increasing mobility of people, and the global reach of certain aspects of life, means that this is not always the case. Cognitive rather than physical distance in this sense is increasingly recognized as the basis for understanding what separates individuals and communities from one another. In this regard, the infinite landscape of virtual space is strewn with individuals and communities separated by their norms, values, interests, and understanding.

References

Bell, B.S., and Kozlowski, S.W.J. (2002) A Typology of Virtual Teams: Implications for Effective Leadership, *Group and Organization Management*, 27(1), 14–49.

Blanchard, A., and Horan, T. (2000) "Virtual Communities and Social Capital," in *Social Dimensions of Information Technology: Issues for the New Millenium*, D. G. Garson (Ed.), London: Idea Group Publishing, pp. 6–21.

Braha, D. (2002) Partitioning Tasks to Product Development Teams. *DETC '02, ASME 2002 International Design Engineering Technical Conferences*, Montreal, Canada.

Burt, R.S. (1997) The Contingent Value of Social Capital, *Administrative Science Quarterly*, 42, 339–365.

Burt, R.S. (2000) The Network Structure of Social Capital, *Research in Organizational Behavior*, 22, 345.

Chudoba, K.M., Wynn, E., Lu, M., and Watson-Manheim, M.B. (2005) How Virtual Are We? Measuring Virtuality and Understanding its Impact in a Global Organization, *Information Systems Journal*, 15(4), 279–306.

Daft, R.L., and Lengel, R.H. (1986) Organizational Information Requirements, Media Richness, and Structural Design, *Management Science*, 32, 554–572.

Espinosa, J.A., Cummings, J.N., Wilson, J.M., and Pearce, B.M. (2003) Team Boundary Issues Across Multiple Global Firms, *Journal of Management Information Systems*, 19, 157–190.

Giddens, A. (1993) *New Rules of Sociological Method*, Oxford: Polity.

Granovetter, M.S. (1973) The Strength of Weak Ties, *The American Journal of Sociology*, 78, 1360–1380.

Griffith, T.L., Sawyer, J.E., and Neale, M.A. (2003) Virtualness and Knowledge in Teams: Managing the Love Triangle of Organizations, Individuals, and Information Technology, *MIS Quarterly*, 27, 265–287.

Hertel, G., Geister, S., and Konradt, U. (2005) Managing Virtual Teams: A Review of Current Empirical research, *Human Resource Management Review*, 15, 69–95.

Hertel, G., Konradt, U., and Orlikowski, B. (2004) Managing Distance by Interdependence: Goal Setting, Task Interdependence, and Team-based Rewards in Virtual Teams, *European Journal of Work & Organizational Psychology*, 13, 1–28.

Jarvenpaa, S.L., Knoll, K., and Leidner, D.E. (1998) Is Anybody Out There? Antecedents of Trust in Global Virtual Teams, *Journal of Management Information Systems*, 14, 29.

Kirkman, B.L., and Mathieu, J.E. (2005) The Dimensions and Antecedents of Team Virtuality, *Journal of Management*, 31(5), 700–718.

Lee, N., and Hassard, J.S. (1999) Organization Unbound: Actor-Network Theory, Research Strategy and Institutional Flexibility, *Organization*, 6, 391.

Lipnack, J., and Stamps, J. (1997) *Virtual Teams: Reaching Across Space, Time, and Organizations with Technology*, John Wiley: New York.

Martins, L.L., Gilson, L.L., and Maynard, M.T. (2004) Virtual Teams: What Do We Know and Where Do We Go From Here?, *Journal of Management*, 30(6), 805–835.

Miles, M.B., and Huberman, M.A. (1994) *Qualitative Data Analysis: An Expanded Sourcebook*, Sage: Thousand Oaks, CA.

Nahapiet, J., and Ghoshal, S. (1998) Social Capital, Intellectual Capital, and The Organizational Advantage, *Academy of Management Review*, 23, 242.

Panteli, N. (2003) Virtual Interactions: Creating Impressions of Boundaries, in *Managing Boundaries in Organizations: Multiple Perspectives*, N. Paulsen and T. Hernes (Eds), Palgrave Macmillan: Hampshire.

Poole, M.S., and van de Ven, A.H. (1989) Using Paradox to Build Management and Organization Theories, *Academy of Management Review*, 14, 562.

Powell, A., Piccoli, G., and Ives, B. (2004) Virtual Teams: A Review of Current Literature and Directions for Future Research, *ACM SIGMIS Database*, 35(1), 6–28.

Ramesh, V., and Dennis, A.R. (2002) The Object-Oriented Team: Lessons for Virtual Teams from Global Software Development. *System Sciences, 2002. HICSS. Proceedings of the 35th Annual Hawaii International Conference on System Sciences*, pp. 212–221.

Schwarz, C., Davidson, G., Seaton, A., and Tebbit, V. (Eds) (1988) *Chambers English Dictionary*, Chambers: Cambridge.

Shields, R. (2006) Boundary-Thinking in Theories of the Present: The Virtuality of Reflexive Modernization, *European Journal of Social Theory*, 9, 223–237.

Siggelkow, N., and Levinthal, D.A. (2003) Temporarily Divide to Conquer: Centralized, Decentralized, and Reintegrated Organizational Approaches to Exploration and Adaptation, *Organization Science*, 14, 650–669.

Sproull, L., and Kiesler, S. (1986) Reducing Social Context Cues: Electronic Mail in Organisational Communication, *Management Science*, 32(11), 1492–1512.

Turoff, M. (1997) Virtuality, *Communications of the ACM*, 40(9), 38–43.

Watson-Manheim, M.B., Chudoba, K.M., and Crowston, K. (2002) Discontinuities and Continuities: A New Way to Understand Virtual Work, *Information Technology and People*, 15, 191–209.

Virtuality beyond organizations

CHAPTER 9

Building social identity through blogging

Patchareeporn Pluempavarn
and Niki Panteli

Introduction

The emergence of the internet has given opportunities for new virtual spaces to be developed and new communication tools to facilitate virtual interactions. These spaces and tools have enabled the emergence of online communities. Not only is the number of virtual communities increasing rapidly, but there is also an increase in the variety of community forms. One prominent new type is the blogging community. Blogs emerged around the late 1990s and are now a recent and important web-based form of communication, which has gained widespread popularity and mainstream use (Schiano et al., 2004). Recent estimates from blogcensus. net (NITLE Blog Census, 2006) place the number of blog sites at over 2.8 million. Blogs are frequently modified web pages in which dated entries are listed in reverse chronological sequence (Herring et al., 2005). They have been highlighted extensively in the popular media and have entered political campaigns, news organizations, businesses, and classrooms. Despite the fact that their popularity has grown exponentially, there is limited knowledge about how individual members identify themselves with such communities.

The study presented in this chapter will examine how bloggers' identities are influenced by the identities of the online communities that they participate in, and how bloggers themselves can influence their online communities. In doing so, this research adopts the theoretical framework of the characteristics of the social identity theory. In what follows, the theoretical underpinnings of the study are discussed, first with a review of the literature on virtual, online communities, and thereafter the concepts of identity and social identity are presented. The nature and characteristics of blogs and blogging communities are then identified and the research method used in the study is discussed. The findings show that there is a reciprocal relationship between bloggers' social identity and the identity of online communities, and that the characteristics of blogs enable this mutual influence to take place.

Virtual communities

Fernback and Thompson (1995, p. 8) define virtual communities as "social relationships forged in cyberspace through repeated contact within a specified boundary or place that is symbolically delineated by topic of interest." The words "online" and "virtual" have similar meaning and are used interchangeably. Rheingold (1993, p. 5) also defines virtual communities as "social aggregations that emerge from the [internet] when enough people carry on … public discussions long enough, with sufficient human feeling, to form webs of personal relationships in cyberspace." Commenting on the strength of the bond within virtual communities, Rheingold posits that:

> People in virtual communities use words on screens to exchange pleasantries and argue, engage in intellectual discourse, conduct commerce, exchange knowledge, share emotional support, make plans, brainstorm, gossip, feud, fall in love, find friends and lose them, play games, flirt, create a little high art and a lot of idle talk. People in virtual communities do just about everything people do in real life, but we leave our bodies behind. (1993, p. 5)

Although some people prefer to use their real names online, most internet users prefer to identify themselves by means of pseudonyms, which reveal varying amounts of personally identifiable information. In some online contexts, including internet forums, multiuser dungeons (MUDs), instant messaging, and massive multiplayer online games, users can represent themselves visually by choosing an avatar, an icon-sized graphic image. As other users interact with an established online identity, it acquires a reputation, which enables these users to decide whether the identity is worthy of trust.

Invisibility and, in some cases, a certain amount of anonymity are aspects of online identity. Its early development and historical and future importance were observed by Sherry Turkle (1995). She stated that internet identities involve simulations, experimentation, and taking things (and people) at interface value. It is this particular sensory communication, in taking each other at interface value, that results in an identity that is specific to the online environment (ibid.).

Accordingly, a study on the social identities within these groups is crucial to understand the communication interactions and influences between individuals and the blogging communities.

Identity and social identity

The concept of identity has been used in many disciplines throughout the social sciences, including psychology and philosophy, and also in the organizational and management fields. Generally, identity means "the characteristics, feelings or beliefs that distinguish people from others" (*Oxford Dictionary*, 2000). In the management field, identity has been found to be important because organizational identities influence people's perception of their work and behavior (Whetten, 1998).

The concept of identity is linked to the self-concept or self-identity. Self-concept is a person's mental and conceptual awareness, including physical, psychological, and social attributes. It has at least three major qualities to consider: it is learned, it is organized, and it is dynamic (Capozza and Brown, 2000). Therefore, an individual's identity is not static, but contextual and multifaceted.

An individual's identity entails both social and personal types. Social identity "results from the categorization of the world into ingroup and outgroup and the labelling of oneself as a member of the ingroup" (Tajfel, 1982, p. 2). On the other hand, personal identity includes the unique characteristics of the individual and their interpersonal relationships rather than intergroup comparison (ibid.). For the purpose of this study, in gaining a better insight on blogging communities, group membership and group identity will be discussed by using the social identity theory (SIT).

The most substantial contributions to the study of identity have grown out of the development of SIT, which was pioneered by Henri Tajfel and John Turner in the 1970s (Abrams and Hogg, 1990). This theory considers social identity as a core factor in an individual's self-concept. Tajfel (1984) defines social identity as "the individual's knowledge that he/she belongs to certain social groups together with some emotional and value significance to him/her of the group membership" (Abrams and Hogg, 1990, p. 2). Just as individuals strive to maintain a positive self-concept as unique personalities, they will attempt to achieve or maintain a positive social identity, an evaluation of the in-group as worthy, positive, and high in prestige. Social groups, as collections of individuals all strive to maintain a positive self-concept, perform a similar evaluative function by seeking to compare themselves positively against other groups. They typically do this by choosing a set of categories that allow them to compare themselves favorably with various out-groups.

Accordingly, SIT is concerned with individuals as a part of a social group, how they identify with the group, behave, and adopt shared attitudes to outsiders. Tajfel (1984) first sought to differentiate between those elements of self-identity derived from individual personality traits and interpersonal relationships (personal identity) and those derived from belonging to a particular group (social identity). Each individual is seen to have both personal and social identities, and each informs the individual as to who they are and what their identity entails. According to the social context, the salience of many identities for an individual will vary. Tajfel (ibid.) then postulates that social behavior exists on a spectrum from the purely interpersonal to the purely intergroup. Where personal identity is salient, the individual will relate to others in an interpersonal manner, dependent on their character traits and any personal relationships existing between the individuals. However, under certain conditions social identity is more notable than personal identity in self-conception, and, when this is the case, behavior is qualitatively different: it is group behavior.

Social identity involves three central ideas: categorization; identification; and comparison (McGarty et al., 1994). Individuals categorize objects in order to understand them. In a very similar way, they categorize people (including themselves) in order to understand the social environment. If they can assign them to categories it tells them things about people. Similarly, they find out things about themselves by knowing what categories they belong to. Individuals define appropriate behavior by reference to the norms of groups they belong to, but they can only do this if they can tell who belongs in their group.

Individuals identify with groups to which they perceive themselves to belong. Identification carries two meanings. Part of who they are is made up of their group memberships. Sometimes they think of themselves as group members and at other times they think of themselves as unique individuals. This varies situationally, so that they can be more or less a group member, depending upon the circumstances. What is crucial is that thinking of oneself as a group member and as a unique individual are both parts of self-concept. The first is referred to as social identity, the latter is referred to as personal identity. In SIT, the group membership is not something foreign, which is tacked onto the person, but is a real, true, and vital part of the person's character. In-groups are ones that individuals identify with, while out-groups are those with which they do not identify.

The third aspect that is involved in SIT is the notion of social comparison (Festinger's, 1975). The basic idea is that a positive self-concept is a part of normal psychological functioning. The idea of social comparison is that, in order to evaluate ourselves, we compare ourselves with similar others. Individuals can gain self-esteem by comparing themselves with others in their group, and they can also see themselves in a positive light by seeing themselves as a member of a prestigious group. Tajfel (1982) stated that group members compare their group with others in order to define their group in a positive way. Two ideas follow from this. One is positive distinctiveness. The idea is that people are motivated to see their own group as relatively better than similar (but inferior) groups. The other is negative distinctiveness, where groups tend to minimize the differences between the groups, so that their own group is seen favorably.

As blogs are created and shared online, the interaction and communication between the blogger and his/her audience are internet-mediated. Within these online communities bloggers can create a virtual identity, which may be different to their often concrete and co-located social identity. We explore this type of online or virtual social identity below with particular reference to the characteristics of blogs.

Blog and blogging

A blog is considered to be a new kind of asynchronous computer-mediated communication (CMC). It can be used in a variety of ways, but often as a personal journal or ongoing commentary about oneself (Herring, 2004; Huffaker, 2004; Halavais, 2002). Blog posts are primarily textual, but many include photographs and other multimedia contents. Though there are different types of blogs (Blood, 2002; Herring, 2004), most are interlinked in that they provide links to other sites on the internet. Many also are interactive, in that they invite and post commentary on their contents, which in turn provide a discussion on blog entries. Readers can leave a comment on a post, which can correct errors or contains their opinion on the post or the post's subject. Most of the research in this area identifies the characteristics of the blogging phenomenon. For example, research conducted by Herring et al. (2005) classifies blogs by their various purposes, such as knowledge sharing, social interaction, and self-expression. In addition, due to their informal and dynamic means of sharing information, it has also been argued that blogs can support communities of practice (Silva, Mousavidin, and Goel, 2006).

Compared with other forms of CMC, blogs have distinctive technological features that set them apart (Herring, 2004), including an ease of use because users do not need to know web programming languages in order to publish on the internet, and opportunities for others to provide comments for each blog post. Such features are especially important for constructing online identity (Huffaker and Calvert, 2005). The reasons for this are threefold. First, the lack of expertise needed to create or maintain blogs makes the application more accessible, regardless of gender and age. Second, the ability to record blog posts creates a way to track previous impressions and expressions; thus, constructing identity can be a continual referential process. Finally, when blog software offers ways to provide feedback or link to other bloggers, this can foster a sense of group relationship. In short, blogs represent a new medium for computer-mediated communication and offers insights in the way bloggers present themselves online, especially in terms of self-expression and group relationships, both of which impact the construction of identity.

In order to differentiate their blogs from others, users create and express their unique characteristics through their blogs in forming their identity – the total conception that people have of who they are. For example, Cohen (2005) conducted empirical studies of photoblogs. They tried to position photographs, photography, and photoblogs in a complex relationship with one another. They found that photoblogs incorporate, and in turn are incorporated by, at least four significant entities: the self of photographer; a potential audience; activities (taking photographs); and the technologies that operate in and around these entities. Further, Schiano et al. (2004) conducted an ethnographic study of blogging as a form of personal expression and communication. They characterize a number of blogging practices, and consider blogging as personal journaling. They found that blogs are important as individualistic, intimate forms of self-expression and communication, and found blogging to be a versatile medium, which can be used in a similar way to an online diary, personal chronicle or newsletter and much more. Another ethnographic study of blogging is by Nardi, Schiano, and Gumbrecht (2004), which focuses on blogs written by individuals or small groups, with limited audiences. They discuss bloggers' motivation, the quality of social interactivity that characterizes the blogs they studied and the bloggers' relationships to the audience. They consider the way bloggers relate to the known audience of their personal social networks as well as the wider "blogosphere" of unknown readers. They then make design recommendations for blogging software based on their findings.

According to Nardi, Schiano, and Gumbrecht (ibid.), the relationship to the known and unknown audience is the key for bloggers to maintain and characterize their blogs. By blogging and interacting with other bloggers, individuals with similar interests are able to form a specific group or community, and to identify themselves with that particular group. Individuals can be members of different groups, depending on their interests. However, by trying to differentiate itself from others, each group will form unique characteristics, including their own rules and norms. These unique characteristics can be seen as the identities of their specific community, which may exercise an influence on the group members' identities, which are social identities. We explore these issues further with the following empirical data.

The research site

A blogging site has been carefully chosen for this study. One of the researchers has a keen interest in photography, and a blogging site with this interest was recommended by a friend. After exploring and reading other blogger reviews about the site, the researchers decided to participate in the site, which is called "Multiply." This site has been open to the public since March 2004 and it is very popular among amateur photographers because it offers a good service for posting photographs. Other reasons for choosing this blogging site include: Multiply calls itself as "social-networking" site, which encourages bloggers to build their own network and links with the community; the number of bloggers participating in the site is still smaller than the pioneer or former blogging sites, which make it easier to join and participate than enter a large-scale site because there are not too many people who already have their own network; the site provides a variety of features, such as uploading music, videos, and photographs, reviews of films and restaurants, a calendar, and links to other blogging and sites.

Methods

In order to gain richness in our data, qualitative methods were used. The open nature of the methods enables the researchers to gain a wide range of data, which is useful in understanding the various aspects of complex phenomenon (Saunders, Lewis, and Thornhill, 2003). Documentation, interviewing, and participant observation were the main methods adopted. The latter in particular has played a key role in the research. With participant observation, the researcher participates in the activities of the people who are observed to become a member of their group and try to get the basis of "what is going on" in the selected social settings.

For the purpose of this study, one of the researchers joined the site and for several months (March–July 2006) she participated in the community's activities, posting blogs, videos, photographs, and making comments on others bloggers. For this part of the project, the researcher adopted the complete participation role by not revealing her identity as a researcher. From July, the researcher adopted the participant observer role by revealing her identity as a researcher. This was done by posting a welcome message in her personal blog with a clarification of her status and the purpose of this research. However, the researcher still participated in the same activities with new people and people within the social network that had been established while adopting the participant role.

Giving her personal interest in photography, the researcher not only posted on her own personal site but also participated in the three photographic groups (Greatest Photos, Photography and Europe Travel) to avoid being influenced by and attached to an individual group. The researcher visited the site almost everyday and posted blogs, photographs, and comments for others. At the end of the research period, the researcher had posted five blogs, one video, five events in calendar, 120 photos, and 86 comments.

Further to these, semi-structured interviews were used to collect primary data. Some of the questions were prepared in advance (e.g., "When and why did you start blogging?") in order to collect core data and to allow the interviewees to talk about their experiences, express their thoughts and opinions, while other questions were asked to gain more insight into users' experiences with the blogging community (e.g., "Can you give me an example of what you have just said?"). Following a posting on the Discussion Forum, seven bloggers volunteered to take part in the study. The interviews were undertaken via instant messaging (IM) by arrangement, due to the geographical dispersion between the interviewer and the interviewees.

Results

Multiply.com and its features

Multiply (http://multiply.com) was launched in March 2004. It calls itself a "social-networking" site. It currently has approximately 3 million registered users (Girard, 2006). Although its traffic is miniscule compared to MySpace, which has over 75 million users, Multiply members generate more than 10 million e-mail alerts and other messaging to the network members in a three-month period. Users are actively sharing digital photo albums, blogs, restaurant and film reviews, and classified and calendar events. This represents the activity of Multiply's members.

Multiply's founder, Peter Pezaris, stated that, while social-networking sites were gaining popularity as an easier way to meet new people, there was a problem with blogs; everyone was writing them but no one was really reading them. Therefore, the philosophy of Multiply is to take the slower approach and gradually expand its network, in the hope of building strong relationships. Compared with MySpace or Facebook, it focuses on customer loyalty more than the number of people within the network (Business2blog, 2006). The relationships in smaller, specialized networks such as Multiply tend to be more substantial and long-lasting than those forged in larger networks, according to Charlene Li, principal analyst at Forrester Research (Girard, 2006).

On Multiply, users can create a personal web page with a blog, upload photos and videos, post reviews, and have a personal calendar; everything that users would expect from a social-networking site (Metz, 2006). But with the fierce competition in the market and because they are free of charge, these blogging sites try to attract new users by introducing unique services not offered by other competitors. As Multiply is focusing on providing a relevant and enriched environment, it offers users a relationship identity label (a security and privacy tool) and live replies (a real-time comment tool). Multiply includes various features, as shown below.

- *Blogs*: On the first section of the user's personal site, he/she can post a running blog. This feature also enables users to add their blog, importing it from Livejournal, Blogger, and Typepad. Blog posts are listed in reverse chronological order. The composing device is similar to composing e-mail. Users can edit font style and color, and can include emotion icons and links. Users can also upload up to three images and create polls in their blogs.
- *Photos*: Multiply gives users a choice of photograph uploaders. There are three uploading tools, which are a Java-based uploader, an ActiveX uploader, and an HTML uploader. Moreover, the user can also add unlimited photographs from other sites such as Shutterfly, Yahoo Photos, Flickr, Kodak Gallery, ImageShack, or any web page with a URL.
- *Videos and Music*: The user can upload unlimited video and music files using HTML tools, and can also add video from YouTube and Google Video.

- *Calendar, Reviews, and Links*: The user can personalize their site with these features. Users can set event lists in their calendar, review and rate films or restaurants, and post links in their sites.

Multiply tries to link its services with other popular sites, for example, linking its blog service with Blogger, photos with Yahoo Photos, and video with YouTube. Peter Pexaris, president and founder of Multiply, believes that this is one of the strengths of its services (Multiply.com, 2006). Moreover, Multiply members have the ability to control who is a part of their network, and what content their network can view. The user can make their photos available to the general public, MySpace style, or the user can limit access to certain e-mail addresses with the master list of contacts. Furthermore, every contact in a user's list will have a relationship label. When the user adds someone as a contact, the user can choose from 50 different relationships types – cousin, wife, sister, brother, schoolmate.

At the beginning of 2006, Multiply launched a new feature called "Live Replies," which is a messaging component that allows users to discuss their media, such as blogs, photographs, and video, in real-time. When multiple users are viewing a blog entry or photo album, replies added to the thread instantly appear on the screen, turning the correspondence into live chat, similar to IM or a chatroom client. This feature, plus the user's content, generates lively discussion and active feedback from people in the user's network.

In addition to personal sites, Multiply provides groups services, sorted by categories. Members can choose to participate "in-groups" or create new groups, depending on their interests, and one can be member of more than one group. There are over 4,000 groups on the site and the number of members in each group ranges from 0 to 7,120. Group members can post photographs, video, links, journals, music, and reviews. The features in-groups are similar to the member's personal page.

The researcher selected three English language-based groups or communities in which to participate: Greatest Photos; Photography; and Europe Travel. The first two groups belong in the hobbies and crafts category, and the third is in the places and travel category. The reason for choosing to participate in these communities is the researcher's personal interests in photography. These groups are different in size and purpose. Details of the groups are presented below:

- *Greatest Photos* (ilovephotos.multiply.com): This is a group for posting pictures taken by members, and for giving and receiving feedback. This group was created in March 2005 and there are now 414 members. Most of the media posted in the site are photographs, of which there are approximately 750.

- *Photography* (photograph1.multiply.com): This group was created in August 2004 and has 876 members. It focuses on the techniques of taking a photograph, discussing what camera the member uses (digital or film) and composition and lighting. It focuses more on the professional aspect of photography. Around 1,500 photos are posted on the site for professional comments, and there are 100 written posts asking about photography techniques, and posing photo-related questions. Personal sites are also introduced.
- *Europe Travel* (europetravel.multiply.com): This is the largest group of the three selected communities. It has 5,151 members. It focuses on places and attractions, how to travel, and places to stay in Europe. The reason that it has also been selected is because many people also post photographs of places to which they have traveled, and so the group is similar to other two groups in this way.

Analysis

Combining the data from observation and the interviews, there are many interesting points to present. To begin with, the reasons or motivations for joining a social-networking site and creating a personal site are discussed. Most people said that they knew about Multiply through their friends, for example, Interviewees 1 and 6. Others wanted to give comments to their friends, who were Multiply members, and they therefore needed to register before publishing their comments. They then continued using the services. Interviewee 4 found Multiply by searching for reviews in other IT sites because he needed a place to store and present his work. After trying the services for a month, he decided to pay to be a platinum member. Interviewee 2 wanted to share his life with his family and friends because he works away from home, while Interviewee 7 is a professional freelance photographer. He uses this site as a showroom/gallery of his work for others to see and to decide if they are interested in hiring him.

There seem to be different reasons for the bloggers to join the different communities within Multiply. One is the ability to meet new friends of a range of ages and in a variety of locations. Another reason is that they want to meet people who have similar interests, and exchange information with these people. In Multiply, there are many groups for users to choose from, and every group has it unique characteristics. For example, Photography is the group that focuses on commenting on members' photographs, discussing photographic techniques, and sharing up-to-date information about photography issues, while the photographs in Europe Travel are focused on places and attractions in Europe. A user can be a member of more than one group, depending on his or her interests. The member duration in each group also depends on users and experiences gained from participating in the group. Most interviewees said that, at first, they needed to explore a group by looking at previous posts before deciding to become a member of that group. In some cases, more than one group was explored. After a period of time, they decided which group was the best match with their interests. Users may post in one group more than another, depending on the content they have. Most of the users will screen their contents first before posting it in the group site. They feel an attachment to groups and members within the groups.

Comparing the individual sites and their blogging features with other CMC tools, many interviewees agreed that having the site is an easy way to keep in contact with others, especially family and friends. With the collaboration of technologies, this social-networking site adopts good points from other CMCs. Many of these features make communication more convenient, such as automatic alerts to users' contact list when there is new media posted, and it is very suitable for communication between people who are geographically dispersed. However, one of the limitations of Multiply is that the audience needs to sign up, create an account, and be included in the social contact list of members in order to respond to the posted media. Therefore, most of the interviewees use both their blogging sites and other CMCs in order to communicate with others.

Most of the interviewees started their social networks with a person they knew first, such as a member of their family, a friend or a business contact. This online network then has enabled them to communicate on a broad scale with the people they already know, either directly or indirectly. According to the interviewees, the relationship identity label is a very useful feature of Multiply because they can divide their contacts according to how close they are and they can also select who can see each media they have uploaded. This gives them control on how they interact with other community members.

Discussion

Blogs have been chosen in this study, for in-depth investigation, not only because this CMC tool has gained widespread popularity but also because of the social interaction that occurs within blogging communities. Our aim has been to explore the relationship between blogs and social identity creation. As the literature suggests, individual identity consists of personal and social identities. At first, bloggers may create a blog dependent on their personal identities or characteristics. At the same time, the presence of their first created site tends to be influenced by their friends or people who invited them into the blogging site. Some bloggers may observe how others organize their sites and read what others have posted. Unlike other types of online communities where users can hide their real identity, in blogging communities users can actively choose not only to reveal their identity but also to develop it further. In what follows, we use the three main elements of social identity that were found in the literature in order to understand the emergence of social identity within the blogging phenomenon.

Categorization

Several bloggers enter the sites with the purpose of finding new friends outside of their real social network. They need to explore which communities they want to enter based on which will match their interests. Most bloggers act first as an observer, before deciding to enter specific communities as members. While observing, the bloggers categorize the communities into perceived and unique characteristics, and then choose to participate in specific groups. After that, they introduce themselves to the communities and start participating by posting photos, journals, or comments in order to create interaction, communication, and discussion. Their actions will be based on the norms of the group that they participate in and those they feel they belong to. Accordingly, it is found that bloggers' own social identity influences their blogging choices and actions but this in turn is influenced by the group actions as they begin to spend more time within the group.

Identification

After participating in the group for a while, the blogger may feel attached to the group and their identity will be affected by the group. These social identities can be shown in users' personal sites. For example, if they are a member of a specific group, over time the content of their personal site will be similar to the group site's content. On the other hand, group identities can also change due to the content that members have shared on the group site. For instance, several members in Europe Travel group posted information about their home country; therefore, the group was used by members not only to reveal their national identity but also to promote their country's tourism and the group was perceived to be more of an information provider.

Comparison

Moreover, bloggers can be members of more than one group, depending on their interests. Each group that has different characteristics and identities may have a different degree of influence on the blogger. When posting photographs, journals, and comments in specific groups, most users screen their content before posting as a way of ensuring that this matches with the identities that they perceive the group to have. Therefore, in different groups, one blogger may post different content in a different style related to that specific group. For example, comments in the Photography group will focus more on photographic techniques such as composition and lighting, while comments in Greatest Photos are mostly complimentary and entertaining. These show the perception of group members toward the characteristics or identities of each community. On the other hand, these actions also reflect members' identities, which were affected by the social interaction within the groups.

Conclusion

It follows from the findings of this exploratory study that the content of each blogging site, when contextualized, provides rich information about the blogger, related to their identity. Participating in blogging communities also has an effect on the bloggers and their identities, which, as shown above, can be seen in the blogger's posted content, both in their personal blog and group site. Further, the identities of blogging communities are also affected by the members' activities within the group. In what follows, we discuss the implications of the study for theory and practice.

Implications for theory

The concept of identity and social identity has diverse meanings in different disciplines throughout the social sciences. While this study focused on the social identity within blogging communities, there are also some important insights from this work that can contribute to understanding the role and impact of social identity within the virtual world in general. There are three areas in particular that illustrate these contributions. First, this study confirms the importance of using social identity in the virtual context. It shows that social identity exists not only in the real world but also in the virtual world. In addition, social identity is shaped by the members within the community, as well as exercising an influence on the group members' identities.

Second, there has been little discussion in the literature about the relationship between social identity and online communities, especially new and emergent types of online communities, like blogging communities. In this study, we found that by blogging and interacting with other bloggers, individuals with similar interests gradually start to form a specific group or community and identify themselves with that particular group. Individuals can be members of different groups, depending on their interests. However, by trying to differentiate itself from others, each group will form unique characteristics, including rules and norms of its own. These unique characteristics can be seen as the social identities of the specific community.

Third, our study has shown that that blogging communities are virtual communities that center around human cooperation, as indicated by Panteli and Dibben (2001), but also the individuals' ability to choose the communities they want to join, as well as to choose their degree of involvement in these communities. It follows that virtual communities are fundamentally a pattern of human interaction and choice. In this way, virtual communities are not just communities that use CMC, but rather they are created, produced, and maintained by and within the use of CMC – and this is a matter of human choice. Our study has shown that this choice depends on the extent to which individuals identify themselves with a specific online community.

While several important contributions about the existence of social identity within online communities have emerged from this study, continued work on this topic is needed. Due to the time-limitation of this research, the longitudinal study approach may be used in the future research of blogging. The comparison between different blogging communities is also another approach in order to gain more understanding about this emerging phenomenon.

Implications for practice

While many organizations nowadays are engaging more in virtual aspects, such as virtual teams, work-from-home employees, etc., into their work practices, the online social aspect of their employees has not been seriously considered. As people's virtual and real lives are occurring together, and also more and more people are going online, organizations should consider how to encourage social interactions of their members within their virtual spaces.

As such, in order to meet their members' social needs for online communities, organizations might consider providing social virtual spaces such as blogs. As shown in the study, such virtual spaces can reduce many barriers, such as geographical and physical factors between members, and enable the development of a common social identity. Further more, online communities such as blogging communities can be manipulated in two different ways, on the one hand, to create organizational identities and, on the other hand, to be shaped by members' social interaction. It follows that organizations and managers should take an interest in online communities because these virtual spaces can and do have an important effect on their employees' identities.

References

Abrams, D., and Hogg, M. (1990) "An Introduction to the Social Identity Approach," IIn D. Abrams and M. Hogg (Eds), *Social Identity Theory: Constructive and Critical Advances*, Harvester Wheatsheaf: London, pp. 1–9.

Blood, R. (2002) Introduction, in J. Rodzvilla (Ed.), *We've Got Blog: How Weblogs are Changing Our Culture*, Perseus: Cambridge, MA, pp. ix–xiii.

Business2blog (2006) B2Day: Multiply (Like Social Networks). Available from: http://business2.blog.com/business2blog/2006/06/multiply_ like_s. html (accessed: 07.09.2006)

Capozza, D., and Brown R. (2000) *Social Identity Processes: Trends in Theory and Research*, Sage: London.

Cohen, K. (2005) What does the Photoblog Want?, *Media, Culture and Society*, 27(6), 833–901.·

Fernback, J., and Thompson, B. (1995) *Virtual Communities: Abort, Retry, Failure?* Howard Rheingold: Albuquerque, New Mexico. Available from: http://www.well.com/user/hlr/texts/VCcivil.html (accessed 09.09.2006)

Festinger, L. (1975) *A Theory of Social Comparison Processes*, Bobbs-Merrill: Indianapolis.

Girard, N. (2006) Networking Site Touts "Tiered" Privacy. Available from: http://news.com.com/2102-1038_3-6097834.html?tag=st.util.print (accessed 09.09.2006)

Halavais, A. (2002) Blogs and the "Social Weather," Internet Research 3.0, Maastricht, the Netherlands.

Herring, S., Scheidt, L., Wright, E., and Bonus, S. (2005) Weblogs as a Bridging Genre, *Information Technology and People*, 18(2), 142–171.

Herring, S.C. (2004) Slouching Toward the Ordinary: Current Trends in Computer-mediated Communication, *New Media & Society*, 6(1), 26–36.

Huffaker, D.A. (2004) The Educated Blogger: Using Weblogs to Promote Literacy in the Classroom, *AACE Journal*, 13(2), 91–98.

Huffaker, D.A., and Calvert, S.L. (2005) Gender, Identity, and Language Use in Teenage Blogs, *Journal of Computer-Mediated Communication*, 10(2), article 1. Available from: http://jcmc.indiana.edu/vol10/issue2/huffaker.html (accessed 09.09.2006)

McGarty, C., Haslam, S.A., Hutchinson, K.J., and Turner, C. (1994) The Effects of Salient Group Memberships on Persuasion, *Small Group Research*, 25(2), 267–293.

Metz, C. (2006) Multiply Review, *PC Mag*. Available from: http://www.pcmag.com/print_article2/0,1217,a=180274,00.asp (accessed 01.09.2006)

Multiply Website (2006) Available from: http://multiply.com (accessed 07.09.2006)

Nardi, B.A., Schiano, D.J., and Gumbrecht, M. (2004) Blogging as Social Activity, or, Would You Let 900 Million People Read Your Diary?, *CSCW*, ACM, Chicago.

NITLE Blog Census (2006) Available from: http://www.blogcensus.net/?page=Home (accessed 16.07.2006)

Oxford Dictionary (2000) *Oxford Advanced Learner's Dictionary*, Oxford University Press: Oxford.

Panteli, N., and Dibben, M.R. (2001) Revisiting the Nature of Virtual Organizations: Reflections on Mobile Communication Systems, *Futures*, 33(5), March, 379–391.

Rheingold, H. (1993) *The Virtual Community Homesteading on the Electronic Frontier*, Addison-Wesley Pub: Reading.

Saunders, M., Lewis, P., and Thornhill, A. (2003) *Research Methods for Business Student*, 3rd edn, Harlow: Prentice Hall.

Schiano, D.J., Nardi, B.A., Gumbrecht, M., and Swartz, L. (2004) Blogging by the Rest of Us, Conference on Human Factors in Computing Systems, CHI'04 Extended Abstracts on Human Factors in Computing Systems 2004, Vienna, Austria, April 24–29, ACM Press, New York, 1143–1146.

Silva, L., Mousavidin, E., and Goel, L. (2006) "Weblogging: Implementing Communities of Practice," In IFIP, E. Trauth, D. Howcroft, T. Butler, B. Fitzgerald, and J. Degross (Eds), *Social Inclusion: Society and Organizational Implications for Information Systems*, Vol. 208, Springer; Boston, pp. 295–316.

Tajfel, H. (ed.) (1982) *Social Identity and Intergroup Relations*, Cambridge University Press: Cambridge.

Tajfel, H. (ed.) (1984) *The Social Dimension: European Developments in Social Psychology*, Cambridge University Press: Cambridge.

Turkle, S. (1995) *Life on the Screen: Identity in the Age of the Internet*, Phoenix: London.

Whetten, D.A. (1998) *Identity in Organizations: Building Theory through Conversations*, Sage: London.

CHAPTER 10

Playing together in cyberspace: Collective action and shared meaning constitution in virtual worlds

Anthony Papargyris and Angeliki Poulymenakou

Extensions to the life-world: MMOGs as context for collective action

Massively multiplayer online games (MMOGs), represent a new genre in the online games industry. They are immensely popular and many MMOGs report millions of subscribers. These games are considered to be the evolution of text-based multi-user dragons (MUDs). The first MUD was developed in 1979 and allowed text-based communication between players in numerous chatrooms. With the introduction of graphics, the first MMOG was launched in 1984 and, since then, many new titles have been introduced into the market. At the moment, there are over 100 commercial MMOGs released and about 94 more in the stage of development or beta testing.[1] MMOGs are different from other types of online games, such as internet games (i.e., chess) or network role-playing games (i.e., tournaments). MMOGs are "active" 24/7 and available for a player to enter and interact with. Most commercial MMOGs require a monthly subscription, where players assume the role of a fictional character (also known as avatar or persona). Each character is capable of performing various activities based on a series of skills. The higher the level of a trained skill, the better the character can handle virtual tools and gain access to special areas of the game environment (e.g., more difficult missions). The game usually comes with a skill-tree, so that players can develop and monitor the careers of their characters, a virtual currency for in-game trading activities, and various social events and fan festivals, which bring players and developers to meet each other. Additionally, each MMOG is supported by an official website, where the developers broadcast the game's rules and mechanisms, news, upcoming features, and events to the player-base. The site also contains a forum, where players and game developers come together and discuss various in-game issues. The role of the game developers is primarily to add and maintain new content to the game's scenario, but also to preserve and guarantee the social order inside the virtual world. To this end, they act as the game's referees, and they maintain an interpretive authority, which players grant to them as properties of their "god"-like status (Fine, 1983).

To the extent that MMOGs represent novel contexts for social interaction, many researchers have entered these virtual worlds to study issues such as disembodiment and identity construction (Holmes, 1997; Turkle, 1997), individual practices of communication and socialization (Ducheneaut and Moore, 2004), online and game-based learning (e.g., Prensky, 2001), politics and law (Lastowka and Hunter, 2004), and virtual economies (Castranova, 2003; Kollock, 1998). In MMOGs, players enjoy experimenting with their crafted virtual bodies, as modern "puppet-masters"[2] who project their intentions through their virtual characters. However, inside MMOGs, many players go beyond just "playing the game." MMOGs constitute an information-intensive and complex environment that simulates many aspects of the physical world. As a result, players form virtual teams and communities, sometimes known as guilds, practice e-governance, and try to manage their collective knowledge, organize their collective actions, freely share knowledge and information, voluntarily create new content, and participate in the game's design. In this study we are particularly interested in the study of collective action among players. The main motive behind this research was the fact that MMOG players around the globe manage to overcome interaction barriers in order to act collectively.

We began our inquiry in MMOGs puzzled by this question. How do people in a persistent virtual world achieve an intersubjective understanding (i.e., shared meanings) of their own or collective actions? Following Kellogg, Carroll, and Richards (1991), we define persistence to refer to "endowing objects with the ability to maintain and utilize historical and state information about their user interaction and other events pertinent to their responsibilities" (p. 420). The quality of persistence gives a sense of continuity, stability and durability to what people can achieve by playing the game. In a sense, MMOGs are conceived as "real" spaces of human interaction, open to all potential visitors[3] to immerse themselves.

Moreover, the concept of "intersubjective understanding" should be understood broadly and not as simply the achievement of consensus. In this study, we use the term "intersubjective understanding" to reflect on the strategies and instruments that facilitate the shared meaning, of individual and collective actions. Similarly, we use the notion of collective action to annotate social actions oriented toward other players, or actions where players do something together. Such collective actions may be cooperative or collaborative, friendly or antagonistic, routine or nonroutine, rational or irrational, emergent or collectively organized and projected. Nevertheless, we start with the premise that in every form of collective action, participants should share a "system of meaning" (e.g., Weick, Sutcliffe, and Obstfeld, 2005; Weick, 1995; Van Maanen, 1979). As social theory suggests, this shared meaning is taken for granted and thus it can serve as a reference schema upon which they can make sense of each other (i.e., identities, roles, and capabilities), the situation or context where the action emerges (i.e., on an ontological or historical level), and the collective action itself (i.e., the action's resources and outcomes). Hence, we are not interested in the individual's motives or incentives behind their collectively oriented actions, but rather in the social instruments the participants employ in order to communicate their meanings to others, and on the various strategies they use in order to establish such a shared system of meaning.

Yet the social interaction through a technological medium, and the experience of others inside the virtual world of the game, challenges the emergence of an intersubjective understanding among players. This in-turn makes any effort of acting collectively extremely difficult. To our understanding, the problem of the achievement of intersubjective understanding in a virtual world is threefold. First, there is the problem of players' cultural heterogeneity, in terms of cultural, national, cognitive, and gender/age diversity – and how they can achieve an intersubjective understanding of the game's situation and context. Second, there is the problem of the mediated experience, that is, how players are experiencing and collectively project their technologically mediated actions. Third, and as an extension of the previous two developments, lies the problem of the envisioned others, that is, how people cope with anonymity and manage to identify other coparticipants in terms of individuals' capabilities and responsibilities during an episode of collective action.

This study draws on an ethnographic research in a MMOG named EVE Online (or simply EVE), relying on participant observation and engagement in collective activities. Our observations are enriched by the collection and study of data collected from in-game chat logs, game news, developments' blogs, posts in game's main forum, but also from videoconferences and on-site observations of players during their engagement in online gaming (i.e., in internet cafés). Finally, face-to-face and chat-based, semi-structured, issue-focused interviews of key informants were used in order to gain a rich insight of the average player's profile, but also to seek the motives behind some notable episodes of collective action. Through these approaches, we could gain a reflexive understanding of what it is like to be a MMOG player (Hine, 2000).

The unit of our analysis includes both individuals and guilds of players. Guilds were treated as well-organized groups, able to form and sustain a sense of collective identity, and to provide structures and opportunities for organized or spontaneous collective actions. On the 26 March 2004, the lead researcher created two accounts and two characters. The first goal was to experience the life of a newcomer to the virtual world of EVE. The researcher soon became a member of a large multinational guild (we will identify this guild as Group A); after some time we had the chance to meet some of the guild's members face-to-face. During the researcher's "career" in this guild, he had the chance to become director in one of the group's chapters, and, after four months of intense participation in the group's commons, he became co-CEO. After about six months, and a few internal disputes, Group A disbanded and most of its 124 members joined other guilds. At this point the researcher became a member of a large nationally based (Greek) guild (Group B). We continued our research with Group B until the end of our participation in EVE at the end of February 2007.

In order to analyze our research findings, we draw on Alfred Schutz's theory of social action (Schutz, 1967) and we use the metaphor of the "life-world." Through the lens of the life-world, we can better focus on the relevance of the taken-for-granted shared meaning (or the social stock of knowledge in Schutz's terms) among individuals that act collectively. Moreover, we further elaborated our research findings using the theory of Communities of Practice (Wenger, 1998; Lave and Wenger, 1991), in order to understand the significance of peripheral practices of negotiation of meaning relevant to collective action within and around the boundaries of the virtual world and a guild. The findings indicate that players acting collectively in a MMOG share an enjoyment but also an agony to construct a shared meaning of the virtual game setting, and employ various instruments and strategies in order to negotiate their understandings. Such instruments include various metaphors, the game's rules, and the players' roles, while common strategies include petitions, propagandas, and peripheral discussions.

In the next section we outline the main features of Schutz's theory of social action, by focusing on the structures of the life-world that facilitate intersubjective understanding, which provide a foundation for the projection or execution of collective action. We then move our attention to collective actions in MMOGs, and to the problems that emerge through the transition from the physical to the virtual reality. We then briefly present the case of our research in EVE. Following that, in the last two sections of this chapter, we analyze and discuss our research findings, and provide some implications for the theory and practice of virtuality.

Social action and the social constitution of shared meaning

The exploration of interrelations between actors and the constitution of meaning of their actions have been a major research direction in many branches of philosophy, sociology, economics, and cognitive science. While it is impossible to address here all the implications of the term "collective action," it is worth mentioning that most studies on collective action have focused on the motivation and incentives behind the logic of collective action (e.g., Olson, 1965) and on the organization of people that act collectively (e.g., Kollock, 1998). Indeed, there is a large body of studies where notions such as distributed cognition (Hutchins, 1996), transactive memory (Wegner, 1986), perspective-making and perspective-taking (Boland and Tenkasi, 1995), and communities of practice (Wenger, 1998), emphasize the social structures that enable collective acting or knowing (Cook and Brown, 1999). Most of these studies converge on the point that actors engaging in social actions (i.e., on collective actions) have some level of a *shared system of meaning* on which a meaningful (collective) action can be performed or be understood (Weick, 1995; Van Maanen, 1979). Of course, the shared meaning reflexively transforms during the progress or after the completion of a collective action.

Building on Weber and Husserl, Alfred Schutz argues that the essential function of social science is to be interpretive, that is, to understand the subjective meaning of social action. The concept "social" is defined in terms of the relationships between the behaviors of two or more people, and the concept "action" is defined as behavior to which a subjective meaning is attached. A "social action" is therefore an action that "is oriented toward the past, present, and future behaviour of another person or persons" (Schutz, 1976, p. xvii). In his theory, Schutz tried to formulate a concept of meaning, and a more specific concept of *the meaning of an action*. He concludes that meaning derives from passive and active experiences in our consciousness. He refers to these experiences as "Acts," or as products of a series of actions, that ascribe meaning only when we recall and identify them as completed projects. Each person uses his biographical experiences to construct interpretive schemata that will allow him to ascribe meaning in retrospect or prospectively to future experiences:

> My *action as it takes place* presents itself to me as a series of *existing* and *present* experiences, experiences that are coming to be and passing away. My *intended action* presents itself to me as a series of *future* experiences. My *terminated completed act* (which is my expired action) presents itself to me as a series of *terminated* experiences which I contemplate in memory. The meaning of my action consists not only in the experiences of consciousness I have while the action is in progress, but also in those future experiences which are my intended action and in those past experiences which are my completed action. (Schutz, 1967, p. 39)

A central theme in the Schutzian theory of social action is the notion of the *life-world*. Life-world is generally defined as the "province of reality which the wide-awake and normal adult simply takes for granted in the attitude of common sense" (Schutz and Luckman, 1973, p. 3). The life-world is conceived as an intersubjective meaning-context, a taken-for-granted, and self-evident reality, which people modify by acting and operating not only within but also upon. In turn, the life-world modifies our actions. Through the concept of the life-world, Schutz emphasizes the intersubjective nature of social reality, as well as the importance of social distribution of knowledge and the stock of knowledge to hand (Schutz and Luckman, 1973; Natanson, 1962; Schutz, 1967). The *social distribution of knowledge* refers to the previous experiences and interpretations an individual holds, that help him or her to make sense of everyday life and actions. Such knowledge is acquired directly by engaging in meaningful actions, or by sharing it with others that, for example, were present at a past event. The *social stock of knowledge*, emphasizes the achieved intersubjective "commonsense" assumptions that a collective shares, and which allows them to organize and engage in collective actions. The stock of knowledge is built on sedimentations of actually former present experiences that were bound to situations (Schutz and Luckman, 1973). Schutz argues that in cases of social encounters with "others," people act or project their social actions in relation to the thesis of the *reciprocity of perspectives* (Schutz and Luckman, 1973; Natanson, 1962). In sum, this thesis implies that people assume and take for granted the existence of intelligent fellow individuals as given, and thus the objects of the life-world are accessible through their knowledge.

In retrospect, Schutz's theory of social action provides a rich account of conceptual tools in order to interpretively analyze episodes of individual or collective social action and shared meaning constitution.

Negotiation of meaning

As we saw earlier in the short presentation of the Schutzian theory of action, social interactions play a crucial role in the development of the social distribution of knowledge. It is through this interaction that people can objectify, communicate, and typify, the nuances of "meaning of an action" (Berger and Luckmann, 1967). In a similar vein, Wenger (1998) argues that inside the social boundaries of a community, shared understanding can be achieved through the *negotiation of meaning*. He perceives this as a process through "which we experience the world and our engagement to it as meaningful" (p. 53). It is only through this ongoing social process of interaction, that participants can gradually achieve an intersubjective understanding of their practices. Wenger emphasizes "the meaningfulness of our engagement in the world is not a state of affairs, but a continual process of renewed negotiation" (ibid., 54), and through this negotiation, he highlights the importance of participating in collective actions, and the process of reification (or typification in Schutz's terms) of a situation.

Wenger's theoretical formulations are bracketed inside the theory of situated learning or "legitimate peripheral participation," a theory that suggests that "learning occurs through centripetal participation in the learning curriculum of the ambient community" (Lave and Wenger, 1991, p. 100). According to this standpoint, communities are perceived as "communities of practice," where members are in a continuous state of *mutual engagement* in a common practice (i.e., sharing know-how through narrations) (Wenger, 1998; Brown and Duguid, 1991).

In our research context, we use the notion of negotiated meaning, in the same manner to Wenger, in order to "convey a favour of continuous interaction, of gradual achievement, and of give-and-take" (1998, p. 53). Nevertheless, our main research question frames our inquiry into the virtual settings of MMOGs. In the next section, we indicate the problems and challenges that emerge from the transition of a collective action into a virtual world.

Meaningful virtual worlds and the virtualization of action

Virtual reality presents a new medium for people to interact and communicate. As Heim (1993) points out, virtual environments introduce a new information-intensive interface, where people can immerse and interact with ideal "forms". Virtual environments are not a merely computerized representation of physical reality. They move beyond simulations and are designed in order to *reconstruct* physical spaces (Heim, 1998; 1993). More related into action, Lévy (1998) describes virtual environments as the *virtualization of an action*. For example, the hypertext reconstructs the notion of a text or a book, and thus, also alters the role of the reader and the action of reading. The text becomes a web of texts linked together, the reader becomes a navigator within this new complex of meaning, while the action of reading requires by the reader to conquer new spaces and develop new choices and velocities (Lévy, 1998). Lévy analyzes the process of virtualization as an exodus, a mode of being, and a deterritorialization from the "here and now" (ibid.).

Indeed, modern information-intensive technologies may cause a temporal transition from our private space to a public space and vice versa. The body transcends and escapes itself; it is simultaneously "here and there." In another recent work, Green (1997) also devotes considerable attention to the problem of embodiment and representation in virtual environments. Green highlights the importance of imagination to be "the driving force in the production and consumption of digital world" (p. 61). He also argues that the meaning of embodiment (or disembodiment) within a virtual environment emerges through significant representations and use of signs, but also through a continuous negotiation "through the possible forms of action and interaction between digital bodies in digital spaces" (ibid., p. 70).

In accord with these critical stances, we perceive the virtualization of action through engagement or participation in MMOGs to pose several challenges, three of which are particularly relevant into our research. In the next paragraphs, we explore each one of these challenges in parallel with previous studies on each subject.

The problem of players' cultural heterogeneity

Due to the nature of MMOGs, millions of users from geographically distributed locations, with different cultural and intellectual backgrounds, age, and gender, meet online and attempt to act cooperatively. During our research on MMOGs, we conducted a quantitative study, mainly on the study of usability of the MMOG user interface and mechanics. The questionnaire was available to players for a period of almost two months, in an English, Spanish, German, and Greek version. A total of 1,081 players responded in this study, mainly from UK (18.9 percent), USA (17.9 percent), and Germany (10.7 percent) (see Table 10.1). From our survey, we also found that most of the players are adults (40.8 percent are between 26 and 36 years old and 11 percent between 36 and 50 years old). Additionally, 52.8 percent reported playing on an average of – three to four hours per day, while 12.3 percent more than six hours per day. These findings are in line with Nick Yee and his Dedalus Project,[4] which reports similar distributions. Apparently, this diversity inherits an endogenous problem in apprehending, negotiating, and collectively explicating the game's context or situations. Consequently, this challenges the achievement of a social stock of knowledge.

Indeed, contemporary research on multicultural communication (e.g., Hinds and Kiesler, 1995) or cultural diversity literature (e.g., Watson, Kumar, and Michaelsen, 1993) report significant barriers that prohibit communication, knowledge sharing, and decision-making (Bhagat et al., 2002). Studies in global organizations report crucial cultural and ethical

Table 10.1 National players' distribution in EVE Online

Country	Percentage of players (n = 1081)
UK	18.96
USA	17.95
Germany	10.73
The Netherlands	4.16
Canada	3.89
Greece	3.70
Sweden	3.33
Hungary	3.15
France	2.87
Poland	2.50
Denmark	2.04
Russia	1.94
Spain	1.94
Australia	1.85
Belgium	1.76
Italy	1.48
Ireland	1.02
Norway	1.02
Other	15.73

barriers, which block communication between geographically distributed and multinational diverse employees (e.g., Pan and Leidner, 2003). On the contrary, as a large portion of the literature suggests, cultural heterogeneity in teams is not always addressed as a "problem" since this very plurality and variety of perspectives, values, and skills benefit team performance and efficiency in decision-making situations (e.g., Maznevski, 1994; McGrath, 1984). Nevertheless, most of these studies try to predict the effects of cultural and multinational diversity on group's performance and efficiency in decision-making. However, the rhetoric of achieving intersubjective understanding moves beyond explaining the variants and functional effects of cultural diversity.

In Schutz's study of the "stranger" (1944), that is, a person who enters a new social environment and faces an unfamiliar "cultural pattern of group life," he highlights the agony of the stranger to interpret the new social environment. In doing so, he starts to interpret his new social environment in terms of his social distribution of knowledge and "thinking as usual." But soon old concepts are inadequate. So a newcomer will start peripherally to observe and then engage in social actions in order to acquire new knowledge that will serve as a reference scheme of interpretation and expression. Lave and Wenger (1991) make a similar argument when they highlight the process of transition from the periphery to the core of a community with the notion of legitimate peripheral participation. Through repetitive participation in joint activities, core community members and newcomers intersubjectively construct the learning curriculum of the collective, until the newcomer is familiarized with the "cultural pattern of group life" (i.e., language, history, institutions, and systems of orientation and guidance). It is only after this period of "enculturation," where participants can establish a coherent and consistent, yet intersubjectively shared stock of knowledge, that they can further socially orient their actions.

The above study of the "stranger" is relevant to cases where newcomers in a MMOG meet a new group of players with an already established "cultural pattern of group life." In the extreme case, where all participants are identified as newcomers (i.e., in the early days of the game's launch), "strangers" that intend to act collectively will either form temporal teams and experiment the negotiation of their stock of knowledge, or they will rely on game developer's interpretation of the game's rules and suggestions on the game's storyline development, in order to form a sufficient understanding of the virtual world. In the first case, players are trying to reduce the heterogeneity by locating others with the same national identity. MMOGs usually provide special spaces that serve as meeting points, where players can publicly broadcast their national identity and meet others with the same nationality. In the second case, players will rely on the game developer's interpretative authority to make sense of the game's formalized rules and storyline, through which they can further apprehend the virtual context in general or their role-playing situation in particular.

The problem of the mediated experience

Undoubtedly, the players of a MMOG experience the game in relation to a technological medium, a computer network, that "links" all players together, and that creates a virtual world of the game. As a result, they are experiencing the virtual world and their action upon it through a technological medium. This mediation can distort or transform their experience of the world. For example, in mediated experiences, virtuality is perceived as a disembodied experience away from the "here and now." Thus, spatiotemporally speaking, virtuality gives a sense of telepresence, as "the extent to which one feels present in the mediated environment, rather than in the immediate physical environment" (Steuer, 1992).

From an interpretative sociological point of view, and using the Schutz's theory of social action, a virtual world constitutes nothing else but a *finite province of meaning*, with distinctive logical, temporal, corporal, and social dimensions and boundaries. In other words, the virtual world presents itself to each visitor as a subjective meaning-context. People can transcend the boundaries and "enter" this reality and act within or upon it, by experiencing the resistance of others or virtual objects. In Schutz's terms, a transition to another province of meaning may result in a crisis for the individual, due to the very lack of familiarity with the new reality. The more this new environment represents something different or alien to the player's life-world, the more difficult it is for him to explicate and apprehend this new world. However, as newcomers, every player that wishes to "stay and play the game" will have to cope with this, in many cases, this hostile uncertainty and unfamiliarity. Schutz and Luckman (1973) name such situations as "great" transcendencies. Individuals in such transcendences are facing the new reality, and they are essentially counted in their familiar stock of knowledge, which serves as a point of reference and relevance. Individuals can then search for an indication (i.e., signs) and symbols that will assist him to explicate the new reality in a meaningful manner.

The problem of the envisioned others

As an extension of the previous two developments, we face another problem; that of the envisioned others. Despite the multiplayer nature of

MMOGs, players have no direct contact with other coplayers. Instead, they are only capable of envisioning them through their virtual selves' (usually called avatars or characters) performance inside the virtual world. Consequently, identifying real people behind the inherent anonymity of the virtual world is not a straightforward process. Although this is not a place to unfold the main developments on the sociological study of identity (for an extensive review, see Cerulo, 1997; Jenkins, 2004), at this point it is worth mentioning that identity is about similarity and difference, through a process of comparison and categorization of others, in association with us. As Jenkins put it, "it is a systematic establishment and signification" between individuals and/or collectives, "of relationships of similarity and difference" (2004, p. 5). Through these continuing relations between self-image and public image, individual identification emerges (Goffman, 1959). Thus, identity is not just perceived by others, but it is actually constituted through an ongoing social process of "being" and "becoming." However, in MMOGs the constitution of individual or collective identity is quite different.

Indeed, research on identity construction (and manipulation) inside virtual worlds highlights the striking discrepancies between the constitution of "real" and "virtual" identity (Holmes, 1997; Turkle, 1997), while other studies have focused on ways in which online participation enables alternative and decentered identities through mechanisms of anonymity, pseudonymity, and alternative embodiment. Not surprisingly, many researchers report on many cases of identity deception and manipulation (e.g., Donath, 1999). Indeed, Caillois by referring to game's roles, asserts that "wearing a mask is intoxicating and liberating" (2001, p. 75). In a similar vein, Turkle argues that "when people adopt online personae, some feel an uncomfortable sense of fragmentation, some a sense of relief, some the possibilities for self-discovery, even self-transformation" (1997, p. 260).

Schutz and Luckman recognize such situations as "medium transcendences" where "the present experience points to [an 'other' person], which in principle can never be directly experienced," except via the media (1983, p. 110). Schutz used the Husserl's concept of *appresentation* in order to describe how agents overcome whatever transcends them. Appresentation is defined as the process in which an element of an external experience stimulates a more complete or richer internal experience of the "whole" of that thing. This is achieved on the basis of the prior experience of it, and thus, appresentation, is conceived by Schutz as a performance of consciousness that is essential to the life-world experience. The conscious process of appresentation facilitates agents to construct a general image of an envisioned other. In turn, and following the *reciprocity of perspectives*, agents take for granted that the envisioned other will share a few provinces of meaning with him. We believe that the main instrument for such an identity construction is the appresentation of other's virtual presence (through a virtual character). The character's characteristics (e.g., gender, name, and role) form the basis for any further negotiations of meaning through performance regarding the player's true identity.

EVE Online: a case of massively multiplayer online game

The virtual world of EVE

EVE is developed by CCP Games and was launched in May 2003. It was the first MMOG that used a single server for its players to interact, and holds the record with 32,534 concurrent accounts logged on to the same server. Currently, there are more than 117,000 subscribers, while in May 2006 the game was introduced as a beta version in the Chinese market. In EVE, each player pays a monthly fee for one account, and each account can have up to three characters. The official language used in EVE is English, while there are many abbreviations used to communicate emotions (i.e., using the /ME command players use smiles such as ☺), and other meaningful actions (i.e., AFK stands for "away from keyboard" and states the absence of a player from his terminal).

According to the storyline, the virtual world of EVE is "located" in a distant galaxy with thousands of sectors where players can travel. Players are grasping the role of a spaceship pilot, and they can either follow scenario-based missions, or play their own fantasy. They can engage in tasks involving mining, fighting, completing missions, manufacturing, and trading. Every transaction inside EVE is based on a virtual economy, with explicit financial rules and a virtual currency. Indeed, it is this freedom given to players that enables them to create their own experiences with the virtual world, and enhances the way that players are engrossed and immersed into the virtual world. Players are free to choose where they will play the game alone or form temporal teams (gangs), and more permanent groups (guilds or corporations). However, the game's storyline, and the completion of complex tasks strongly motivate players to join more permanent corporations or alliances (Papargyris and Poulymenakou, 2005). Here is how Charles Dane, EVE's community manager, describes the game's lack of explicit objectives:

> I feel EVE is one of the few sandbox games, where players are given the toys to play with, and do as they like as long as they are willing to suffer the consequences of their actions. It is not a theme park MMOG where everything is provided for you. (SeanMike, 2006)

The game provides various synchronous and asynchronous communication mechanisms, including a multichannel chat system, e-mails and private messages. In-game interactions are regulated by explicit rules that forbid players from harassing other players, by using "grief tactics" such as the use of hateful, racist, sexually explicit, threatening or harmful comments. Additionally, players can also use the game's website, where they have access to a huge knowledge base, a news center, and a forum for asynchronous communication with the rest of the game community. Beyond the official website, many players build their own fun-sites and blogs, and provide space for the community to exchange experiences, tips, and histories. Other players are engaged in the game at a much deeper level and develop custom applications that help players customize their characters, or better organize and interpret the in-game content. A case of such a popular application widely used by most of the players is a voiceover IP (VoIP) application that facilitates real-time oral communication. Such applications are extremely helpful for assisting groups of players to better organize their collective actions.

The users of the game receive a continuous bombardment of information. It is absolutely crucial for them to process information from multiple sources and make critical decisions. They have to pay attention to the game's users and the game flow, multiple chat channels, and various parameters that affect their character's navigation into the virtual world. At the same time, they have to carefully listen to the VoIP conversations and coordinate their actions with the rest of the team. Most experienced players use printouts with detailed maps where they can project their awareness of their teams' spatial location and trajectories.

Shared meaning construction and negotiation in EVE

As a newcomer in a new gaming environment, one tries to familiarize oneself with the game's mechanics, storyline, rules, and objectives. The game offers an online tutorial that explains the basics of the user interface, while it allows rookie players (they are also called "newbies") to participate in the "rookie help" chat channel. In this channel, veteran players voluntarily offer their expertise and answer any questions newcomers may have. In order to assist newcomers, CCP have launched a special volunteer program, where a group of volunteers graciously share their free time in order to assist fellow players in the world of EVE. They answer questions, help resolve minor problems and act as goodwill ambassadors throughout the community. The most frequently asked questions in help channels concern the games rules and policies ("what-if" questions), storyline and scenarios ("what is the impact of doing something" type of questions), tips and workarounds ("how can I do something" or "how does something work" types of questions).

Apart from the tutorial, in order to get the newcomer to learn the game's storyline as well as some more advanced aspects of the game, they are motivated to engage in storyline missions. These missions are specific scenario-related tasks where players are prompted to engage in some "purposeful action." Completing the missions results in a reward (usually a financial one), while any failure to complete results in some kind of punishment (usually in the players standing toward the agent who issued the mission). Newcomers also learn how to navigate inside the EVE world by using a virtual map, and by communicating with other players in order to find out in which sectors or solar systems there is something they need. Due to the digitized nature of the VE, participants can easily capture and reproduce still images of their current location. This is extremely helpful, since in such a way it helps them communicate spatial information to others instantly. In order to better organize their activities, all players use the GMT time zone as a point of reference during their communications.

In time, newcomers may decide to form or join a corporation. Membership in a corporation will help them to develop a sense of identity and belonging. Indeed, the rest of the corporation encourages the newcomer to engage in meaningful practices and provides access to its knowledge repository (usually this takes the form of a private website, where the community keeps track of their activities, strategies, and tactics). Additionally, every large guild usually adopts a hierarchical system of management, with a CEO, and many directors managing the various activities of the group (e.g., requiting, training, manufacturing, and logistics, etc.). The game provides a mechanism for managing a guild through a common wallet, hangars for storing goods, a unique name and a flag, which serves as an emblem, shares and a voting system, and the capability for the guild to rent or build a station. However, the politics and decision-making mechanism inside the guild are determined by the CEO. When one of the authors became a member in Group A, he had to carefully read and agree to follow the guild's "code of ethics" and constitution. The in-game guild member's actions and progress were monitored by senior members, while promotions to higher levels of management were granted by the CEO. This is how the CEO encouraged new members to mutually engage in joint activities:

> New members are now required to register for the forums to remain a guild member in good standing, This is part of a better guild communication strategy we would like to promote and encourage. Squires need to register as easy as that. If they don't, no promotion. (Excerpt from an e-mail to all members of Group A)

Guild members' continuous engagement, participation, and socialization intrinsically motivated newcomers to become part of the community's cultural context, and to familiarize them with the community's language, politics, norms, rituals, and history. Fortunately, the guild used the English language in the everyday communication. Nevertheless, mutual engagement in Group A's joint activities was not always an easy process. For example, minor communication issues arose, especially during discussions of complex group activities (e.g., the guilds promotion plan to encourage recruitment, or colonizing new regions of space). Consequently, we observed many misunderstandings. Nevertheless, it was those very episodes of dispute that forced members into processes of negotiation of meaning regarding the collective actions and the meaning of the collective. A vivid case of such negotiation of meaning took place during the discussion of merging Group A with another larger one, and through this merging, becoming of a member of a large alliance of guilds. During the discussions on this topic, we noticed that the more abstract a concept was (i.e., alliance), the easier it was for misunderstanding to occur.

During our participation in Group B, the process of our "enculturation" was faster. This was due to the lack of any communication problems, as well as due to our growing social distribution of knowledge, especially in terms of the game's mechanics, rules, and dynamics. Indeed, when we became members of Group B, we found that the "cultural pattern of group life" was familiar to us. Group B also had a central CEO with a few directors for managing the collective. Due to smaller geographic distribution of its members, most of them had the chance to meet each other during nationwide social events. The level of trust between several members was so high that some of them were sharing their accounts and characters with others. Moreover, the collective identity of Group B seemed to be more coherent, due to the tendency of its members to engage only in one type of collective activity, that of Player versus Player (PvP). Members identifyed themselves as proud "warriors" and they were frequently engaged in detailed narratives of their past battles. This specialization and collective will to master the PvP aspect of the game, also provided more time between players to discuss and analyze their previous shared experiences and to indicate any tactical errors.

PvP is a one of the most popular competitive activities in EVE. The motivation behind such team-scale conflicts is usually territorial and reputational issues, since the winner will gain higher status among the entire EVE community of players. The action of PvP is complex in terms of the resources needed for its execution, and because it requires absolute synchronization and alignment between the members of a group. It is collectively considered and projected in advance. Discussions during the planning phase of a battle include strategic and tactical movements, as well as the political impact to the game's social order. Due to the importance of PvP events to a guild's history and reputation, usually only experienced players are allowed to participate in task execution. In cases of emergency, less experienced players may participate as well, but in less critical roles (e.g., scouting or logistics). Nevertheless, in Group B, we noticed continuous training programs, where old veterans and new players were participating in joint activities of PvP. There, newcomers were experiencing the intensity of the battle, by learning how to collectively evaluate a situation, and to make strategic decisions on their own initiative. Additionally, experienced players used the group's forum to write detailed guides, where they explained core tactics as well as human, informational, and material resources needed in different cases of engagement. Especially in an effort to legitimize a PvP tactic, they engaged in peripheral discussions with the rest of the group. In such discussions, members usually refer to past cases of real-life combat situations (e.g., the Napoleonian battles), military textbooks (e.g., Sun Tzu's *Art of War*), as well as past episodes of PvP. Through storytelling, they narrate their greatest moments of their virtual life, legitimize their actions, and in general, share their knowledge on handling difficult situations collectively.

A large PvP battle usually is remembered as a significant point in game's history since it may change the course of the game's storyline. Players are prompted to capture their battles on video and make them available to the rest of the community. Through these video files, others can study strategies of engagement and revise the group's tactics. However, a significant use of battle "kills and losses" reports and video files is as propaganda material between the players' community. This is how an experienced player put it:

> Ultimate victory is achieved at the strategic level. Kills & losses are also relevant as they are the only measure of progress we have available, and are an indicator of the level of commitment of the various participants. Kills and losses are also obviously the fuel of propaganda and morale, which do play a major role at the strategic level. (Excerpt from personal field notes)

Propaganda is indeed a common strategy between players who wish to reinforce their individual or collective identity. Many players with some expertise on computer graphics and video editing, can engineer fake evidence and present them as authentic. Unfortunately, in mediated experiences within MMOGs, determining "real" and "nonauthentic" virtuality is far from clear. As a result, many players are leery of others' reports, unless the involved parties of a situation claim a report to be true. However, this process of objectification through testimony of the involved parties can last several days or weeks. In an effort to establish the identity of a dispassionate observer, many players take on the role of a journalist, and report on epic battles between strong opponents. They also engage in extensive novelization of different aspects of the game's storyline, by adding additional background information to the game's logic. These players are considered to be fully immersed in the role-playing aspect of the game, since they try to explicate the very meaning of the existence of the virtual world.

Finally, it is worth mentioning here a notable consequence of misleading MMOG group opinions through propaganda: the generation or reinforcement of stereotypes. Such a case is the stereotyping of the "Chinese player," one who is envisioned to live in China, and cheats by playing the game not for fun but for gaining real money. It is true that some players are using macro-programming techniques in order to "farm" an area of the virtual world, and to prospect by selling, for example through eBay, their accumulated virtual resources for real money. Due to the fact that in China there are many companies that employ players to farm MMOGs, there is a strong tendency among players to consider that all "farmers" are Chinese. Another example of stereotyping is the legitimization of propaganda. As a player observed:

> Propaganda is not bad at all! On the contrary, it is one of the most efficient strategies for a gang to gain a tactical advantage over the enemy. Like all warfare, PvP is based on deception too. Sun Tzu told

that ages ago and trust me, he was right. I wish we had a video-editing expert in our guild. (Excerpt from a chat with a player from Group A)

And later in our discussions he/she kept arguing "This is common knowledge in EVE. Don't get upset. Besides this is just a game."

To conclude, we believe that such stereotypes generated inside virtual worlds sediment in the player's stock of knowledge and transcend the boundaries of the virtual into the real world, sometimes in exaggerated forms. In general, we observe that the habitualized online practices and meaning transcend the virtual boundaries of MMOGs, and become relevant and applicable in everyday reality. The individual stock of knowledge, enriched with interpretative schemes from mediated experiences inside a virtual world, would in turn reflexively affect the player's experience of reality, thinking, and behavior. In terms of a player's life-world, through continuous interaction with virtual worlds, physical and virtual reality collide and then coincide into a habitual and meaningful whole.

On negotiating the meaning of a collective action in EVE

As we already discussed in the second section of this chapter, mutual engagement into collective action presupposes that agents are sharing a sufficient level of shared meaning regarding the action's context, but also the action's resources and outcomes. The findings indicate a strong tendency among agents to be on a continuous alert and to engage in negotiations of their life-worlds, and their individual stock of knowledge with the rest of the participants. This process of negotiation of meaning affects different levels of individual and collective understanding of the collective action's context and meaning. Additionally, during the process of negotiation, they employ different conceptual instruments and strategies that facilitate the establishment of an intersubjective understanding through the form of a taken-for-granted social stock of knowledge.

We may summarize these two ideas by saying that shared meanings of collective actions are socially constructed through the negotiation of the meaning of: (1) the virtual reality, (2) the virtual identity of the participants in a persistent virtual environment (PVE), and (3) the actions these participants perform. Table 10.2 lists these types of negotiations, while it indicates the accompanied instruments and strategies players furnish during such processes.

Table 10.2 The three processes of negotiation of meaning in an episode of collective action in a PVE

Aspects of shared meaning (SM) required in collective actions (CA)	Instruments that facilitate the symbolic constitution of SM	Strategies that facilitate the common-sense constitution of SM
The SM of the game context or a situation	Metaphors and game's rules (common sense and logic)	Petitions, narratives, and novelization
The SM of the participants (agents) of a CA	Players' roles (fantasizing)	Propaganda and stereotyping
The SM of the CA itself	Metaphors (appresentation)	Peripheral discussions

The first type of negotiation of meaning concerns the constitution of shared meaning regarding the intersubjective understanding of a context where collective actions emerge or are projected. In the cultural heterogeneity of virtual world, shared meaning emerges through the negotiation of meaning of metaphors and regulative rules. In the case of MMOGs, our findings indicate that players rely on common sense and aspects of their social distribution of knowledge, in order to explicate the contextual information, properties and dynamics. Nevertheless, the plurality of different life-worlds prohibits players from taking for granted such emerging systems of shared meaning per se. In advance, they rely on the interpretive authority of the game's referee (i.e., the community manager). It is the presence of a game developer or a community manager that serves as a referee and thus constitutes the ultimate interpretative authority. Additionally, our findings suggest that common sense in a MMOG virtual world is also reinforced by logic, and a reliance on the interpretation of game rules. In many MMOGs, the game's rules are a popular topic of discussion and negotiation between players and game developers (see Fine, 1983, pp. 107–122) and this was the case here. This is why a common strategy for negotiating meaning of the virtual world is the petition. Through petitions, players protest and request a referee to resolve a situation where different common-sense interpretations of a game's rule cause uncertainty and conflict between players.

In general, players experience the game as a boundary-crossing experience; an immersion into a finite province of meaning. They collectively explicate the virtual world in terms of what they already know and this is why newcomers automatically tend toward mimicry. Through trial and error, players are experiencing the game environments, and engaging in the collective social action of explicating a new and unfamiliar environment. In all of these levels of negotiation of meaning in the virtual world, players rely heavily on the use of spatiotemporal metaphors. Metaphors serve as carriers of meaning and reference schemata for explicating the new and unfamiliar province of meaning. Players are using metaphors as symbols to assist them in the boundary-crossing between the real and the virtual world. In time, metaphors brought from the real world acquire new descriptive meanings of social actions in the PVE. Indeed, metaphors and indirect speech act as a way of proceeding from the known to the unknown (Nisbet, 1969, p. 4). Especially in virtual environments, metaphors are considered to play an important role on constructing the "reality" of the "virtual" (Schultze and Orlikowski, 2001). Nevertheless, communication and negotiation of meaning through metaphors is not a straightforward process. This is due to the fact that in order to successfully use a metaphor in a communicative act, the speaker and the listener should share the "same principles" (Searle, 1993; Turner, 1974). Only then can the listener perform an ontological mapping (Lakoff, 1993) across conceptual domains of reality and virtuality, and separate the speaker's utterance meaning from the word or sentence meaning (Searle, 1993). In EVE, most metaphors refer back into the sci-fi literature. Consequently, the core of the game's content contains many abstract concepts that are hard for new players who are not sci-fi fans to understand.

In the second type of negotiation of meaning, players try to identify others. Other players are generally perceived as strangers, although a general categorization may apply. For example, players that come in a MMOG from other similar games tend to identify themselves as "refugees." because without a membership into a guild they feel "homeless." In this process of negotiation of meaning, players rely on their fantasizing and appresentation to envision other players. They use the in-game roles to identify other players, and usually they ignore others' real identity or the reasons and motives that brought him/her into the virtual world.

In a similar study, Turkle notes, inside a MMOG, "you can completely redefine yourself if you want. ... You can be whoever you want, really, whoever you have the capacity to be" (1997, p. 184). However, our research findings show that most players are reluctant to abandon their true identity, norms and beliefs. For example, even the fact that the game's scenario legitimizes the role of piracy, many players do not become pirates, since they perceive piracy as grief behavior. As one of the interviewees stated:

> I don't want to become a pirate. I don't see any fun in camping at star-gates and shooting helpless and unarmed pilots for money. Due to my trained skills and my experiences in the battlefield, I consider myself to be a well-skilled fighter. Thus I prefer to go practice and compete

my combat skills in a real PvP situation. I would hate myself if I ever become a pirate. (Personal interview with a player)

In sum, we conclude that, in PVEs, individual or collective identities are crafted symbolically thought the assignment of in-game roles. Jenkins argues convincingly that all identities are social identities, and that identification is a matter of meaning, and that "meaning always involves interaction: agreement and disagreement, convention and innovation, communication and negotiation" (2004, p. 4). However, in PVEs like games, "the game seems like the very image of life, yet an imaginary, ideal, ordered, separate, and limited image" (Caillois, 2001, p. 75). Nevertheless, our observations indicate that EVE's players are not engaged in esoteric dilemmas of being and acting as a person or a digital persona (e.g., an avatar). They behave in a meaningful way as they would in the physical world, and through their collective actions they socially construct the gaming virtual world to be an "authentic shared fantasy."

Finally, in the third type of negotiation of meaning, players try to make sense of an episode of collective action, mainly in terms of the information or human resources required for action, and the action's outcomes. As in every game, individual or collective action inside EVE is governed by the game's rules. In the case of EVE, the community manager acts as a referee and in some cases he can even ban a player's account. Such incidents are not common but when they occur, the player's community conceives it as a death penalty. At this point, important instruments for shared meaning constitution are the metaphors used in the explication of the virtual world. Additionally, the collective's action projection, execution, or meaning and significance to the virtual world's storyline is being negotiated through peripheral discussions and reference to commonly known real-life situations (e.g., Sun Tzu's *Art of War*).

Concluding remarks

This research examined collective action in a virtual world of a MMOG, in order to better understand how agents in an episode of collective action achieve an intersubjective understanding. Such understanding can refer to simple elements of the virtual world (i.e., rules and procedures) but also into more complex forms of collective action (i.e., PvP and fair play). By using the theory of social action proposed by Schutz, and the concept of the "life-world," we studied episodes of collective action inside the virtual world of EVE. Through the lens of the "life-world," we can reject the polarized dilemma between the physical and the virtual reality. Instead, we can study the virtual and the physical to blend in a multiplexed experience. In sum, through our analysis, we identified the basic instruments and strategies that players deploy in order to negotiate and progressively construct a shared system of meaning. However, we strongly believe that this research is far from complete, and future research should seek deeper understanding of the emergent roles, rules, and actions that people furnish collectively in order to socialize virtual spaces. Indeed, the study of virtual worlds can prove to be a goldmine for researchers and practitioners.

Implications for theory and practice

In the pure theoretical domain, social and political scientists can use virtual worlds as a social laboratory, a space where they have the great opportunity to observe and study individual and collective patterns of behavior online. Through such observations, researchers could test social theories and develop new ones, toward the better understanding of virtuality in general and the interpretation of human performance in particular. Virtual worlds like MMOGs provide a means for significant transcendence. Through MMOGs, players transcend not only spatiotemporal boundaries of the physical world, but also national, cultural, economic, and political boundaries. This liberation from confined life-worlds produces new challenges and ambitions, and a strong tendency to reexamine the very structure of a virtualized action. This is a never-ending process, since a virtual world is always under construction. It grows to a larger space of interaction by adding new content, but it also grows through players' imagination and as a place to construct a meaningful world of experience. As such, several observations can be made for the apparent limitedness of a virtual space of interaction.

Indeed, MMOGs, as any game, are characterized by their spatiotemporal seclusion and limits (Huizinga, 1955) and it is only through the players' repeated actions that we (the observers or players) can make sense of the virtual world as a meaningful one. Indeed, a game has only an intrinsic meaning (Caillois, 2001). However, despite the limits of meaningful actions in a scenario-driven MMOG, and the problems with shared meaning, players extend the confined meaning of their shared fantasizing by negotiating their "life-worlds" and celebrating through a collective agony their ability to transcend the imaginary boundaries of the virtual world. To an extent, the study of collective action in MMOGs can give us two insights: on the one hand, it highlights the limits of virtuality, since virtual worlds are reconstructions of the physical world, governed by formalized and strict rules and scenarios that define what players can and cannot do. On the other hand, it juxtaposes the virtual world as a province of meaning where the game's scenario provides the seed for social action. The virtual environment gives a sense of safety and liberty, where players can experiment with new forms of action and identities. Such actions are conceived as the virtualization of everyday actions found in the physical world. But it is this very virtualization of an action that provides the liberty to an agent to reconstruct the action's structure. In turn, the virtualization of an emergent action in a global and virtual setting like a MMOG, challenges the agents to redefine their stock of knowledge, not only through an explication of the confined meaning of a game world, but also through the transition from the local to a more global perspective of the world and everyday life.

Although MMOGs present the best case at hand of virtual worlds, future developments in the computing industry will allow individuals to customize or create their own personal virtual worlds. That is, virtual spaces will emerge where they could experience their fantasies and myths on demand. Whatever the future holds, we believe that virtual worlds can prove to be an ideal laboratory for Information Systems (IS) designers and analysts. MMOGs reflect a unique form of virtuality where individuals enthusiastically use their networked computers to "enter" the virtual world and play. Despite the high complexity of MMOGs systems (in terms of both content management and user interface familiarization) individuals are encouraged and motivated to adopt and learn the new system. As recent research in hedonic computing (Brown, 2005) indicates, IS researchers can learn many things from the experience of enjoyment by interacting with playful technologies such as MMOGs. Moreover, practitioners can adopt and use some well-tested practices and procedures of complex transactional and governance systems that MMOGs players already use in their everyday virtual lives.

Acknowledgment

We are grateful to Paul C. van Fenema for his helpful comments and suggestions on an early version of this chapter.

Notes

1. source: http://www.mmorpg.com/gamelist.cfm/gameId/0
2. As we explain later in our analysis, the culture of fantasy and science-fiction (sci-fi) genre in literature or film plays a crucial role in understanding

MMOGs. Here, the term "puppet-master" originates from the film *Ghost in the Shell*, a Japanese cyberpunk manga in 1991. In this futuristic thriller, the "puppet-master" was a hacker who could manage to remotely hack a person's cyber-brain and gain access to her/his actions.
3. Ontologically speaking, virtual worlds are usually treated as synthetic, yet objective realities, where people can "enter," "visit," or even "colonize," and navigate through the environment's spatial attributes and affordances.
4. http://www.nickyee.com/daedalus/gateway_demographics.html

References

Berger, P., and Luckmann, T. (1967) *The Social Construction of Reality: A Treatise in the Sociology of Knowledge*, Penguin: London.

Bhagat, R.S., Kedia, B.L., Harveston, P.D., and Triandis, H.C. (2002) Cultural Variations in the Cross-border Transfer of Organizational Knowledge: An Integrative Framework, *Academy of Management Review*, 27(2), 204–221.

Boland, R.J., Jr., and Tenkasi, R.V. (1995) Perspective Making and Perspective Taking in Communities of Knowing, *Organization Science*, 6(4), 350–372.

Brown, B. (2005) Hedonic Computing: The Computer Science of Leisure and Enjoyment, Paper presented at the The Virtual – A Room without Borders?, Rosenön, Stockholm.

Brown, S.J., and Duguid, P. (1991) Organizational Learning and Communities of Practice: Toward a Unified View of Working, Learning and Innovation, *Organization Science*, 2(1), 40–57.

Caillois, R. (2001) *Man, Play and Games*, trans. M. Barash, University of Illinois Press: Urbana and Chicago.

Castranova, E. (2003) On Virtual Economies, *Game Studies*, 3(2). Available from: http://www.gamestudies.org/0302/castronova

Cerulo, A.K. (1997) Identity Construction: New Issues, New directions, *Annual Review of Sociology*, 23, 25.

Cook, S.D.N., and Brown, J.S. (1999) Bridging Epistemologies: The Generative Dance between Organizational Knowledge and Organizational knowing, *Organization Science*, 10(4), 381–400.

Donath, S.J. (1999) "Identity and Deception in the Virtual Community," In M. Smith and P. Kollock (Eds), *Communities in Cyberspace*, Routledge: New York, pp. 29–59.

Ducheneaut, N., and Moore, R.J. (2004) The Social Side of Gaming: A Study of Interaction Patterns in a Massively Multiplayer Online Game, Paper presented at the Computer-Supported Cooperative Work (CSCW), November 6–10, Chicago.

Fine, G.-A. (1983) *Shared Fantasy: Role-Playing Games as Social Worlds*, trans. B. Robert, 2nd edn, University of Chicago Press: Chicago, London.

Goffman, E. (1959) *The Presentation of Self in Everyday Life*, Doubleday: New York.

Green, N. (1997) "Beyond Being Digital: Representation and Virtual corporeality," In D. Holmes (Ed.), *Virtual Politics – Identity and Community in Cyberspace*, Sage: London, Thousand Oaks, New Delhi, pp. 59–78.

Heim, M. (1993) *The Metaphysics of Virtual Reality*, Oxford University Press: New York, Oxford.

Heim, M. (1998) *Virtual Realism*, Oxford University Press: New York, Oxford.

Hinds, P., and Kiesler, S. (1995) Communication Across Boundaries: Work, Structure, and Use of Communication Technologies in a Large Organization, *Organization Science*, 6(4), 373–393.

Hine, C. (2000) *Virtual Ethnography*, Sage: London, Thousand Oaks, New Delhi.

Holmes, D. (1997) "Virtual Identity: Communities of Broadcast, Communities of Interactivity," In D. Holmes (Ed.), *Virtual Politics – Identity and Community in Cyberspace*, Sage: London, Thousand Oaks, New Delhi, pp. 26–45.

Huizinga, J. (1955) *Homo Ludens: A Study of the Play-Element in Culture*, Beacon Press: Boston.

Hutchins, E. (1996) *Cognition in the Wild*, MIT Press: Cambridge, MA.

Jenkins, R. (2004) *Social Identity*, trans. B. Robert, 2nd edn, Routledge: London, New York.

Kellogg, A.W., Carroll, M.J., and Richards, T.J. (1991) "Making Reality a Cyberspace," in M. Benedikt (Ed.), *Cyberspace: First Steps*, MIT Press: Cambridge, pp. 411–431.

Kollock, P. (1998) Social Dilemmas: The Anatomy of Cooperation, *Annual Review of Sociology*, 24, 183–214.

Lakoff, G., and Johnson, M. (1980) *Metaphors We Live By*, University of Chicago Press: Chicago.

Lave, J., and Wenger, E. (1991) *Situated Learning: Legitimate Peripheral Participation*, Cambridge University Press: Cambridge.

Lévy, P. (1998) *Becoming Virtual: Reality in the Digital Age*, trans. B. Robert, Plenum Trade: New York, London.

Maznevski, M.L. (1994) Understanding our Differences: Performance in Decision-making Groups with Diverse Members, *Human Relations*, 47, 21.

McGrath, J.E. (1984) *Groups: Interactions and Performance*, Prentice Hall: Englewood Cliffs, NJ.

Natanson, M. (Ed.) (1962) *Collected Papers I: The Problem of Social Reality*, Martinus Nijhoff: The Hague.

Nisbet, R.A. (1969) *Social Change and History: Aspects of the Western Theory of Development*, Oxford University Press: London.

Olson, M. (1965) *The Logic of Collective Action*, Harvard University Press: Cambridge, MA.

Pan, S.L., and Leidner, D. (2003) Bridging Communities of Practice with Information Technology in Pursuit of Global Knowledge Sharing, *Strategic Information Systems*, 12, 17.

Papargyris, A., and Poulymenakou, A. (2005) Learning to Fly in Persistent Digital Worlds: The Case of Massively Multiplayer Online Role Playing Games, *ACM SIGGROUP Bulletin*, 25(1), 8.

Prensky, M. (2001) *Digital Game-Based Learning*, McGraw-Hill: New York.

Schultze, U., and Orlikowski, W.J. (2001) Metaphors of Virtuality: Shaping an Emergent Reality, *Information and Organization*, 11(1), 45–77.

Schutz, A. (1944) The Stranger: An Essay in Social Psychology, *The American Journal of Sociology*, 49(6), 499–507.

Schutz, A. (1967) *The Phenomenology of the Social World*, trans. G. Walsh and F. Lehnert, Heinemann Educational Books: London.

Schutz, A. (1976) *The Phenomenology of the Social World*, trans. G. Walsh and F. Lehnert, Heinemann Educational Books: London.

Schutz, A., and Luckman, T. (1973) *The Structures of the Life-World* (Vol. 1), Northwestern University Press: Evanston, IL.

Schutz, A., and Luckman, T. (1983) *The Structures of the Life-World* (Vol. 2), Northwestern University Press: Evanston, IL.

SeanMike (2006) EVE Online Interview – Charles Dane, Online Community Manager [Electronic Version]. *GamersInfo.net* from http://www.gamersinfo.net/index.php?art/id:1255

Searle, J.R. (1993) "Metaphor," in A. Ortony (Ed.), *Metaphor and Thought*, 2nd edn, pp. 83–111, Cambridge University Press: Cambridge.

Steuer, J.S. (1992) Defining Virtual Reality: Dimensions Determining Telepresence, *Journal of Communication*, 42(4), 73–93.

Turkle, S. (1997) *Life on the Screen: Identity in the Age of the Internet*, Simon and Schuster.

Turner, V. (1974) Dramas, Fields and Metaphors: Symbolic Action in Human Society, Cornell University Press: Ithaca, NY.

Van Maanen, J. (1979) "On the Understanding of Interpersonal Relations," in W. Bennis, J. Van Maanen, E.H. Schein, and F.I. Steele (Eds), *Essays in Interpersonal Dynamics*, Dorsey Press: Homewood, IL, pp. 13–42.

Watson, E.W., Kumar, K., and Michaelsen, K.L. (1993) Cultural Diversity's Impact on Interaction Process and Performance: Comparing Homogeneous and Diverse Task Groups, *Academy of Management Journal*, 36(3), 590–602.

Wegner, D.M. (1986) "Transactive Memory: A Contemporary Analysis of the Group Mind," In B. Mullen and R.R. Goethals (Eds), *Theories of Group Behavior*, Springer-Verlag: New York, pp. 185–205.

Weick, K.E. (1995) *Sensemaking in Organizations*, Sage: Thousand Oaks, London, New Delhi.

Weick, K.E., Sutcliffe, M.K., and Obstfeld, D. (2005) Organizing and the Process of Sensemaking, *Organization Science*, 16(4), 409–421.

Wenger, E. (1998) *Communities of Practice: Learning, Meaning, and Identity*, Cambridge University Press: New York.

CHAPTER 11

Luminal possibilities for the study of virtual systems, global effects, and local practices

Mike Chiasson

Introduction

There has been considerable attention and research on virtuality in various disciplines. The field of Information Systems (IS) has been especially interested in the impact of virtual systems on management practices: virtual teams, organizations, markets, etc. This research has provided us with many ways to think about the global effects of information and communications technology (ICT) – the assumed producer of virtuality – on local practices. These local practices include: working practices, communication, trust, and collaboration.

However, this work often contains various assumptions about the nature of the local and global, and the role and influence of ICTs on virtuality. For example, some studies suggest that ICTs supporting internet chat and e-mail, are capable of bringing participants in touch with a range of new people and cultures, creating a "global village" of like-minded people, sharing common concerns. In contrast, other studies, building from similar assumptions but different directions, suggest that participants' local settings inhibit the limitless and productive use of ICT, restricting the benefits of virtual teams, virtual work, and organizational knowledge sharing.

In both cases, the relationships among the local, global, virtuality, and ICTs are largely assumed. These typical relationships suggest an exponential increase in the number of individuals whom could work together and influence each other (a form of global), which can then prompt unrestricted possibilities for individual practice change (the local). In the first case, the global capability of ICTs to allow contact between many other individuals expands the range of the individual to influence and be influenced by other local practices and ideas. In the second case, the global possibilities of ICTs can reorganize work and knowledge sharing by overcoming the restrictions of local settings. Despite a different emphasis, the assumptions about ICT and virtuality are the same – that ICT produces numerous virtual and global possibilities for individuals to affect and be affected by others, and to transform their local circumstances and working arrangements.

The purpose of this chapter is to explore these typical assumptions about the local, global, virtual, and the role of ICTs in virtuality. The result is an expanded range of possibilities for research and practice in virtuality research. In doing this, I expose a number of *luminal* spaces for virtuality – possible spaces *in-between* the global, local, and ICTs, in producing and forming the virtual. In the process, I draw upon several theorists and philosophers who provide a number of alternative approaches to the study of virtuality.

I conclude with one luminal possibility for virtuality research, which arises from Shields (2003), and his assumptions about the local, global, virtuality, and various electronic and nonelectronic mediums. This luminal possibility suggests that the virtual is not tied to any particular electronic medium, but is produced by absorbed individuals, necessarily operating in concrete and local circumstances. The result is a *locale* produced by the absorbed individual using various channels – electronic and nonelectronic – to influence and be influenced by topics, groups, and individuals that are always virtual, even in face-to-face encounters. This suggests an important role for the individual in creating *locales* from this stitching together of virtual concepts and topics (global) in their concrete settings (local).

The chapter is structured as follows. I examine and expose the sets of characteristics often associated with global, local, virtual, and ICTs. I then provide typical assumptions about how these characteristics are associated with the local, global, and virtual, and the role of ICTs in each. I then relax these assumptions by exploring alternative luminal spaces "in-between" the local, global, virtual, and ICT. I then draw conclusions about one revised luminal space for virtuality research and practice.

Characteristics

There are various characteristics that help in defining the local, global, and virtual. These include, but are not limited to: *space* (present or absent), *time* (same-time vs not-the-same time), *absorption* (attention vs inattention), *substance* (real vs nonreal), and *identity* (strong vs weak). Depending on the nature of local, global, and virtuality, they determine the luminal possibilities for various social and material effects realized within and beyond specific settings.

In terms of *space*, we could say that a person or thing is either *present* or *absent* to another person or thing. For example, a person is either in your house and within your direct vision, or they are not. When it comes to space and the assumptions about the local, global, virtual, and ICTs, the presence and absence is important, if not definitive. For example, virtuality often implies that a thing or person can be *absent* and yet still be *present* to another, through various mediums – for example, a letter, television, computer, etc. More often these days, virtuality is tied to particular information and communication technologies, which allow a person to influence another across global *distances*. This suggests that ICTs allow individuals to influence others without needing to be physically present. In contrast, the local is often characterized by a restricted and *present* space, often associated with face-to-face communication. While this may seem obvious, there are a number of challenges to these typical assumptions, which will be raised in later sections.

In terms of *time*, a person or thing is either interacting with someone at the *same time* (synchronous) or *not – at the same time* (asynchronous). Again, when considering the nature of local, global, and virtual, the issue of time is assumed in typical definitions. For example, virtual systems allow the storage of a message by a sender, which can be read and retrieved at a later time by the receiver. Again, typically this asynchronous communication could be considered a global influence on local practices by supporting the increased ability and effect of communication on others across time. Asynchronous communication is also often associated with *absent* space, given that the sender of an e-mail message, for example, is often absent.

Absorption of an individual's attention to a topic, group or individual is an important but less-discussed aspect of the local, global, and virtual. In terms of absorption, many consider face-to-face (present) and same-time communication to be the richest for absorbed communication. For example, media richness theorists argue that face-to-face communication is a richer medium for the exchange of important nonlinguistic signals, such as body and facial gestures. Other researchers point to the lack of cues in ICT-based communication as an important influence on group communication – anonymity, lack of hierarchical structures, inflaming remarks and insult, and the possibility of aggressive posturing. Given the absorption and richness of face-to-face communication, effective communication is often associated with local, present, and same-time communication, and less so with global, distanced communication through ICTs (often considered "virtual" communication).

Often associated with local, global, and virtual is *substance* – whether a thing or person is *real* or *unreal* (i.e., often associated with the term *virtual*). Again, this characteristic corresponds strongly with local, global, and virtual. For example, electronic communication may be considered *unreal* because of other characteristics already mentioned – lack of absorption, asynchronous communication, and absence. On the other hand, face-to-face involves the real and local, and as suggested by the Greek philosopher Socrates in his critique of writing (the form of the virtual at the time), can be trusted because the person speaking is present and can be questioned.

Somewhat related to absorption is the issue of *identity*. A more complex characteristic than the others, a person's identification with a group, symbol, etc. is either *strong* or *weak*. This characteristic is often tightly organized around our other concepts – the local often associated with a strong identity, and the global with a weak identity. However, given some individuals' absorption with online games, strong identity may be as likely to occur in virtual systems as nonvirtual.

We explore the typical relationships among these characteristics next.

Common relationships among the local, global, virtual, and ICTs

As already suggested in the previous section, typical assumptions about local and global characteristics, and their relationships to ICTs, are produced along dichotomous dimensions of the previous characteristics. For example, the *local* is considered to include: *present* space, *synchronous* time, *attentive* individuals, *real* substance, and *strong* identity. The *global* is often the opposite: *absent* space, *asynchronous* communication, *inattentive* individual absorption, *unreal* substance, and *weak* identity. In many cases, virtual systems are associated with the global and use of ICTs, and non-virtual systems with the local and use of face-to-face communication.

The reasons for these typical positions arise out of dichotomous conceptions of virtual and nonvirtual channels – traditionally *face-to-face* versus *other* electronic channels, such as the telephone, e-mail, internet chat, etc. Face-to-face is considered rich because it includes absorbing possibilities in the local: present, synchronous, attentive, real, and strong. *Virtual* channels, typically ICT-based channels, have characteristics that produce a lack of absorption: the person is *absent*, communication is *asynchronous*, the receiver can be *inattentive*, and there is an *unreal* (i.e., *virtual*) substance to communication and presence. This increases the chances for a *weak* identification among the communicating individuals.

From this, we can discern two general approaches to virtuality, which, despite different conclusions, share similar assumptions about the local, global, and ICTs, as outlined above. The first suggests that virtual systems (usually referring to ICT) extend the possibilities and advantages of the local (present, synchronous, etc.), typically *face-to-face* communication, but they risk *losing* the inherent advantages of face-to-face communication. These advantages include: trust, rich interaction, knowledge sharing, etc. The task then is to design virtual systems that can recover the advantages of the local (i.e., face-to-face) communication. This depiction represents a broad summary of media richness theory and design approaches to ICT-based communication.

A second approach that appears to contrast with the first, is that virtual systems (i.e., electronic communication) extend the ability of people to interact with each other, without local constraints, because the ICTs allow a simple and pure form of communication. For instance, the internet and its global connectivity is purported to allow the production of a global village of participants, united by shared concerns and interests. This is facilitated by the ability of electronic (virtual) systems to bypass social and political constraints in their local settings, which allow for democratic and open dialogue. In assuming this, it suggests that ICTs can *better* support the selection and absorption of individuals into topics and actions that matter to them, beyond local constraints. This scenario suggests a utopia, such as an ideal speech situation, in which participants are able to self-organize and transform the specificity and arbitrariness of the local, through a global space supported by ICT. Organized events, such as the rallies against global trade, are examples of how the local is transformed by global activism, organized through electronic systems. Rheingold provides earlier and later examples of virtual community action and solidarity (1993; 2002).

Speculation and conclusions from the first approach suggest a strong connection between face-to-face and local communication, while the second argues that individuals are better absorbed and unfettered through electronic communication systems. While the argument in the first approach would maintain that the local is a place for authentic and productive dialogue, which needs to be designed into electronic and virtual systems, the second argues that electronic systems currently support unfettered collection of interests, which are more authentic and productive because they transcend the confines of face-to-face communication. Despite these differences, both share similar technological and channel imperatives of the same kind, in assuming both face-to-face and ICT-mediated communi-cation have certain outcomes and characteristics.

In response to the assumptions in both approaches, speculations from a third approach could move beyond both to argue a looser connection among local, global, virtual, and ICTs. Some existing research suggests this is possible including most of the work in this book. For example, it has been found that e-mail systems can be just as rich for communication as face-to-face (Lee, 1994), and that text-based e-mails sustain and reinforce power through cues (Panteli, 2002). This challenges the inherent richness found in face-to-face versus ICT-based communication, because elec-tronic communication systems depend on the rich interpretations and social construction of the individuals. This position reveals a weak link in our polarized characteristics – that ICTs do not necessarily imply inatten-tion and weak identity. As suggested already, electronic communication channels can produce absorbed communities of individuals (Rheingold, 1993; 2002).

Regardless of whether we resolve the first and second approach through the third, the deconstruction of both using this and many other approaches suggests a need to explore the many luminal spaces between the local and global, and the role of information and communication technologies in producing revised and new communicative spaces.

Our exploration raises questions about whether locality, as defined by absorption, can only depend on face-to-face communication, or whether it can and is being created online. It also raises the question whether communication is simply text and symbols, which can be captured and transported to form authentic virtual communities, and the typical mapping of local and global characteristics into face-to-face and ICTs. In illustrating the loose bonds here, some researchers have shown that electronic and face-to-face channels both increase in use by individuals who use ICTs, in order to reinforce and further develop interpersonal relationships (Woolgar, 2002). For example, a person who uses a mobile phone often increases their face-to-face contact with the individuals they call.

A key to our initial steps beyond traditional definitions may lie with Coyne (1995), and his critique of the technological determinism in virtual reality research, which aims to build technical systems that require a realistic rendering of the concrete world. Drawing on Heidegger, he argues that individual *attention* and *absorption* is the reality and locality of participants. If so, the connection between locality and face-to-face com-munication in producing a "rich" channel for individual absorption, is not required, as anyone reading a book can attest. The same is true of virtual reality systems, which show that the production of a completely accurate representation is not required for individual absorption. For those who have played simple text-based role-playing games, the individual is able to construct a rich reality around and beyond the text. Thus, if our focus is on absorption and, in a Heideggerian sense, immersion in one's tasks, neither electronic or face-to-face channels per se determines absorption. It depends not on *space* or *substance*, but on the individual and their willingness to engage.

Neither does absorption require *same-time* communication, as anyone reading a book can attest. Many individuals often prefer a book to its film, suggesting that a brain can do more to paint a rich picture from text, than a director can from a singular and restricted version. A good book can also absorb the individual more than the spoken word, as board attendees sending texts on mobile phones during a meeting demonstrate.

This does not imply that a new electronic system does not meet with skepticism and suspicion during its initial period. For example, Socrates believed that the absence of a person meant that written words could not be believed, questioned, interrogated – and therefore carried little authority and weight. Following this argument, some have recently argued that verbal testimony is possibly the only true form of knowledge (Flyvbjerg, 2001; Welbourne, 2001), and that the privileging of speech over text remains (Coyne, 1995). However, we would argue that the level of trust and absorption in the medium is not determined by the medium, but by sociocultural norms. More and more these days, people are trusting and being more absorbed by ICT-based communication than by face-to-face communication, if the construction of virtual lives on Second Life and the increase in internet shopping are any indication.

At this juncture it becomes clear that a simple rendering of local, global, and virtual through face-to-face or electronic channels is only possible under limited circumstances. Locale and locality, defined by individual absorption and attention, can be supported and established in either electronic of physical spaces. So where does this leave us as researchers and practitioners? More specifically, what is the local, global, and virtual, and how do they relate to face-to-face and ICTs?

Alternatives

In many ways, we have already explored a number alternative research and practical approaches to the local and global. My next task is focused on alternative luminal possibilities among the local, global, and virtual in ICT research and practice.

If locality is about individual absorption and attention, then, despite our being situated in particular physical circumstances, our lives are filled with topics and languages that exist both within and beyond us. This definition does two things. First, it suggests we have always been virtual, since language and thought have allowed individuals to communicate thoughts and ideas beyond their physical settings for many thousands of years. Second, it suggests that the new electronic channels have extended and transformed the portability and reach of concepts and ideas for people to be absorbed by, but not the possibility of being absorbed by concepts and people beyond our immediate setting. Anyone interested in world events on the television news could vouch for us. The task then for virtuality research is to study the time and context-dependent selection and use of ICT and nonelectronic communication systems to select and stitch together virtual topics, groups, and individuals of interest that inhabit their locales of interest, which allow them to live certain lives and to work in certain ways.

This changes virtuality research to examine how and what absorbs individuals in their local settings, from both electronic and nonelectronic systems use. The virtual is not a separate unreal influence, through electronic systems, that intertwines with the real (Robey, Schwaig, and Jin, 2003), but is a symbolic system like many other things in an individual's setting, which interacts with other symbol-producing systems in an individual's setting.

In addition, if we have always been virtual, electronic systems are not the only or even predominant source of the virtual, but have added to the reach and transmission of virtual concepts and ideas that influence individual locales. The printed word, language, symbols, mental images, even social stereotypes of the individual facing you, are all virtualities that invade and create the real for the individual.

Given this, Shields (2003) suggests that virtuality is as old as the spoken word. Building on the dictionary definition of "that which is so in essence but not actually so" (p. 2), his model of how the virtual interacts with the real crosses the *present* (actual) and the *future* (possible), with the *real* and the *ideal*. The result is a simple model of virtuality layers, among the *concrete* (*real, actual*), the *possible* (*real, future*), the *virtual* (*ideal, present*), and the *abstract* (*ideal, future*).

For example, a "virtuous" person mixes various virtual, concrete, possible, and abstract categories. The "virtuous" person is associated with *concrete* behaviors, suggesting that others may perceive them as "virtuous" – a *virtual* concept applied to understand and simplify their concrete behaviors. This *virtual* concept both highlights and simplifies these *concrete* behaviors, but it is also further transformed by the *abstract* concept of virtuousness, which informs the future behaviors of the individuals, and the concept of virtuousness. This then suggests *possible* behaviors that we would anticipate in the future.

Given this example, what distinguishes the *virtual*, and its mobility across space and time (global) is not tied to an electronic device, but to the concepts and ideas that inform *concrete* practices. Referring back to our discussion of the local, global and electronic systems, I would suggest that all four elements – the virtual-concrete-abstract-probable – are mixed together during any meaningful moment for an individual – through an active mixture of electronic and nonelectronic channels. For example, a person using a real-time text chat system to communicate with a coworker is producing a *virtual* representation of her: a set of ideal words that the communicating individual and others use to paint a picture of her, formed from concrete symbols and words on the computer screen. The computer text is a *concrete* expression of linguistic characters, put together in an attempt to stimulate another's absorption and interpretation. In this sense, meaning is always a combination of the concrete text and the ideal concepts, consistent with the *signifier* and the *signified* in structuralist philosophy. But this isn't the only virtual system, in the concrete-virtual-abstract-probable sense. Both users are also using a computer system that has a keyboard, computer screen, and mouse – the *concrete* (*present* and *actual*). But the computer system is also a *virtual* system because of its *ideal* and *present* influence on the construction of meaning through its relaying of abstract symbols, in text.

This communication between individuals via information and communication technologies can also inform speculations on their concrete and future (i.e., *probable*) activities, but also the future and ideal (i.e., *abstract*) possibilities for this future. For example, both users may be communicating in order to organize future meetings – a concrete and future *probable* event. This specific and future event is also informed by the ideal and future concept of a *meeting*, which suggests an ideal structure, which may be drawn upon in order to shape the structure and format of the meeting.

Through these examples, we can see how the *virtual* is represented – as an *ideal* and *actual* influence on the present – such as a "virtuous" person, or as a pure and idealized form of communication through its concrete rendering in a physical device called a "computer," which is itself an idealized notion of concrete outcomes that predates its use for communication. In doing so, the *virtual* is an *ideal* and *present* concept, which influences the *concrete* technical and social activities around it.

Expanding beyond the domain of electronic communication, Shields (2003) provides other examples to illustrate the relationships among the virtual, concrete, abstract, and probable. In the case of the *virtual* and *concrete*, he examines how *rituals* are used in Christian worship to invoke and draw out an *ideal* God within *concrete* practices, such as *prayers* and *symbols*. As another example of the *concrete* and *virtual*, a feeling of déjà vu can be considered a concrete experience influenced by a *virtual* form.

He also suggests other mediating systems such as *symbols* which can mediate the *virtual* and *abstract* by informing the *virtual*. Reversing the direction, *myths* can render the *virtual* into the *abstract*, which allows us to speculate on many instances of future activities.

Overall, Shields is arguing against a separation between the real and virtual in many typical assumptions about them, consistent with Burbules (2004):

> The problem with this view [that the virtual is illusion and the real is not], is that it assumes an overly sharp separation between the "virtual" and the "real" – the real seems to be a simple, unproblematic given that we perceive and interact with directly, while the virtual means something more like "synthetic" or "illusory". Yet any reality we inhabit is to some extent actively filtered, interpreted, constructed, or made; it is not merely an unproblematic given, while the virtual is not merely imaginary. The virtual should not be understood as a simulated reality exposed to us, which we passively observe, but a context where our own active response and involvement are part of what give the experience its veracity and meaningfulness. Hence the virtual is better seen as a medial concept, neither real nor imaginary, or better, both real and imaginary. (p. 163)

Given this approach, electronic mediums such as e-mail, chat, videoconferencing, etc. only affect the complexity and reach of virtual and concrete possibilities for interaction, but not its historical role. It is the sheer number of virtual possibilities that now confront the individual today, which electronic systems have provided, that has changed, and not virtuality itself. Shields (2003) argues that the relationship between the virtual and real has a long history. For example, the replacement of the spoken word with text is a shift toward *virtual* symbols, which "re-present" the speaker. This shift also includes what are often considered to be nonvirtual systems: pictures, texts, printing press, telegraph, and the telephone. This long history of the virtual suggests a transformation in our thinking about virtuality research.

Going even further, some argue that even our interpretation of a spoken word is a virtual construction. Within this approach to the virtuality of language and text, the concrete element only plays an initial role in stimulating the constructed and virtual reality of engaged participants.

The computer then simply extends the already long-standing capability of humans as symbol-producing and symbol-consuming creatures. The computer represents only the latest medium in a long history of the distancing of people from the immediacy of the spoken word. It complicates but does not upset the virtual-concrete-abstract-probable interactions that occupy our world. The computer and the internet are therefore only an evolutionary trend in symbolic virtuality (Shields, 2003).

Given this approach, the relationships among the global, local, virtual, and electronic mediums are revealed with new luminal spaces among them. This allows for the development of new theoretical and practical examinations of the various mediating systems, including electronic systems, which promote attention and absorption by individuals. No longer are we constrained to study how the advantages of face-to-face communication can be recovered in virtual systems. No longer do we bypass the face-to-face to focus on the unrestricted possibilities in electronic communication. Shields's claim is that individuals achieve meaning beyond the concrete, and have always done so. In this sense, we have never been local or global, but global thinkers acting locally, and local thinkers acting globally. This raises a number of important implications for research into the local and global in IS virtuality research.

Implications for research and practice

This deconstruction of the characteristics of the local and global, and virtual systems, illustrates a number of new possibilities for virtuality research and practice. The first is that our focus in virtuality research should be on the absorbed and attentive individual striving for meaning. Using Shields's framework, we can research how chains of virtual-concrete-abstract-probable interactions are put together by active individuals, through electronic and nonelectronic channels. In asking this revised question, we are exploring not the local, but the *localities* produced within local (i.e., concrete) and global circumstances (i.e., virtual-abstract symbols). The virtual is no longer imprisoned within an electronic medium, but includes the ideal-present concepts that influence and are influenced by the absorbed individual. We do this by observing concrete behaviors produced in particular circumstances (the concrete), talking and influenced by others through electronic text (virtual), exploring and transforming future meetings and actions (probable), with the intent of forming new social movements, friendships, and contacts (abstract).

Despite my deconstructive critique, these conclusions are not particularly unique. A "virtuous cycle" of intertwining between the virtual and the real has already been suggested by Robey, Schwaig, and Jin (2003). However, differing from their congruent and incongruent approach to the virtual and real, I suggest that a focus on the absorbed and attentive individual, and their concrete and virtual systems, would be more productive. It is the absorbed individual who produces his or her *locales* in various concrete-virtual circumstances. According to Burbules (2004), even face-to-face communication has this virtual-concrete dynamic. The result is that the communication mediums are pushed into the background.

Second, and consistent with Burbules (ibid.), electronic systems are recast as symbolic systems that provide symbolic mobility across time and space. These symbols are both virtual (i.e., representations of language) and concrete (i.e., printed symbols on a screen). In this sense, they represent a global influence in that they are carried across large distances and times through their concrete representation of language. However, it is when they encounter absorbed individuals who read and use symbols that they render concrete-virtual localities.

Third, despite removing our focus from the electronic or nonelectronic media, we cannot ignore the fact that communication channels do affect and restrict an individual's concrete practices of use. Thus, electronic systems, to varying degrees, prescribe their use. For example, a chat tool requires certain keyboard and technical practices in order for the individual to participate. These concrete practices may also restrict their virtual possibilities.

In addition, certain socio-technical affordances of the medium may influence concrete behaviors. As one example, Introna (2001) argues that a lack of proximity through computer systems allows a receiver to disregard and remain undisturbed by the real faces of the senders. Drawing upon Levinas, he suggests that the face-to-face encounter matters in terms of invoking our compassion and attention to the other. Computer systems afford and allow individual and collective disregard for people in concrete situations, especially if the virtual images abstract-away the harsh realities of a concrete situation.

In concluding then, the local includes *concrete* practices and words, the global includes *virtual* words and concepts that emerge from and affect the concrete, and the intersection of the two by absorbed individuals produces *localities*. These are influenced by both electronic and nonelectronic communication channels, which render new virtual possibilities and dynamics for the individual. They contribute to a world that has always been virtual. While electronic systems may dictate both the concrete and virtual to some degree, it is the active role of individuals, engaged with topics, communities, and other individuals, that is the focus of virtuality research and practice. Our current focus on the electronic machine as the virtual-global, and the face-to-face as the concrete-local, has limited the range of topics and approaches we have used in our research.

In focusing on those concrete and virtual places where an individual is an absorbed participant, we move beyond typical assumptions about the local and global, and a relatively uniform effect of electronic and nonelectronic systems on this communication. In becoming an absorbed participant, communicating with others, the mediums influence the possibilities of absorption and thus the shape and contours of the relationship. But they do not deterministically define the relationship and its characteristics. In doing so, our focus turns to the localities produced through and across electronic and nonelectronic systems, by absorbed individuals.

References

Burbules, N.C. (2004) Rethinking the Virtual, *E-Learning*, 2(2), 162–183.

Coyne, R. (1995) *Designing Information Technology in the Postmodern Age: From Method to Metaphor*, MIT Press: Cambridge, MA.

Flyvbjerg, B. (2001) *Making Social Science Matter: Why Social Inquiry Fails and How it Can Succeed Again*, Cambridge University Press: Cambridge.

Introna, L. (2001) Virtuality and Morality: On (not) Being Disturbed by the Other, *Philosophy in the Contemporary World*, 8(1), 11–19.

Lee, A.S. (1994) Electronic Mail as a Medium for Rich Communication (Using Hermeneutic Interpretation), *MIS Quarterly*, 18(2), 143–157.

Panteli, N. (2002) Richness, Power Cues and Email Text, *Information & Management*, 40(2), 75–86.

Rheingold, H. (1993) *The Virtual Community: Homesteading on the Electronic Frontier*, Addison-Wesley: Reading, MA.

Rheingold, H. (2002) *Smart Mobs: The Next Social Revolution*, Basic Books: Cambridge, MA.

Robey, D., Schwaig, K.S., and Jin, L. (2003) Intertwining Material and Virtual Work, *Information and Organization*, 13, 111–129.

Shields, R. (2003) *The Virtual*, Routledge: London.

Welbourne, M. (2001) *Knowledge*, McGill-Queen's University Press: Montreal-Kingston.

Woolgar, S. (2002) *Virtual Society? Technology, Cyberbole, Reality*, Oxford University Press: Oxford, New York.

CHAPTER 12

Virtuality: time, space, consciousness, and a second life

David Kreps

Introduction

Virtuality and reality are today sometimes seen as opposites (Sotto, 1997). Yet a look beneath the surface of the concept of virtuality leads us into a much more complex understanding, not only of what virtuality is or might be, but of reality itself. We are left, indeed, unsure of the opposition, and even uncertain of our future in an increasingly virtual world. Are the real and the virtual truly as opposed to one another as might at first appear? Does virtuality threaten to starve us of the merits of a more "grounded" or "substantial" reality? This chapter – perhaps the most philosophical and abstract in this current collection – questions whether the real and the virtual are really so opposed, and, in the course of the arguments in examining this issue, questions whether virtuality can indeed be regarded as any kind of threat to the mental health or psychological development of those engaged in it – or indeed to a society that embraces it – and posits that virtuality may even be inherent in the nature of what it is to be human.

The path of traditional logic, from its Socratic origins to the programming languages underpinning today's computer and information systems, has been shadowed by an alternative path of more intuitive, holistic thought, from its Lucretian origins to the post-structuralist ideas of philosophers like Gilles Deleuze. It is to this latter path that we shall turn, in order to shed light upon the nature of virtuality as an information system.

Let us begin with a restatement of the obvious. The word "virtual" was defined by Charles Peirce in 1902 as follows: "A virtual X (where X is a common noun) is something, not an X, which has the efficiency (*virtus*) of an X" (Commens, 2006). This piece of very classical logic we shall examine in greater detail in the course of this chapter. Michael Heim defined "virtual" as: "A philosophical term meaning 'not actually but just as if'" (Skagestad, 1998; also see Sotto, 1997). In that sense virtuality is akin to simulation – defined as a sham or counterfeit of the "real" thing (Merriam-Webster). The word "virtuality," was probably first used in the context of interactive computer systems by Theodore Nelson (coiner of the term "hypertext"), back in 1980 (Skagestad, 1998), and since that time – especially over the course of the 1990s, and since – the word has been used a great deal. Virtuality on interactive computer systems relies on two new technologies: digital telecommunications and the graphical user interface (GUI) – be it 2 or 3D. Yet it is arguable that virtuality is in fact something inherent in the human condition, in human consciousness itself, and that information and communication technologies (ICTs) are merely a recent expression. This chapter, however, does not set out to explore what expressions of human virtuality may be found in history prior to the advent of ICTs. Rather, it sets out to explore the concept of virtuality itself, in relation to the concept of reality, and the implications for an information society capable of highly convincing computer-graphic virtuality.

The theoretical backdrop for our discussion is provided by Gilles Deleuze, arguably father of post-structuralism, and his rediscovery and revitalization of the ideas of Henri Bergson, the early twentieth-century French philosopher. These ideas present for us an insight into the nature of reality *as perceived* by human beings, and enable us to conceive of virtuality as *an effect* of human perception. We shall apply these concepts first to Gibson's concept of the "Matrix", in the realm of science fiction, and then to the extraordinary and growing phenomenon of "Second Life," a "metaverse" that is growing on the Internet, populated roughly 30 percent by US citizens, 13 percent French, 10 percent German, 8 percent UK, and the rest made up by a further 96 countries around the world (Linden Labs, 2007). This 3D virtual world of over 11 million individuals (TechCrunch, 2007) has to date exchanged over $5 million for the local currency, "Linden dollars." There are 258 islands on Second Life, generating between $200–$300 per month each in revenue for the company, as well as another 103 square kilometers of mainland real estate, which costs $3–$10 per square meter. Such a growing economy reflects what can only be described as a real experience, albeit mediated by one's avatar, in this virtual world. In this chapter, we will seek to find whether the real and the virtual are really so opposed, and whether virtuality may indeed have important lessons for us in the Information Society.

Consciousness, space, and time

First, however, we must catch up on some philosophy. Many thinkers have addressed the problem of consciousness, notions of space and time, and the nature of reality. This is not the place to revisit all of these ideas, but to explore a specific line of argument: that virtuality is inherent in the nature of what it is to be human. The argument begins with a consideration of the holistic, exploring the evolution of vitalism and one of its most famous proponents, Henri Bergson, before turning to Gilles Deleuze and contemporary critical theory.

Holism

On the subatomic/microcosmic scale, and on the planetary-macrocosmic scale, we deal with wholes. On the scale of individual human bodies, we tend to work with an older, rather different, reductionist, and scientific approach. Is this just an example of postmodern pragmatism – fitting the right model to the right thing – or is there potentially some future problem that might arise from this disjunction?

Consciousness, indeed, is of crucial importance in this argument, both with regard to scale, and with regard to the disjunction between reductive and holistic approaches. The holistic approach is a particular skill of consciousness that has been largely sidelined by the more reductive rationality of modern, "Enlightenment" science. What Dreyfus describes as "holistic discrimination and association" is, in essence, "an ability to intuitively respond to patterns without decomposing them into component features" (Dreyfus, 1986, p. 28). Moreover, in his book championing *Mind Over Machine*, Dreyfus states categorically that "Intuition or know-how, as we understand it, is neither wild guessing nor supernatural inspiration, but the sort of ability we all use all the time as we go about our everyday tasks" (ibid., p. 29). This capacity to intuit, to grasp things holistically, is a skill which has been acknowledged in our society "only in women, usually in interpersonal relations," and been "adjudged inferior to masculine rationality" (ibid.).

Yet holistic grasp, one might argue, is precisely the sort of skill we might be applying to our interactions with a metaverse such as Second Life. Understanding the whole experience in a gestalt[1] moment might indeed be prerequisite to its appeal to so many people, who might otherwise quickly tire of the business of creating and dressing their avatars, meeting other avatars, and typing questions and responses, acquiring land, and setting up home, etc. (Avatars in Second Life are the online representatives of the individuals engaging in this virtual world; there are numerous ways in which one's avatar can be customized to give one an element of individuality in one's virtual self.) Holistic grasp, as we shall see, proves crucial to the apprehension of Bergson's – and thereby Deleuze's – ideas on the nature of human consciousness, and thereby, the concept of virtuality.

Vitalism

Now the holistic and reductive approaches can be seen as merely the latest in two very long and opposing traditions in the West, streams that have wound around each other, contradicted each other – even sometimes usurped each other's arguments. The vitalist tradition in western thought, for example, albeit something of a countertradition, is easy to find, and has not been completely consigned to history by modern science as one might expect. In brief, vitalism has tried in various ways over the centuries to demonstrate that there is something unique about life, about living beings, that sets them apart from nonliving things. Right up to the middle of the nineteenth century, even most mechanists used some vitalistic ideas in their work. Modern chemistry, however, sought successfully to completely discredit any notion of "substantival vitalism" – the idea of some physical/material essence unique to living beings. But "holistic vitalism" – focusing mainly upon consciousness as the unique attribute of the living – has never been properly contested by a scientific tradition because it has been unable to address the fact of consciousness, itself, and relies largely upon what some would describe as a lower form of thinking (ibid.).

The continuity from nineteenth-century vitalism to its modern, holistic-ecological/diversity-led cousin, requires two missing pieces: the neo-vitalism of Bergson, and Deleuze's revisiting of Bergson at the hinge of the post-structuralist turn. Here, we will find that it is precisely consciousness, and the intellectual courage to properly address it, that sets the vitalistic countermetanarrative apart from the scientific-materialist, mechanistic metanarrative of the ongoing Enlightenment project. Consciousness, moreover, will prove to be a lynchpin of the real and the virtual, as we shall see through the following philosophical exploration.

Bergson

To discuss the nature of virtuality, we must now turn to a brief discussion of the nature of reality itself. In his famous 1907 book, *Creative Evolution*

(1944) Bergson adds his voice to the general reappraisal and resurgence of the vitalist tradition at that time, outlining his concept of the *élan vital* ("creative impulse" or "living energy"). The *élan vital*, he argues, lies at the heart of evolution, in place of the Darwinian concept of natural selection. It is a monist philosophy, a reunification of the sundered worlds of Nature and Culture. Importantly, Bergson is explicit in stating that this *élan vital* is a force whose existence cannot be scientifically verified – a crucial break from the traditional "substantival" vitalists, who contended that there must be some fluid or other organic material at the spring of life. These earlier vitalists believed that there must be some divine force outside of matter, driving it. Bergson's *élan vital*, however, is a property of matter itself. This is consistent with his reconception of materiality in the concept of the *durée réelle* – or "real duration." For Bergson material objects do not exist separate from a "fourth dimension" of time, in which events involving these objects occur. In Bergson's universe time and matter are indistinguishable, the flow of unfolding evolution is the continuous movement of a space-time whole that is quite simply indivisible in the way that reductive mechanists persist in doing. Bergson even differed with Einstein on this crucial point, challenging the theory of relativity in ways only the later quantum physicists would dare.

So Bergson presents us with a panoramic reassessment of the real: time and space, holistically grasped as a unified whole, driven forward by an *élan vital* that is a property of matter itself, intrinsic to the movement of unfolding reality. Further, he contends that this universe "is best understood on the model of the development and elaboration of consciousness." Moreover, albeit by a reductive route, "[a]ccording to at least some historians of science, modern physics has discovered that Bergson was right" (Burwick and Paul, 1992, p. 4). The reader may wish to look to the writings of Fritjof Kapra, and the work of Llinas mentioned later in this chapter, for further exploration of this line of enquiry.

Deleuze

So how, from Bergson's neo-vitalism, do we arrive at today's ecological perspective? What, after all, is all this talk of individual autonomy and human consciousness? What room, moreover, for teleological, vitalistic thinking in critical theory, after the post-structuralist turn, which, as we shall see, Bergson (arguably) may have spawned? Teleological notions are commonly associated by modern biologists with the pre-Darwinian view that the biological realm provides evidence of conscious design by a supernatural creator. But even after most biologists have rejected such creationist viewpoints, the role of teleology in biology has not disappeared, in particular with regard to whether for example such terms as "function" and "design" are permissible in biological terminology. Are such terms: (1) vitalistic (positing some special "life-force"); (2) requiring backwards causation (because future outcomes explain present traits); (3) incompatible with mechanistic explanation (because of 1 and 2); (4) mentalistic (attributing the action of mind where there is none); or (5) empirically untestable (for all the above reasons)? This is not the place to exhaust these arguments. Nonetheless, biologists continue to make use of such teleological terms as "function" and "design" all the time, unconsciously including vitalistic terminology in their thinking, to this day.

At the root of the linguistic turn, at the very foundation of post-structuralism, we find a textual study, a revisiting and contemporary critique and rereading, by one of the first proponents of post-structuralism, Gilles Deleuze, entitled, *La Bergsonisme*, published in France in 1966, and in English in New York in 1988. In the eyes of Paul Douglass, at least, it presents us with the possibility that Vitalism, albeit in its early twentieth-century "neo-" form as propounded by Bergson, can be considered an important source for many of post-structuralism's most pivotal ideas.

In *La Bergsonisme*, as Douglass reads it, "Deleuze has taken up the cudgels for a time-worn cause: namely, the vitalist approach to philosophy" (Douglass, 1992, p. 370). Douglass contends that there is almost a "willed memory lapse" among those discussing post-structuralist thought, in this regard. Anglo-American criticism at least, according to Douglass, seems to have "failed to appreciate post-structuralism as a resurgence of a time-honored movement in western social, psychological, and political theory – especially as a rejection of formal logic and dialectical reasoning." What he means here is what Deleuze describes as a "counter history" of philosophy: "an escape from the games of negation, a turning back against Platonic dialogue, and an embrace with a 'different' philosophical method exemplified in the works of Lucretius, and latterly, Nietzsche and Bergson" (ibid.). Vitalism, in short, is a countermetanarrative to the Enlightenment project. Indeed, many of the issues of post-structuralist thinkers like Foucault and Butler mirror the issues of Bergsonian vitalism: multiplicity, duration, and movement. For Douglass, "The post-structural vocabulary of 'decentring' is actually a sophistication of the [Bergsonian] concept of flux" (ibid., p. 371). Deleuze is especially admiring, Douglass tells us, of Bergson's "critique of the negative and of negation, in all its forms, as sources of false problems" (ibid., p. 372).

Logical negation, as expounded by the Platonists in the Socratic dialogue, is an operation on one logical value, typically the value of a proposition, that produces a value of true when its operand is false and a value of false when its operand is true. So, if statement A is true, then ¬A (pronounced "not A") would therefore be false; and conversely, if ¬A is true, then A would be false. The word "virtual," as the reader will recall from the introduction, was defined by Charles Peirce in 1902 as follows: "A virtual X (where X is a common noun) is something, not an X, which has the efficiency (*virtus*) of an X" (Commens, 2006). This is a typical, *classical* logical argument.

Bergson made a frontal attack on this traditional logic. Bergson stung the establishment with an unorthodox method that claimed "to mediate between idealism and realism, subjectivism and objectivism, and even between physics and metaphysics" (Douglass, 1992, p. 372). This very refusal to engage with formal logic and dialectical reasoning formed the central thrust of Bergson's turn of the century work, *Matter and Memory* (Bergson, 1990) – a pivotal text for Deleuze because it sidesteps the dualisms of dialectic, proposing something different:

> Matter, in our view, is an aggregate of "images." And by "image" we mean a certain existence which is more than what the idealist calls a representation, but less than that which the realist calls a thing, – an existence placed halfway between the "thing" and the "representation." This conception of matter is simply that of common sense … . For common sense, then, the object exists in itself, and on the other hand, the object is, in itself, pictorial, as we perceive it: image it is, but a self-existing image. (Ibid., pp. 372–373)

Here, in this quotation from Deleuze, we see what we would regard, in modern terminology, as the virtual, placed at the centre not only of human consciousness but of the nature of reality itself. Matter is presented as having two simultaneous coterminus faces – the one objective and measurable by reductive science, the other human perception – the "measuring" of it. We can see, no less, the virtual world of Second Life as both a perceived reality to the resident, and as a set of pixels on an objectively real screen.

Deleuze extrapolates from this concept of the image-reality Bergson's "determination to escape the history of philosophy by short-circuiting dialectical oppositions" (ibid., p. 373). In place of such oppositions – like that between the real and virtual – Bergson uses a terminology of "composite images," "multiplicities," or "aggregates," and the truly radical nature of Bergsonian analysis, as read by Deleuze, resides in this notion of multiplicities. "That discussion," moreover, Douglass notes, "inevitably focuses on tensions inherent in a constantly evolving cosmos that is not merely analogous with, but finally indistinguishable from, what we call 'consciousness'" (ibid., 371). The notion of multiplicities in composite and continuous form, embracing material, objective reality, and human perception of it, into one unfolding consciousness, presents us with an apparent conclusion that the "virtual" is not a "sham" of the "real," but another (and perhaps the only) face of it, and the creation and apprehension of that which is "virtual" is inherent in the nature of what it is to be human.

> Like Bergson, Deleuze
> sees man as the endpoint of creation, for he enfolds all, and durations that are inferior or superior are still internal to him. Man therefore creates a differentiation that is valid for the Whole, and he alone traces out an open direction that is able to express a whole that is itself open. (Douglas 1992; p. 379)

In this sense Virtuality is Reality, Reality is Virtuality, and our distinctions between the two are for intellectual convenience only. Bergson, and his interpretation by Deleuze, brings us here a picture of the holistic, meaning-centered, intuitive consciousness of humanity as being at the center of a time-space universe, cresting a wave of multiplicities that are neither image nor representation, grasping the whole where our intellect, trained by millennia of reductive thought, seeks out dualities.

Grasping such comprehensive virtu-realities/multiplicities with our mind's eye, let us return to the ICT conceptualization of virtuality, à la Pierce and Nelson, and see where it may lead. For if human consciousness is as capable of perceiving the virtual as real, as our tour of Bergson and Deleuze would imply, there might indeed be substantial implications for our future information society.

TimeSpace multiplicities, *The Matrix*, and Second Life

Multiplicities in cyberspace were perhaps first (or at least most famously) and best envisioned by fiction writers. Specifically, Neal Stephenson's cyberpunk novel *Snow Crash* (Stephenson, 1992) and his concept of the metaverse, and William Gibson's *Neuromancer* (Gibson, 1993) and the other books associated with it, set out a cyberpunk world that captures the sense of "reality" in computer-generated "virtual" worlds that Bergsonian multiplicity implies. There was also Sherry Turkle's work, particularly *Life on the Screen* (Turkle, 1993) at this time, reflecting and paralleling the work of the cyberpunk fiction writers.

Gibson's world presupposes a fundamental affinity between carbon-based neural activity and silicon-based digital activity, which makes possible a direct interface between the two. This interface includes the Sense/Net, the "simstim," and "microsofts." This brain/computer direct interface, apparent in all of Gibson's work, enables one to "jack-in" to cyberspace and experience it with all of one's senses in an internalized virtual reality – one literally plugs either chips (microsofts) or "cyberspace decks" into a jack plug set into one's skull behind the ear. One can then either travel in cyberspace using the deck to navigate, or play back "simstim" soaps or films into oneself. This interface makes possible such a thing as a "construct" – like the character Dixie Flatline. He is dead, but a digital recording of him is available that can interact, as if alive, in the simstim environment. But even Gibson includes some doubt about this world: "The sinister thing about a simstim construct, really, was that it carried the suggestion that 'any' environment might be unreal" (Gibson, 1993, p. 197). One might equally say that any virtual environment might be real.

Gibson gives a neat potted history of this hyperreal world, which he dubs, the "Matrix": "The matrix has its roots in early arcade games," said the voiceover, "in early graphics programs and military experimentation with cranial jacks." On the Sony, a two-dimensional space war faded behind a forest of mathematically generated ferns, demonstrating the special possibilities of logarithmic spirals; cold blue military footage burned through, lab animals wired into test systems, helmets feeding into fire control circuits of tanks and war planes.

> Cyberspace. A consensual hallucination experienced daily by billions of legitimate operators, in every nation, by children being taught mathematical concepts. … A graphic representation of data abstracted from the banks of every computer in the human system. Unthinkable complexity. Lines of light ranged in the nonspace of the mind, clusters and constellations of data. Like city lights, receding. (Gibson, 1993, p. 67)

Gibson's world makes a fundamental assumption – almost, one might say, an "absolute pre-supposition" (Collingwood, 1972) – that consciousness, identity, selfhood, etc. can be divorced from, separated from, and exist beyond and outside of the body – a view that is almost Cartesian in flavor. It equates the former with information, in a digital sense, and grants it the quality that information has been granted (in the last century) – of being a pattern, and a pattern only, that has no substance, and is free to flow from place to place along suitable conductors (Hayles, 1999). Given this presupposition, it is possible for Gibson to include a subplot in *Neuromancer* in which a voodoo sect (involving "horses" ridden by "snakes") is able to navigate in cyberspace through a form of ritualistically (and chemically) induced astral travel. The traditional, pre-Darwinian, vitalistic realm of the spiritual world is here directly equated with cyberspace. Take away the presupposition that our mental faculties are translatable from brain-matter to digital information, and move the voodoo context slightly further east, and *Neuromancer* becomes pure Bollywood. The "Wig" explains how, uncannily like a Sardu, "his technique of mystical exploration involved projecting his consciousness into blank, unstructured sectors of the matrix and waiting" (Gibson, 1993).

Yet there seems to remain a fundamental distrust of such a virtual metaverse. Almost in homage to Gibson's work, the Hollywood movie, *The Matrix* (Wachowski, 1999) presents a virtual-reality that is deconstructed before our eyes. Bridging the already familiar Gibsonian elision between the psychic and the digital, human beings encased in pods stacked miles high in underground bunkers have massive jacks inserted into their brainstems and are thus plugged into vast computers, and act out the characters in a gigantic simulation of late twentieth-century American culture – a nightmare indeed. A hero arises to fight for enlightenment and freedom from the chains of microelectronic maya, plucked like some reincarnated demigod from the masses by the outlaw priesthood of the true path. Yet this is no sentimental romance for the eagle and flag. For here in the "Matrix" shine the possibilities inherent in the awareness that all that we are is an act. The notion of cultural performance is here taken to its logical extreme, and the root suggestion that reality itself is an act – a consensual hallucination like Gibson's cyberspace – is presented to us, on the screen.

Now, turning for a moment to the world of neuroscience, one Professor Llinas would have it, from his studies of dreaming and wakefulness, that our brains are in actuality in a constant state of dreaming – "they are continually generating images to manufacture the world inside our heads." He asserts,

> The outside world is a projection, you put it there. It is not happening out there, it is happening inside your head. It is, in fact, a dream, exactly like when you fall asleep. We need to see, we need to perceive, we need to dream actively – because this is the only way we can take this huge universe and put it inside a very tiny head. We fold it, make an image, and then we project it out. (Greenfield, 2000, p. 75)

Imagination and normal vision, it would appear, are separate but overlapping brain processes, and our visual experience "is a kind of mixture of information coming in from the eyes and prior association." In short, "we see things with our brains, not our eyes" (ibid., p. 79). This would appear to be the world of reductive, rationalist, mechanist medical science confirming the philosophical impressions of Bergson and Deleuze.

If this is so, then the world of the metaverse and the "Matrix" is our world – our modern Information Society. We live in a consensual hallucination that is the human interpretation of the universe, and with our minds collectively construct a reality that makes sense of it all, and of us. Is not, after all, this "Matrix," in which Keanu Reaves and his accomplices play out their Game Boy fantasy, a perfect figure for the world of Intellection of which Bergson spoke? Even the "substantival virtualism" (physical neurodigital interfaces) is, in light of neo-Bergsonian multiplicities, unnecessary, for it seems clear that people are already all too able to "picture" themselves in a cyberspatial world, and interact with it, using the nonimmersive interface of keyboard, mouse, and screen, and treat it as a world equally as real as that we more normally associate with physical objects. "Second Life," as its introduction claims, "is a 3-D virtual world entirely built and owned by its residents" (Second Life, 2003). Sweden, in a move that makes it the first nation state to do so, has declared that it is opening an embassy on Second Life (BBC News Website, January 2007). In Second Life, sports manufacturers Adidas and Reebok sell virtual training shoes, Toyota and Nissan sell virtual cars, the BBC has rented an island to stage live music events, Reuters has a permanent Second Life reporter, and generally people do what they do in the real world – but without leaving their chair. You can chat, as with many other online meeting places, but you can also go dancing, attend lectures, gamble … have sex. Second Lifers can make and sell goods in exchange for Linden dollars. As the BBC News website reported in November 2006, "Some estimates put the economic value of Second Life in 2005 at $64 million (£33 million)."

Yet the world of Second Life is not without its detractors – notably http://www.getafirstlife.com/, which lampoons the site by advertising the wonderful – and oh so cool – possibilities of physicality in the real world. "Find Out Where You Actually Live" it offers, with a link to Google Earth. "Fornicate With Your Actual Genitals" it exhorts – notably with no hyperlink. "What's this body thing, and what do I do with the dangly bits?" it asks, in the Frequently Asked Questions list. Clearly, there is a good deal to criticize with the ungrounded virtuality of Second Life. Yet clearly, too, it has its followers – over 3 million of them – and with Entropia and others following it, and IBM employing its first metaverse evangelist tasked with spreading the word on 3D worlds among the company's employees, such virtual worlds seem not only here to stay, but a likely growing part of our future information society (BBC News website, November 2006).

It takes little imagination to forecast how Second Life might be accessed, through a range of VR headsets, gloves, and other wearable computing costumes, in the not so distant future – and what activities residents might get up to in such clothing. Flexible plastic screen technology promises contact lens access to virtual worlds with the prospect of sitting in a real boardroom with both "present" and "telepresent" board members, whose highly accurate 3D avatars appear to all intents and purposes to be sitting next to one another on the sofa. No doubt the technology that arrives in the boardroom will first have been developed for the virtual bordello, but the potential for mixing real and virtual in our everyday experience becomes more and more apparent as time goes by.

Implications for theory and practice

There is little doubt that theories of virtuality in contemporary society stand to be greatly enriched by the notions of consciousness raised in this chapter. Experiences of practical applications of virtuality are potentially much more deeply understood when this perspective is adopted – and the potential enhancements (and dangers) of such experiences more clearly envisioned. Equally, the design of practical applications of virtuality may benefit from an understanding of the human ability to engage in, and deem as completely real, what in other perspectives might be viewed as "merely" virtual environments. In particular, perhaps, the somewhat counterintuitive realization that "immersion" through blinkered vision and haptic interfaces is by no means requisite for a very full engagement with virtual worlds is something the builders of virtual worlds may take note of! Equally, the implication that such immersion might engender an engagement so total that "reality" becomes dangerously far away from immediate consciousness may also become a fruitful area of research.

One is reminded of the current debate around the use of mobile phones while driving, wherein the popular notion would have it that a hands-free kit makes everything alright, because one then has one's hands on the wheel and can properly attend to the controls of the car. However, according to research as far back as 1998, it is indeed not the engagement with the controls of the phone that is at issue, but the mental state of the driver engaged in a conversation with someone outside of the car (Haigney and Taylor, 1998; McEvoy et al., 2005). The virtual presence of the driver in a nongeographic, telecommunications space that takes up a part of her/his consciousness inevitably relegates the more motor-centered and learned behavior of driving to a deeper and less attended part of consciousness, rendering the driver quite literally unsafe to drive, and statistically four times more likely to be involved in an accident (McEvoy et al., 2005). There are important lessons here for all theorists and practitioners in virtuality. Consciousness and its relationship with time and space can be ignored at our peril in any number of situations.

Conclusion

The discussion above shows that such multiplicities, despite the scorn of GetAFirstLife, promise rich and all-too-human experiences of a world at once both real *and* virtual. As we have seen from our tour through the alternative, intuitive-holistic conception of reality, the real and the virtual are arguably not so opposed as the more rationalist perspective might lead us to believe.

Now, in truth, Bergson's philosophy carries with it both great dangers and great responsibilities. If the intellect is indeed to be demoted from its rationalist pinnacle, if our intuitive faculties are truly the greater, then a gigantic doorway is opened. As Irwin Edman says in his fascinating foreword to the second edition of Arthur Mitchell's translation of *Creative Evolution* published in 1944 for the Random House Modern Library, "The *élan vital* means a renaissance to a poet; to a barbarian it means brute power" (Bergson, 1944, p. xvi). In the world of intuition, as Levi-Strauss amply demonstrates on many occasions in his studies of world mythology (1992), at the threshold of every door there is a guardian – a gargoyle. It is my reading of the fall of Bergson's philosophy from favor, in the postwar period, and his consignment to a "repressed content of modern thought" (Burwick and Paul, 1992, p. 4), that the Nazis were the demon at the gate, and that having defeated them and retreated from that gate back into the primacy of intellection, the western world is loath, as yet, to risk that road again. The popularity of Husserl and some of the other postwar phenomenologists contributed to this demise – more by historical accident than anything else, and it is only Deleuze that has brought us the recent revitalization of Bergson's thought.

Finally – and this is the point that Bergson ultimately wished to make – the intuitive faculty, making choices at the crest of the unfolding present, is the means to our individuality, the means to creating personhood. If our experiences, and the choices we make in them, derive from the "virtual," as opposed to the real, are they any the less our experiences? Do we through virtuality create our personhood in a way that is any the less individual compared to the route through reality? These are questions to explore more fully in another paper, but clearly the basic process of individuation and human experience, as understood through Bergson's ideas, does not fundamentally differentiate between the real and the virtual, indeed makes no such distinction, and the future information society promises a fascinating range of possibilities for both. Short of sounding like a metaverse evangelist myself, I would conclude that the 3D virtual worlds of Second Life, Entropia (2005), and their copyists, will have an increasing role to play in our lives.

Note

1. A collection of physical, biological, psychological or symbolic entities that creates a unified concept, configuration or pattern which is greater than the sum of its parts. http://en.wiktionary.org/wiki/gestalt

References

BBC News Website http://news.bbc.co.uk/1/hi/world/europe/6310915.stm (accessed January 2007)

Bergson, H. (1896) *Matter and Memory*, Zone Books, 1990.

Bergson, H. (1907) *Creative Evolution*, Random House: New York, 1944.

Burwick, F., and Paul, D. (Eds) (1992) *The Crisis In Modernism: Bergson and the Vitalist Controversy*, Cambridge University Press: Cambridge.

Collingwood, R.G. (1972) *An Essay on Metaphysics*, University Press of America: London.

Commens (2006) http://www.helsinki.fi/science/commens/terms/virtual. html

Deleuze, G. (1966) *Le Bergsonisme* [Bergsonism], trans. C. Boundas (1988), Zone Books: New York.

Douglass, P. (1992) *Deleuze's Bergson: Bergson Redux. The Crisis in Modernism: Bergson and the Vitalist Controversy*, Cambridge University Press: Cambridge.

Dreyfus, H. (1986) *Mind Over Machine: The Power of Human Intuition and Expertise in the Era of the Computer*, Free Press: New York.

Entropia Universe (2005) http://www.entropiauniverse.com/en/rich/5000. html

Gibson, W. (1993) *Neuromancer*, HarperCollins: London.

Greenfield, S. (2000) *Brain Story*. BBC.

Haigney, D., and Taylor, R. (1998) Free Road Safety Resource provided by Royal Society for the Prevention of Accidents, http://www. rospa.com/roadsafety/info/mobile_phone_studies.pdf

Hayles, N.K. (1999) *How We Became Posthuman*, University of Chicago Press: Chicago.

Levi-Strauss, C. (1992) *Introduction to a Science of Mythology*, Penguin: London.

Linden Labs (2007) *Second Life Virtual Economy Key Metrics*, available from http://secondlife.com/

McEvoy, S.P., Stevenson, M.R., McCartt, A.T., Woodward, M., Haworth, C., Palamara, P., and Cercarelli, R. (2005) Role of Mobile Phones in Motor Vehicle Crashes Resulting in Hospital Attendance: A Case-crossover Study, *British Medical Journal*, Aug, 331, 428.

Second Life (2003) http://secondlife.com/whatis/ (accessed January 2007)

Skagestad, P. (1998) *Peirce, Virtuality, and Semiotic*, Paper given at 20th World Congress of Philosophy, Boston, at the University of Massachusetts – Lowell, http://www.bu.edu/wcp/Papers/Cogn/Cogn Skag.htm (accessed January 2008).

Sotto R. (1997) The Virtual Organization, *Accounting, Management and Information Technology*, 7(1), 37–51.

Stephenson, N. (1992) *Snow Crash*, Bantam: New York.

TechCrunch (2007) http://www.techcrunch.com/2007/02/10/second-life-census/

Turkle, S. (1993) *Life on the Screen*, Simon and Schuster: New York.

Wachowski, A., and Wachowski, L. (1999) *The Matrix*, Warner.

CHAPTER 13

The virtual and virtuality: Toward dialogues of transdisciplinarity

Jeremy Hunsinger

In confronting the issues surrounding virtuality and its study in the future, we need to think about the plurality of perspectives and communities that support them. In pursuing this line of thought, we must confront the contradictions found in our knowledge and understanding of the virtual. These contradictions can be resolved by considering the possibility of radical otherness found in virtuality and its implications for our future knowledge, for a basis of dialogue about transdisciplinarity, and for the inclusion of the whole plurality of perspectives available in specific contexts. The argument continues through three phases. The first is a consideration of two incommensurable perspectives on virtuality. With that contradiction in hand, I propose a more general position that takes a metaunderstanding of those two perspectives. From this understanding, an analysis of the possibility of the development as a discipline is problematized in relation to the boundary work and territorialization of the field. Finally, the resolution to the constitution of boundary work is presented as creating an inclusive transdisciplinary dialogue, which will help us create and sustain a legitimate research program of virtuality studies.

A question of perspective

The nature of the virtual is teeming with plural meanings. The meanings we choose to use as the basis of our interpretations of virtuality have deep implications for our current work and our future collaboration. When approaching the virtual, scholars from diverse disciplines have found that conceptually "the virtual" wrestled with the profound challenges to their ideological or disciplinary constraints that the concept presents. However, in many of the abstract areas of the disciplines, one could argue that there is nothing other than the virtual; theoretical mathematics or metalogic, for instance, which examine questions of the virtual almost exclusively. However, the virtual is no longer limited to those theoretical disciplines. As the technical realm has opened up a new arena of the virtual in recent years, the whole of the human disciplines (arts, psychology, sociology, business, etc.) have engaged virtualities as areas of exploration. The nature of the virtual has become more pluralist, and that shift has created a space for new dialogues about the meaning and inclusion of virtuality. The meanings we choose to use as the basis for our interpretations have deep implications for our current and future collaborative work.

The virtual should be understood as those sets of things which have no referent in the real world, yet are virtualized through the projection of identities, institutions, ecologies, and their relations in a world that is mediated, such as through a computer game or other embodiments of a world without referent. Virtuality, then, must be mediated by something such as our minds, or digital or analog systems, because while we might usually think of computer games as one paradigmatic sense of virtuality, the plural realities of textual fictions are as much virtualities as are games or logical abstractions. The virtual is less the expression of the virtuality on the page or on the screen as the distribution of that reality through the memories and actions of its participants. The virtual is the combined and active imaginations and memories through which we engage mediated environments; it is a shared, but plural, projection. As we become more aware of the expansion of the virtual, the actualization of the virtual through the practices of our everyday lives, our economies, and our politics is restructuring research programs and academic centers, as we can see from the emergent interest in social simulation, e-science/e-social science, and digital humanities.

We might consider the following two perspectives of the virtual to exemplify the expanding and fragmented nature of virtuality studies. These perspectives derive from two very different disciplinary perspectives. The key differences in the two perspectives center on their understanding of the relationships between what exists and virtual objects. The first perspective, which we might think of as the synchronic perspective, constructs an understanding of virtual objects as ones that have no referent in the real world; they have no relationships that reach into the real. Building through the structures of reference, this perspective constructs an understanding of the inherent difference between the real and the virtual on the basis of a relation among sets of signs existing in a fixed and static field without temporal relations. This perspective assumes the virtual are immanent and floating signifiers that, while sensible as constructions outside of space/time, cannot be real (Van Fraassen, 1980). Thus the virtual is not real because it lacks either an empirical or positive relation to the world at a certain time. This analytical construction of the virtual assigns relationships in a system of meaning where there can only be one resolved set of conceptual perspectives relating to empirical observations at any point in time, without relations to either the past or future states of that object. In this model, one must think that something either is or is not virtual, and if it is virtual, it cannot be real.

An alternative to the synchronic analysis is the diachronic perspective. It is derived from the Bergsonian and Deleuzian traditions (though certainly the one that I provide is at best a derivation of pragmatic and process philosophies, but also grounded in a materialism). This perspective of the virtual, centers on artifacts and their mediations as related through time, but here the relations are processual and pragmatic, grounded in an open system of concepts. The concepts are defined not by their boundaries or opposites, but by the fluctuating constructions of relations that constitutes knowledge and understanding in those traditions. The virtual in this system of signs operates as a series of relations that are virtualized and constantly in flux; they have become virtual through any number of human, mechanical, or informational processes. These virtualities are real in that they exist as some relation to the world as constituted by our mental processes and material forms. This differs from the first perspective, which requires a fixed relationship at any given time, whereas the construction of the virtual in the second perspective relies on the flow of time to establish the relationship. However, as virtual objects are not actual as compared to potential in a Deleuzian ontology, and are fluxing and transitioning across a myriad of cyborg interpretants, the virtual is perpetually coming into being through those interpretants. The virtual exists as things and as signs to be perceived, and through their perception they are interpreted and understood in relation to other signs.

In the second perspective, the virtual, and virtuality in general, is not actual, in that the actual is what is not fluxing and changing, but is becoming stable. For Deleuze, in *A Thousand Plateaus*, the actual is the system of strata. It is the aggregation and concretion of stable systems that can be modeled in a fixed and linear fashion (Bonta and Protevi, 2004). By contrast with the nature of the actual, for instance, a rock, which will tend toward finding a resting place in a gravitational field, the virtual is different. The virtual rock need not have the defined relations of a rock in the world. It need not react to gravitational fields, nor need it occupy a virtual space. However, there comes a time when, in attempting to grasp the relations through which we come to understand what it might mean for the virtual rock to be understood as a rock, that we might no longer have, in most people's interpretations, a rock at all.

Insofar as the virtual rock is both becoming rock and non-rock concurrently within the context of a plurality of human experiences of rockness, the virtual rock has no direct relation to a rock beyond mediation and conceptualization. The changing nature of the virtual is key to understanding the difference between the synchronic (i.e., same-time) perspective as opposed to the diachronic (i.e., changing through time) perspective on virtuality. In the synchronic and fixed analysis of the virtual, we deal with systems composed in time, but where that composition has ended, and where we are left with a construction of the virtual "as is." In the first perspective on the virtual, the relations are fixed and uncontested in the imaginations of their interpretants. The processes are not ongoing, but are frozen in their states so that they are no longer becoming what they may be. In that they are frozen, the virtual rock "just is" a rock in the analysis. It may be other things too within the framework of rockness, such as part of a building, a weapon, and/or the gallstone of dragon. However, the synchronic mode of virtual has implications for our capacity to understand its nature as it fails to recognize the changing relationships of virtuality through time.

The importance of understanding the problems caused by having plural and divergent understandings of the virtual and virtuality cannot be stressed enough. The two perspectives of the virtual influence the research that is performed on virtuality topics, and if the virtual world becomes the domain of any fixed theory or perspective, elements of the possible knowledge of the virtual will be lost. The Enlightenment ideal of the unification of knowledge into hierarchical categories governed by divergent theoretical and empirical assumptions, which converge into the grand schema, is a process of editing out the parts of the knowledge that do not fit the scheme. Thus, when we consider the alternate perspectives on the virtual, we have to consider the implicit normative systems of knowledge and the edits they require. For the first perspective of the virtual, we must by necessity edit out the relations of time of the second, while the relations of time of the second erases the fixed meanings of the former. Thus, one perspective does not become the other, though they may over time provide points of translation between them.

Understanding the signs

Consider that we might merely think of virtuality as a system of signs, very real signs, but signs that do not map onto reality. In society, both reality and virtuality operate as systems of signs, complementing each other, each bulwarking the understanding of the other. This occurs where real things have references in the virtual, and some virtual things have reference to a real thing, but no virtuality or virtual world has a direct reference to reality or the real world. The signs interoperate and in some cases can be interpolated across virtual worlds and real worlds. Signs in the virtual world are less fixed on their objects and more fixed in the interpretative communities through which they operate. Given the plurality of systems and communities within those systems, we need to take care when constructing our interpretations of these perspectives.

The interoperation and interpolation of signs between the virtual and the real depend on human experiences. The virtual need not rely on those experiences, however; it can become a whole new set of experiences. The experience of information outside of textual, televisual, or other fixed forms that constitute the realm of the "normal" in our cultural milieu generally begins at the edges of metaphors grounded in that milieu. It is not hard to understand the avatar becoming virtual dragon or unicorn as much as it is hard to understand it becoming the virtual circle or square such as in the novel *Flatland* (Abbott, 1992). The virtual as reflected in fictional worlds provides some access to the radical otherness of the circle, but the access is limited by our anthropomorphism of the circle. However, the capacity to understand elements of being a circle is present in our sign systems, whereas more alien experiences are possible. It is in those alienations that a creative construction of concepts, which are fundamentally innovative in breaking the structures and norms of the system of signs, occurs. It is in this breaking, in this transgression, where there is a virtuality that is neither actual, nor actualizable. In science fiction and fantasy texts, for example, there have already been humans becoming dragons, unicorns and circles, and even alien beings, but those transformations have been enclosed in narratives and textualities that are normalized in our lives. This is to say that there is a virtual that is not fantasy, but that is real, and until experienced and interpreted, is misunderstood. This radical other of the virtual constitutes one liminality of the boundary of virtual experiences. It is a point that allows us to see how our understanding works in virtual worlds, because we have to imagine a new self to even begin to comprehend that which has no referent, no interoperation, and no interpolation with our current everyday life and cultural milieu.

That the real and virtual usually have a relationship does not mean that we can ever fully know or grasp a virtuality in our minds either individually or collectively, or from one subjective perspective or distributed perspectives. Our capacity to understand the normal in our cultural milieu is unquestioned, but the virtual provides things outside of these norms. As academics and informed readers, we may be able to come to terms with virtuality as a topic of study, as a series of relationships within the academy and society, and more precisely as a set of quickly formed differences, which may be overcome. However, describing and document-ing the relations of virtuality to our everyday lives will take a plurality of knowledge practices, and thus a plurality of perspectives, disciplines, and methods. This intertwinement of the virtual and the real creates a messy arena for study, in which we can pursue a variety of modes of research.

Could there be "virtuality studies"?

Is there a field that studies virtuality? One way that we identify fields of study is to identify the questions that they address. To some extent, as alluded to above, all fields deal with virtuality. Those fields that study the causes of human action and the nature of human thoughts clearly are studying virtuality as well as reality. Thus, the full breadth of human life is open to question through the rubric of virtuality studies. Most centrally, the virtual has become an implied as a cause of human action, and in that those that study the virtual have extensions into a myriad of fields. Virtual constructs like *will* and *intent* pervade our theory and explanations. In other fields, other virtual constructs are pervasive and map through their concepts and explanations.

The explosion of virtualities across all fields lends itself to the construction of expert knowledge and expert terminologies that could become incomprehensible as a whole, both to its academic and public audience. The unsystematic growth of virtualities has eventually yielded contestation and divergence in the axiomatic and conceptual foundations of virtuality, as we have seen between the philosophical and the media studies perspectives above. This dissensus about the nature and import of the virtual fragments our understanding, and the plurality of nascent disci-plines, either imported from existing disciplines or developing around the topic itself, will quickly reproduce the problems of translation and interpretation among fields of knowledge. By recognizing these ongoing problems in the development and structuring of disciplines in relation to bodies of knowledge, we can see that we need an opening of dialogue about the virtual across these disciplines. This dialogue is necessary to preserve the plurality of knowledge and trajectories for research, to resist the narrowing of the expansive understanding of the virtual, and to sustain the continued interest in virtual worlds.

Virtuality studies is pertinent in many disciplines, which translate some understanding of the virtual into their own work. Disciplines have borders and display a "recognizable continuity" (Becher, 1989, p. 21). Disciplines have boundary workers who seek to encapsulate and defend a territory of knowledge, some of which is heavily contested among the disciplines. This boundary work is often important in demarcating science from non-science and determining who receives the related benefits of belonging within the territory (Gieryn, 1983). The construction and contestation of territory in relation to benefits and public goods also leaves gaps and unclaimed spaces where those goods will not flourish. It is in these less contested territories that interdisciplinary possibilities arise and encapsulate certain issues and topics that are often ignored by the disciplines.

We can see these contestations happening, for instance, in the pluralization of methods and techniques becoming literacies in domains of knowledge. As it has become more difficult to comprehend our everyday life due to the contestation of boundaries and its implications, knowledge has become territorialized as domains of literacy, as domains requiring specific or expert knowledge. We no longer have a sense of being singularly literate, instead we now must possess media literacy, informational literacy, and library literacy, to name a few. Instead of encouraging people to learn how to be generally capable and critical subjects, we now have boundaries that say they can be information literate, but not media literate, or generally literate. The division of the literacies indicates a fundamental misunderstanding of thought in context. Human beings have a capacity for thought, which is singular and applied to contexts, but the division of expertise based on contestations of disciplines and territories implies that not only is our capacity for thought pluralized, it can be divided anew for each technical system and their requisite technicities (Dodge and Kitchin, 2005). Each new literacy maps a set of conceptualizations and productive functions that may be tied to a technical system, but the new literacies are centered on those technical systems, their technicities, and knowledge. Technicities, such as those in virtual worlds, do not create new mental capacities, though they might habituate old ones in new ways. However, it is likely that we will soon see the case where people will not be literate in the virtual, even when they use the virtual everyday in one sense, whether in virtual worlds or not, as literacy is becoming abstracted from the world of everyday social life and contexts (Schroeder, 2001).

The division, abstraction, and territorialization of the world as part of the process of creating and defending knowledge domains leads us to the position where the pluralities of meanings, which were once possible to understand as a whole within our everyday lives, have become impossible to understand outside of the contexts of expertise (Beck, 1992; Beck, Giddens, and Lash, 1995). The development of knowledge within related fields, where the knowledge does not refer to itself or refer to a process of the construction of subjects, is one sign of the development of disciplines. If understanding the virtual becomes a matter of having people who are literate, then we can be assured that there is a field on virtuality studies, and, more importantly, we can be assured that most people who have studied and will study the virtual will not be part of virtuality studies. In short, the disciplinarity of virtuality, I argue, is not yet formed, but if it does form, it will become more than a discipline, it will become a literacy. In becoming a literacy, the study of virtuality will have to relate to literate people, creating new formalisms, and, through those formalizations, creating new norms for the knowledge of the virtual that will further divide research in the field.

A move toward transdisciplinarity

The extensive and open spaces currently inhabited by interdisciplinary studies are important new specialties for the constitution of virtuality studies, because they point to a territory constituted by transversals – those trajectories that cut across and pass through territories and constitutes new wholes, new transdisciplinary areas. There has been a movement toward transdisciplinary research in a variety of fields in the last 30 years. Transdisciplinary research attempts to approach the object of study beyond and across disciplinary and interdisciplinary perspectives. Transdisciplinary research is composed of several independent disciplines, which can be combined into a whole, transdisciplinary field (Dickens, 2003, p. 97). A transdisciplinary field is one defined by the globality of its object of study, combined with the complex, emergent, and changing nature of that object (Genosko, 2002, p. 26). This globality represents a larger whole that can be approached from many perspectives because it cannot be understood completely from any given perspective. As we have seen above, virtuality as an object of study is incomprehensible as a whole from disciplinary or interdisciplinary perspectives, as it does not yet have its own literacy. Realizing that no single perspective will capture the territories entailed by virtuality, we need to develop and integrate inclusive models that can bring understanding to the greater whole without destroying its parts (Genosko, 2002, p. 25). We need to engage in a process of metamodelization; that is, we need to examine and rebuild our models to account for more than disciplinary perspectives. One way to do that is to intervene in the formative disciplinary discourses through dialogue. By engaging our perspectival models with the enveloping discursive strategies of dialogue, the models that we use become transparent. We discover the fissures and breaks of our models, their points of operation, and application, and thus also where they fail to capture knowledges across disciplines. Discussing models at a meta level, and engaging in metamodelization through transdisciplinary dialogue, enables a broader, more applicable mode 2 research model (Gibbons et al., 1994; Nowotny, Scott, and Gibbons, 2001). We need to build a dialogue among scholars of the virtual that enables them to share their conceptualizations and research, not merely on the everyday level of research practices, but a dialogue that includes discussion of the axiomatic and axiological bases of their research. Such a dialogue would be the foundation of a new transdisciplinary research agenda. Granted, virtuality studies is not the only arena where these dialogues might enable research, but in virtuality studies it might prevent future confusions and allow us to construct a sense of agreement that is currently absent.

Inclusivity toward the groups of interested peoples seeking knowledge about virtuality and society is central to the transdisciplinary agenda of creating dialogues in research and development. Once the boundary work is overcome, most fields can be reimagined as transdisciplinary fields. To begin the process of reimagination toward transdisciplinarity, the creation of new discourses must occur, and we must begin to use them to translate among all disciplines with interests in virtuality studies in a way that allows for the general understanding of conceptual and empirical fields. The constitution of these new discourses will borrow heavily from the disciplinary field from which they are constituted. However, these discourses will by necessity have to innovate both linguistically and conceptually in order to map between disciplinary domains or traditions (MacIntyre, 1989).

Translation is not merely the importation of language and concepts; it is the constitution of the meaning of the other that is becoming a part of the whole. Through translation, we not only map concepts and languages, but we map and reconstitute the foundations of cultures and institutions. Translation does not only find the commensurable areas of cultures and communities; it must recognize where the communities and cultures are incommensurate. Translators must find the meanings the cultures and communities do not or cannot share (ibid.). Translation is not merely "samesaying," but it is mapping the plural territories, including their differences and parts, in the contexts of everyday lives, cultures, and communities (ibid.). The study of virtuality needs to move beyond the samesaying of translation surrounding the idea of the "the virtual" and "virtuality" to become a field in which the plurality of perspectives is inclusive toward the possible knowledges to be found. Translation, in virtuality studies, must create a new discourse that over time will participate in the wholes and not merely in the parts. This translated discourse will, over time, become part of the reconstituted whole, which is renewed in response to their presence.

For translation among fields to occur, the dialogues creating the transdisciplinary discourses of virtuality studies need to embrace an agenda of inclusion, so that the number of cross-community interpreters is maximized, allowing for many possible translations in many directions. Plurality of translation is the only means of providing for the plurality of interpretations and thus providing access to the meaning among groups, such as disciplines, that do not hold the same axioms or axiologies. The necessity of plurality and maximization of plurality seems counterintuitive if one accepts the unity of knowledges, but in exploring virtual worlds, one cannot help but realize the plurality of knowledges present. Inclusion of this plurality in the case of translation is by necessity tied to correct performance of translation, a plurality of perspectives brings the robustness necessary to make the interpretation possible. Cross-community, and thus cross-cultural translation, can overcome boundary work and the implicit problems of translation noted in Macintyre's work on translating among traditions (ibid.). The necessary communicative abstraction of translation forms the basis for transdisciplinary research, but once in place the translation through discourse can provide a common language for constructing a public understanding of research. This discourse becomes the home for new axiological systems, new points of agreement about the nature of the transdisciplinary field. This understanding of transdisciplinary research is fundamentally different from interdisciplinary approaches. Were we to engage in interdisciplinary research, we would engage in the systematic appropriation and interpretation of the various disciplinary toolboxes involved into one or more frameworks of understanding that we already possess, whereas in transdisciplinary research we are attempting to construct the new framework through the sharing of research practices, axiomatic understandings, and axiological systems. Interdisciplinary research requires modes of translation as much as transdisciplinary work, but interdisciplinary research is fundamentally different, and that difference is where you also find the difference between samesaying and translation. In other words, interdisciplinary research is a mode of research that borrows techniques and speaks them into a whole, it tries to fill gaps in disciplinary research by redescribing the other disciplinary tools into the project, which is samesaying. Transdisciplinary research cuts across research at a foundational level, which requires not that one discipline translate into another discipline such as interdisciplinary research, but that any discipline that participates translates into a mutually understood model or set of models composed of axioms and axiologies informing our research practices. Interdisciplinary research is based on samesaying, whereas transdisciplinary is based on translation.

The agenda of inclusion makes necessary a study of virtuality that is constituted by disciplinary plurality. We need to train researchers in more than one discipline. We need to have cross-disciplinarity and thus cross-community-trained researchers to perform the act of translation among and for their respective communities. It is not enough to have interdisciplinarily trained researchers to translate methods and knowledge. We have to translate the wholes, not the parts of the disciplines.

As the virtual has expanded throughout everyday life in the last few years, disciplinary and interdisciplinary forms of research focusing on it have become more institutionalized as subdisciplines and specialties. Centers, departments, and sections in universities and research institutes focused on virtual worlds, game studies, medical simulation, business virtualities, and other topics have been created across the United States and around the world. Without collaborative effort toward a dialogue, these various research trajectories will become minor sidelines instead of major practices. For instance, it is already becoming difficult for the digital humanities to address the e-social sciences in a dialogue. Transdisciplinary practices break the normalized disciplinary boundaries, hierarchies, and stratifications normally found in academic knowledge production, by necessity and practice, not by a utopian proposition. Starting the dialogue is possible, but it requires us to move toward people doing similar work in other disciplines and to ask questions about foundations. Transdisciplinary research dialogues are not asking how individual researchers relate to each other, but how they relate to something larger, such as the virtual. The humanities, the sciences, and the special sciences discuss virtuality to some degree, but are we not at a loss about what exactly each group is saying? The agenda of inclusion and the dialogue of transdisciplinarity can help resolve these novel institutionalizations by reconstituting the basis of the institutions and the discourses themselves. In reconstituting these institutions and discourses, we need to be prepared for different institutional forms to arise, different research practices to occur, and different knowledges to be promulgated. Perhaps the transdisciplinary study of the virtual will no longer require the actual research institution in its current form because the communities that constitute the virtual world may be different from those in the real world.

The study of the virtual is becoming fragmentary, and increasingly unintelligible across disciplines and to the general public, as it progresses down narrow disciplinary paths. For laypersons, heavily disciplined or even interdisciplinary expert knowledge can be hard to interpret, and harder to use in any meaningful way. Transdisciplinary knowledge, because it has been recontextualized for the broader audience of multiple disciplines, is more accessible and interpretable due to the need to translate among disciplines. This interpretability and transdisciplinarity will allow the study of the virtual to retain its relevance to a broader audience, encouraging public interest and future growth of the field in ways other than through awesome media spectacles that have previously generated public interest in the virtual. In resisting disciplinarity, we should consider what the centers of our understandings and research about virtuality could become, and how virtuality studies makes sense not just to researchers and experts, but also to a broader audience. Every researcher has a research agenda, a set of questions, problems, and/or issues that they are working toward resolving in some manner. Those resolutions have trajectories and transversal relations that exist within some contexts, some knowledges, and some normative systems. Those contexts, knowledges, and normative systems contain inferences about what is possible, what virtuality studies could become. Recontextualizing our research to make sense of and bring understanding and interpretation to the possibilities and complexities involved in developing an understanding of virtuality can help us progress from disciplinary and interdisciplinary understandings toward a transdisciplinary understanding.

Public reception, relevance, and thus legitimacy are becoming important issues to consider in all research because they are the foundation for the capitalization of research; research and the aims of knowledge production are slowly disappearing from the public view, being replaced by controlled innovation and knowledge management. In an age where search engines can find the top results for any informational topic, it is harder and harder for the public to find the researcher behind yesterday's news of virtual worlds. The desktop computer is already disappearing into ubiquity and becoming an everyday appliance. This is not to say the household and business appliances are not important to our everyday life, our economies, our politics, or our individual research agendas. However, frequently these appliances are understood as part of a system of objects, technical systems, or similar theoretical assemblages that become particularized to certain disciplinary discourses; because of that they embrace disciplinary perspectives that highlight certain issues and seemingly forget others. This disciplinary back burner is the fate of the common appliance in the disciplines; it becomes ordinary, everyday, and thus systematized and normalized until it is forgotten as a separate object of study, though it frequently is and should be periodically be reprised and reintegrated into the growing body of knowledge (ISSC, 2003, p. 3; Herring, 2004, p. 33). We need to be careful not to lose virtuality studies to an embodiment in appliances and infrastructures lost to specialization, commodification, and technological development, or we will lose our topics of study. We need to preempt the disappearance of our topics of study into the everyday by increasing the relevance to researchers and the public they nominally serve. Virtuality studies' relevance and legitimacy varies with its capacity to communicate its findings and their relative importance to its audiences.

As virtual experiences and virtual worlds become part of everyday life, they will become less visible. The networks and infrastructures through which they operate are already very much invisible to the everyday user. As topics of research become less publicly visible, they become less relevant to the audience, and in the end they may even lose their perspectives. This may have tragic consequences for our growing body of knowledge and research practices.

The possibilities of having different research in virtual worlds highlight the directions we can pursue in a transdisciplinary manner. We do not have to use surveys when we have a history of the users' complete actions in a world. Their actions in virtual worlds, much like their actions in the real worlds, reveal as much as the surveys could reveal. Studies in virtual worlds do not have the same limits as studies in real life; this is clear whether the real limits are generated from the newly mutable physical world, the mutable social world, the alternative constitutions of subjectivity, or otherwise. While there is a tendency to map our current practices into the virtual environment, we need to be careful that we are not forcibly importing our reality to that environment in ways that harm the environment or its users. People already import a myriad of discursive frames into virtual worlds, but we do not need to reify those frames by pursuing the constitution of them through their parallel research practices, thus constituting the virtual world to be increasingly parallel to the real world. Perhaps there is, as indicated earlier in this chapter, a chance to see a radical other through reconstituting our research programs. What would it be like, for instance, to be a participant-observer in a world where the actors are constituted as nonunified gusts of air, broken apart and performing actions across great distances? In other words, what if the virtual world was nonindividualist, nonbodily, and/or nontextually oriented. If there is a world that is fundamentally different from our current modes of thought, can we find ways of researching it that does not reconstitute it within our frame of reference without destroying it or radically reconstituting it to fit our models. I cannot imagine that the paradigmatic model of participant-observer would work without our westernized assumptions of subjectivity. Interpretation in virtual environments becomes problematic when we no longer can assume that the environment is a neutral object, much like we cannot assume that in the built environment. Similarly, one can imagine creating a survey of the humans behind the screen, but is this accurately capturing the same being as is represented on the screen? On one level it may be, but we can imagine an interface where an ecology would be manifested by the cooperation of hundreds, if not millions, of people all contributing merely a part of a whole, which might bring into question just who is representing what about whom. We could also imagine an interface that interacted in nondeterministic ways, perhaps representing the subject in ways that limit the inferences we can make about other users. The openness offered by the virtual not mapping into the actual is a significant problem for traditional methods that may not map onto the assumptions, both epistemological and ontological, of our research models.

These epistemological and ontological assumptions are the axiological bases of research; they are claims about the world being measured and our interactions in it. They are as much claims about our own participation and our interpretations in the virtual world. They are bounded in disciplinary and interdisciplinary discourses, founded in traditions of research and understanding. Much like MacIntyre (1989), who argues that moral traditions are grounded in a practical rationality that was generated and still exists in a culturally specific historic trajectory of knowledge that in part explains and determines its possibilities, so are research traditions grounded and bounded in traditions. The functions of legitimizing our research depend on those traditions and their discourses and dialogues for their capacities to convey meaning to others. The virtual is not limited to the same epistemological or ontological systems that legitimize current social and physical research, as those epistemological and ontological systems need not be built into the code of the virtual environment. There may be, for instance, no individual research subjects in a world where avatars are constituted in a plurality of contributions from users. In lacking these shared epistemological and ontological assumptions, we have a new set questions that involve translation, that deal with research moving from the understandings of the possible in the virtual to the real in traditional research and the capacity of making comparisons between the two. If the assumptions of our research tools are no longer certifiably grounded in some manner, then the claims that we are capable of making about the virtual might falter. The different origins of this lack of legitimacy of research constitute yet one more reason to open dialogues with other disciplines and to transition our thinking toward transdisciplinary research in virtual worlds, toward a larger dialogue about our research.

Conclusion and implications

Virtuality and society constitutes a body of knowledge, a growing set of practices, and a set of divergent meanings that embody a place for realizing a common or perhaps an uncommon ground on which to build an audience and an understanding. In coming to terms with the divergent meanings of the virtual, the problems of public understanding and legitimacy of studying the virtual, and the question of a new disciplinarity of virtuality studies, we have come to terms with the questions of pluralities and territorialization in new fields of research. We cannot forgo the questions and possibilities raised in this chapter without admitting an unwillingness to confront thoughts about the future of our understandings of the virtual.

I have argued that, to study the virtual, we need a transdisciplinary agenda. This agenda should be based in an agenda of inclusion and dialogue with an eye toward the future. Transdisciplinarity resolves the problem by establishing the commonality in "unconnected or partially interacting disciplines" (Briggs, 1977, p. 2211). Commonality is what transdisciplinarity pursues, though it pursues that across disciplines through dialogue and model building. Transdisciplinary virtuality studies can create the topic of study, it can realize its objects and the continuance because it develops the axioms, understandings, and discourses that construct relevancy both inside and outside of academia. This way we can create and translate our findings to our colleagues and the public, providing legitimacy to our research and providing for its future. We need to be circumspect as researchers so that our research reaches out not only to our own disciplinary and interdisciplinary communities, but also to the broader audiences. We can with effort recontextualize our research and pursue transdisciplinary research to allow a broader audience to better understand the complex, global, and ever-changing nature of the virtual as a whole, doing work that we will enjoy for years to come.

References

Abbott, E. (1992) Flatland: A Romance in Many Directions, Dover, originally published in 1884.

Becher, T. (1989) *Academic Tribes and Territories*, Society for Research into Higher Education and Open University Press: Milton Keynes, UK.

Beck, U. (1992) *Risk Society: Towards a New Modernity*, Sage: Thousand Oaks, CA.

Beck, U., Giddens, A., and Lash, S. (1995) *Reflexive Modernization: Politics, Tradition and Aesthetics in the Modern Social Order*, Stanford University Press: Palo Alto, CA.

Bonta, M., and Protevi, J. (2004) *Deleuze and Geophilosophy: A Guide and Glossary*, Edinburgh University Press: Scotland.

Briggs, A. (1977) "Interdisciplinarity," in A.S. Knowles (Ed.), *International Encyclopedia of Higher Education*, Jossey-Bass: Washington.

Consalvo, M., Baym, N., Hunsinger, J., Jensen, K.B., Logie, J., Murero, M., et al. (2004) *Internet Research Annual: Selected Papers from the Association of Internet Researchers Conferences 2000–2002 (Digital Formations, 19)*, Peter Lang Publishing: Consalvo, NY.

Dickens, P. (2003) Changing Our Environment, Changing Ourselves: Critical Realism and Trandisciplinary Research, *Interdisciplinary Science Reviews*, 28, 95–105.

Dodge, M., and Kitchin, R. (2005) Code and the Transduction of Space, *Annals of the Association of American Geographers*, 95(1).

Gieryn, T.F. (1983) Boundary-Work and the Demarcation of Science from Non-Science: Strains and Interests in Professional Ideologies of Scientists, *American Sociological Review*, 48(6), 781–795.

Genosko, G. (2002) *Felix Guattari: An Aberrant Introduction*, Continuum: London.

Gibbons, M., Limoges, C., Nowotny, H., Schwartzman, S., Scott, P., and Trow, M. (1994) *The New Production of Knowledge: The Dynamics of Science and Research in Contemporary Societies*, Sage: Thousand Oaks, CA.

Hagoel, L., and Kalekin-Fishman, D. (2002) Crossing Borders: Towards a Trans-Disciplinary Scientific Identity, *Studies in Higher Education*, 27, 297–308.

Herring, S.C. (2004) Slouching Toward the Ordinary: Current Trends in Computer-mediated Communication, *New Media & Society*, 6(1), 26–36.

International Social Science Council (ISSC) (2003) Optimizing Knowledge in the Information Society. Available at http://www.icsu.org/2_resourcecentre/RESOURCE_list_base.php4?rub=9

Jones, S. (1998) *Doing Internet Research: Critical Issues and Methods for Examining the Net*, Sage: Thousand Oaks, CA.

Kiger, J.C. (1971) "Disciplines," in L.C. Deighton (Ed.), *The Encyclopedia of Education v. 3*, Macmillan and Free Press: New York, pp. 99–105.

MacIntyre, A. (1989) *Whose Justice? Which Rationality?*, University of Notre Dame Press: Notre Dame, IN.

Mansell, R. (2004) Political Economy, Power, and New Media, *New Media & Society*, 6(1), 96–105.

Nowotny, H., Scott, P., and Gibbons, M. (2001) *Re-Thinking Science: Knowledge and the Public in an Age of Uncertainty*, Polity Press: London.

Schroeder, C. (2001) Academic Literacies, Legitimacy Crises, and Electronic Cultures, *The Journal of Literacy and Technology*, 1(2).

Silver, D. (2004) Internet/cyberculture/digital culture/new media/fill-in-the-blank studies, *New Media & Society*, 6(1), 55–64.

Toulmin, S. (1972) *Human Understanding*, Clarendon Press: Oxford.

Van Fraassen, B.C. (1980) *The Scientific Image*, Clarendon Press: Oxford.

CHAPTER 14

Is everything virtuality? Exploring the boundaries of the topics

Mike Chiasson and Niki Panteli

Where have we gone?

The contributors to this book have, in different ways, identified and discussed critical issues, and given us insights on the nature of virtuality. These different contributions allow us to reflect on the diverse approaches to virtuality which illustrate the emerging agendas for further research and practice in intra- and interorganizational virtuality.

The chapters in this book have shown that different conceptualizations of virtuality are important and possible. We do not claim to have identified all possibilities for virtuality in this book, and later on we indicate various approaches and topics that have not been covered in the book. In doing so, we show that, as a field constantly under development and revision, as researchers, managers, and users become more aware of the potentials and diversity of virtuality, we embark on revised studies and explorations that lead to new depths and breadth of the field.

This book and its authors have examined various common and uncommon topics in the virtual. The topics include virtual experiences and interactions inside and beyond the organizations, covering both traditional (e.g. virtual teams) and less traditional (e.g. multiuser games) topics in management research. Many of these topics focus on computer-mediated systems, which involve virtual communication and coordination between people. These include relationships between employees and other employees, employees and suppliers, employees and customers, and customers with other customers. The interactivity and involvement of this virtual exchange varies, from straightforward e-mails between employees, to multiuser gaming between customers. The topics associated within the organization include: globally distributed work teams, perceptions of boundary and identity, the role of leadership in virtual team cohesion and performance, the social and psychological efficiency of distributed and virtual teams, the virtuality of shared norms and cultures across distributed groups, the purely technical versus the mixed-mediated practices of virtual workers, and the effects of discontinuities introduced by virtually connecting geographically and identity-separated organizations.

The topics beyond the organization in this book include emerging virtual relationships with customers and between customers, in various communities. Topics here include: the production of social identities in blogging, the emergence of communities during multiplayer online gaming, and the societal evolution or revolution in the virtuality introduced and extended by computer systems. The final chapters examine whether and how virtuality is different and discontinuous with the past, with two chapters arguing for an expansion in virtuality beyond the computer. The final chapter argues for a summary and assessment of key axioms and conventions in the many fields of virtuality research, and a transdisciplinary agenda that allows each to remain as separate yet complementary approaches to virtuality research.

Where haven't we gone?

Given the breadth and range of the book, it may be hard to imagine which topics, approaches, and methodologies have not been used by authors in the book. Despite our intentions, a good portion of the chapters are still focused on intra-organizational virtuality – how information systems support the co-located and distributed enterprise. In terms of theory, much of the work still implicitly or explicitly focuses on the computer as the virtuality-inducing machine. Starting from this initial assumption, a number of chapters explore the challenges, and sometimes lack of challenges that teams experience overcoming geographical, temporal, and conceptual space, compared with face-to-face interaction. A number argue that it is the conceptual space – social, shared culture-language, and psychological discontinuities in people's heads – which is key to knowledge sharing, trust, coordinated action, and the like.

The studies that explore beyond the organization show how some individuals are quite capable and interested in forming substantive communities beyond their physical boundaries. However, what is different here is that these virtual spaces are only possible through electronic systems, and the participants (usually customers) are there to find an alternative social forum. In these instances, virtual systems are not competing with the inertia of existing face-to-face mediums, except for the "first lives" that may suffer from this redirection of attention.

Although some of the chapters employ or cite research examining individual and group levels of analysis, most of the work sits at the organizational level of analysis. Detailed studies of the specific virtual experiences of individuals are touched on in only some of the work.

In addition, most of the research is either broadly qualitative and positivist, or philosophical and interpretive. Although touched on briefly in some of the chapters, most of the work remains uncritical in terms of examining or challenging power, for example.

This raises a number of possibly new and revised topics for virtuality research in the future, beyond the ones explored in this book. Some of these topics are already being studied elsewhere. These new possibilities are produced by common and uncommon assumptions about virtuality, the role (or not) of information technology, and the nature and possibilities for social interaction. All assume that virtuality is an important part of social and even object interactions. Some are perhaps more sensible than others, but we will try to make an argument for each.

1. Computerized games for intra- and interorganizational use. It is possible that structured games could be used to support organizational practices. In fact, we could argue that most information systems and computer software are simulated representations of work, and are thus "serious games."
2. Web-based systems have and will continue to support the co-development of products and services with customers. The open-source movement and customer-led product development point to various possibilities for distributed work with customers. Of interest here are the motivations of participants, and the capabilities required in computer-based systems to support the attraction and coordination of advice and action across employees and customers.
3. Face-to-face talk during meetings, and their intended and realized meaning with participants, provides a place to explore noncomputer mediated virtuality. The assumption here is that computer systems are not required for virtual interaction and symbolism. In fact, the philosophy and method of symbolic interactionism suggests that meaning is constructed around and from symbols. An extension to the topic, to include computer mediation, is to study the use of computer systems before and after meetings. Before-meeting computer-mediated studies could focus on individual interpretations and actions leading to meeting agendas and various interpretations of meanings. After the meeting, researchers could focus on the reporting and distribution of outcomes to both meeting participants and nonparticipants, and the radiating representation and effect of these virtual representations.

4. An examination of employee's e-mails would provide a fruitful place to explore the use of unstructured computerized genres, and the types of social relationships and distributed actions prompted and stimulated by other computerized messaging. Differences in the richness and absorption of the individual in their messaging task may point to histories of inter-action through face-to-face and computer systems, and how these exchanges infuse the richness of current exchanges.

5. Studies of both mobile and fixed telephone conversations with employees would be consistent with previous studies of managerial communica-tion and its effects on distributed decision-making. Here, an electronic medium, which is no longer considered a vital and defining part of virtuality, could be explored.

6. The co-location and distribution of participants in a person's work life, and a study of the mixed face-to-face and computerized communica-tion, could explore how people handle various virtual mediums (yes, face-to-face could be considered virtual) to coordinate and maintain the attention to issues across time. Woolgar points to these issues in his studies of increasing interactions among face-to-face and computerized mediums in his studies of virtual work.

7. Studies of similarly trained professionals, and how this training allows (and doesn't allow) the mobilization and coordination of distributed individuals working for the first time, would be welcome.

8. Studies of how power is produced, mediated, and realized through computerized systems would bring a critical theoretical examination of the enabling and constraining conditions produced within virtual systems.

These represent only the start of many other approaches to virtuality research, some of which have been studied and explored in other disciplines.

Where do we stop?

Is there any end to virtuality research? There certainly is a focus and interest on computer-mediated communication, and the possibilities and limitations of expanding beyond time and space to communicate and coordinate activi-ties. In this sense, virtuality is a working proposition about whether proxim-ity can be reproduced when people are not physically or temporally proximate. However, if the computer medium is our focus of attention, then virtuality provides a limited expansion of the field beyond our original focus on computer-mediation studies before the internet.

Beyond computer-mediated definitions of virtuality, a number of our authors have stretched the definition of virtuality toward symbolic and interpreted parts of life. Given that we are linguistic creatures, this could involve many things not traditionally considered a part of virtuality research, including the reading of a book, watching a movie and talking to someone in the same room. The definition here of virtuality revolves around those symbolic systems that absorb the individual in the activities and concerns of a community. This definition of virtuality potentially implies a dizzying expansion of the topic to include practically anything in social life, which may or may not be productive. Especially to those interested in a cumulative science of virtuality, this may be uncomfortable. On the other hand, to those interested in a postmodern exploration of the topic, this may be comfortable.

In terms of linking these diverse research and practical approaches to virtuality, there are primarily two approaches that have been adopted in the literature. The first is perhaps the most common approach, where independent studies on virtuality are conducted, without reference to the others. While this may suggest an increasingly diverse set of approaches and theories in virtuality research, it has in fact led to a few dominant positions focused either on the recovery of face-to-face (i.e. "real") effects through virtual systems, or the release of participants from real constraints in forming new communities.

A second approach to linking the various studies is to standardize and integrate the concepts and theories in a cumulative tradition that directs and restricts future research, along the lines indicated (but not necessarily suggested) by Kuhn (1996). While increasing the integration and perhaps the acknowledgment of other virtuality studies, the restrictions of a dominant cumulative tradition may restrict the requisite theoretical and methodological variety required to anticipate and produce virtuality.

In response to these two, we (and many of our authors) argue for an appreciation of the diversity of virtuality research theory and practice, so that we can learn from each other in order to produce an independent appreciation of the theories and findings (not a cumulative tradition), so that we can increase the theoretical and empirical diversity in virtuality research, in a heedful and thoughtful way. We thus argue that virtuality research and practice is itself virtual, in that the theories and approaches we employ in understanding virtuality direct our understanding of it, and transform its future possibilities. This approach differs from a cumulative tradition by avoiding the "cleaning house" approach of producing a tight cumulative tradition, and continuing to explore and appreciate the range of theories and approaches, which may be only loosely complementary and perhaps even contradictory with each other. The transdisciplinary approach suggested by one of our authors remains open to the emergent possibilities and surprises of virtual activity.

Appreciating this diversity, virtuality researchers are a virtual community of academics and practitioners, interested in the insights that could arise from the "real but nonmaterial effects" of various virtual influences. Particular communities of practice would be more tightly connected to particular topics and methods, but they would be loosely connected with other communities interested in exploring the material and immaterial nature of virtuality, in its various forms.

Regardless of the field's complexity and its management, everyone's task is commonly spurred by continuing changes to the material conditions of both technology and locality, such as the cost and capabilities of ICTs, which promote distributed coordination, and the local social and technical environments, which challenge and reshape these technological affordances. We believe this book is a representation of this creative and informed expansion, producing what van Binsbergen (1998) suggests: "the opening up of new spaces and new times within new boundaries that were hitherto inconceivable" (p. 875).

In the end, virtuality depends on the active role of the individual to navigate across virtual and real systems, whether traditional or computer-based, in order to think, feel, act and respond in a way that is meaningful to them and others. This may be the universal focus of virtuality researchers and practitioners. These are exciting times, and building upon the virtuality of human life, which has existed for some time, we live in an experimental and increasingly computer-mediated time, which renders numerous virtual dynamics across various systems. Let our research theories and perspectives explore, understand, and shape the people and activities at the end of our virtual looking-glasses.

References

Kuhn, T.S. (1996) *The Structure of Scientific Revolutions (3rd edition)*, University of Chicago Press: Chicago.

Van Binsbergen, Wim (1998) *Virtuality as a Key Concept in the Study of Globalisation: Aspects of the Symbolic Transformation of Contemporary Africa*, WOTRO (Netherlands Foundation for Tropical Research, a division of the Netherlands Research Foundation NWO): The Hague. Working papers on Globalisation and the Construction of Communal Identity, available at: http://come.to/vanbinsbergen

INDEX

absorption, 242–3
abstract, 248–51
appresentation, 224
avatar, 213, 224, 234, 256, 273

Bergson, 257–61, 266
bloggers, 195, 207–8
blogging communities, 196, 209
blogs, 14, 195, 199–201
boundaries, 55, 57, 171, 175–9, 231, 235
boundary crossing, 232
business intensification, 158

case study method, 27, 183
collaboration, 165
collaborative technologies, 25
communication
    electronic, 23, 172, 245
    face to face, 25, 34, 165, 245
    shared, 61
communication media repertoire, 65–6
communities of practice, 219
computer-mediated communication,
        199, 209
conflict, 126
consciousness, 256
continuities, 60, 61, 153, 175
contracts, 166
conventional teams, 102
cost, *see* price
cyberspace, 261, 263

Deleuze, 258–61
discontinuities, 55, 57, 61, 153, 171,
        174–6, 190
distance, 243
distantiation, 153

embodiment, 220
emotions, 83, 98
EVE, 215, 225–6
expectations, 55

global, 3, 156–7, 241
global village, 241
globalization, 1, 2

globally dispersed teams, *see* globally
        distributed teams
globally distributed teams, 22, 24
    development process, 26, 42, 44
grid technology, 151
grounded theory, 133
guilds, 214, 227

hallucination, 264
holism, 256
hybrid teams, 24, 45, 68, 101–2

identification, 97, 120, 198
    see also organizational identification
identity, 97, 120, 195, 197, 224, 230, 234, 244
IFIP WG 9.5, 4
information and communication
        technologies, 241
information technology, 1–2, 13
information systems, 241
intellectual property, 158, 160
interdisciplinary, 151, 159, 279

knowledge, 132, 276

language barriers, 34
learning, 64, 219
life-world, 216, 218, 235
local, 3, 16, 156–7, 241, 244
locales, 252
locality, 166, 246, 248, 252

management, 165
Massively Multiplayer Online Games, *see*
        MMOGs
matrix, 262–3
media richness theory, 245
mental models, 61, 64
metaphors, 216, 232–3
MMOGs, 14, 196, 213, 234–6
mobile phones, 265
motivation, 97, 120
MUDs, 213
multi-tasking, 177–8, 186
multi-teaming, 175–8, 186
multi-user dragons, *see* MUDs